Graham Mott trained as a management accountant and then had fifteen years' industrial experience. During this time he also graduated in economics and accounting at Bristol University on an Electricity Council scholarship. He is now a principal lecturer in financial management at Newcastle upon Tyne Polytechnic, where he has lectured on financial and economic topics since 1969. His particular interest is explaining financial techniques to non-financial managers and other post-experience students. Graham Mott is the author of *Accounting for Non-Accountants* and *Investment Appraisal for Managers*, also available in Pan Books.

Also by Graham Mott
in Pan Books:

Accounting for Non-Accountants
Investment Appraisal for Managers

Management Accounting
A guide to costing and management
accounting techniques

Graham Mott

A Pan Original
Pan Books London and Sydney

First published 1987 by Pan Books Ltd,
Cavaye Place, London SW10 9PG
9 8 7 6 5 4 3 2 1

ISBN 0 330 29727 9

Phototypeset by Input Typesetting Ltd, London
Printed and bound in Great Britain by
Cox & Wyman Ltd, Reading

To Valerie

Contents

Acknowledgements

I would like to thank the following professional bodies for permission to use samples of their past examination questions throughout the text and in Appendix 4 of the paperback edition.

The relevant body for each question is denoted in brackets as indicated below. The suggested solutions are my own and not those of the body concerned except where indicated in the case of (AAT).

Association of Accounting Technicians (AAT)

The Chartered Association of Certified Accountants (Certified Diploma)

The Institute of Marketing (IOM)

The London Chamber of Commerce and Industry (LCCI)

The Royal Institution of Chartered Surveyors (RICS)

The Royal Society of Arts (RSA)

Preface

This book is written primarily for practising managers who need a working knowledge of costing and management accounting techniques. The explanations given are as non-technical as possible and numerous examples are used to illustrate both the principles and their application.

Accounting has a language of its own and many accounting terms, like 'contribution' or 'profit', have a precise meaning which is not always understood. Whether communicating with colleagues or subordinates, managers need to know both the language and the ways in which detailed financial information can be used or misused.

Three of the key functions performed by management are planning, control and decision making. It is no exaggeration to suggest that many plans and decisions are founded on, or influenced by, financial considerations.

This book is in three parts. Part I looks at the origins of costs and their various classifications, leading to the costing and pricing of the firm's output, be that a product, a process or a service.

Part II of the book takes planning and control as its theme. These two management functions are interwoven in the sense that planned standard costs, budgets, divisional objectives, etc. all need to be monitored and controlled to become effective. The techniques of marginal costing, budgetary control and accounting ratios allow this to be done.

Part III explains the financial aspects of decision making and draws heavily on the principles of marginal costing. Some decisions are short term, concerning the best use of existing resources. Other decisions involve capital expenditure which may have a life span of many years. Managers provide the information for these decisions and they need to know how it is used in discounted cash flow techniques. They should also know which factors influence the acceptance or rejection of new investments so that they can more easily identify worthwhile opportunities.

Most of the material in this book applies to any form of business organization, both large and small, in both public and private sectors. Some government departments, for example health, education and social services, are not commercial activities. Their goods or services are not directly paid for by their clients. Even so, many costing techniques have relevance to the costing, budgeting and decision-making roles of public service managers. Nationalized industries are of course now virtually indistinguishable from private sector companies.

I hope you find the book both interesting and useful. If you are a manager you will certainly find the examples given have practical applications to your everyday work.

Graham Mott

Part I
Costing and pricing

Overview

Broadly speaking, there are two main types of accounting which are normally referred to as 'Financial Accounting' and 'Management Accounting' which embraces all types of costing. Financial accounting concentrates on the recording of all financial transactions, the receipt and payment of cash, and keeping track of money owed and owing. This all culminates in the preparation of global financial statements like the profit and loss account, the balance sheet, value added and the sources and applications of funds. Such statements are global in the sense that they either refer to the whole company, or to some semi-autonomous unit within it.

Costing and management accounting, however, are concerned with the detailed analysis of the costs and incomes going into the profit and loss account. This detailed analysis is used to cost out, and hence price, a firm's output of goods or services and is also used to facilitate the planning, controlling and decision-making roles of managers.

It must be stressed immediately that the costs and incomes constituting a profit and loss account are the same costs and incomes that are analysed in detail for costing purposes. For example, a profit and loss account may have one global figure for wages paid to the operations staff. What cost analysis does is to break down that total wage bill to identify the departments concerned, the operations performed and the products or services involved.

All financial information originates from the same basic documents. These include:

- Timesheets or timecards for wage and salary costs
- Stores issue notes or requisitions for material costs
- Invoices for purchases of materials, goods and services
- Invoices for charges to customers
- Budgets and standards for planned activities

The way this information is handled is by the use of a cost coding system that is capable of describing every aspect of each transaction. Cost codes are structured and designed to suit the requirements of individual firms, but they basically consist of a series of numbers that identify costs and income in detail. In some ways a cost code can be likened to the UK telephone numbering system. As both the value and description of any transaction can be expressed in numerical form, the input of cost information to computerized systems is the norm these days.

The term 'management information system' is used to describe any planned system of collecting, storing, processing and presenting information to management so that effective decision making and control can take place. This term suggests one complete system when in reality it is composed of a number of sub-systems and even sub-sub-systems! Financial information is one such sub-system, comprising many sub-sub-systems dealing with trading performance, overhead recovery, product costs and cost control via standards or budgets.

One of the prime tasks of any management information system is to be able to cost out the products or services provided to a firm's customers. This entails the evaluation of labour, material and overhead costs attributable to that output whether it is a one-off product, a mass-produced article, a process or a service.

The objective of any profit-seeking organization will be to recover the total costs of the outputs and to make sufficient profit to satisfy the providers of its capital. This can be achieved either by adding a percentage oncost to total costs as a profit margin, or by aiming for a percentage contribution from every sale sufficient to recover general overheads and to leave the required profit.

These topics are now explored in detail in the following four chapters.

1. Cost analysis and classification

If you have read or studied any branch of accounting before, you may have thought you were studying a foreign language at times. The whole subject is riddled with terms and jargon that often leave the layman confused. This is not helped by the fact that occasionally we have more than one name for the same thing, and we do not always agree precisely on the same definition.

Although this book is not about bookkeeping, the story comes to mind of the accountant who was not allowed to join the top management team. So, to get his own back and make sure he was indispensable, he invented a language and system of recording called 'double entry bookkeeping' that only he could understand!

I hope you will not feel this way about this book, but it is essential that we start by introducing some of the terms and definitions in costing, before going on to put them to use in other chapters. The terms we particularly need to grasp are:

- Cost unit
- Cost centre
- Direct and indirect cost
- Cost allocation
- Cost apportionment
- Overhead recovery and absorption
- Cost classification
- Cost coding

Cost Units and Cost Centres

A 'cost' is any expenditure that can be attributed to a particular thing or activity and may be related to past events or to budgeted activities. The term may apply to one individual item, but is more often a function of price × quantity.

A 'cost unit' is a product or service to which costs can be

charged. The term is not restricted to the final product or service supplied to clients, but includes intermediate products and services transferred internally.

In a polytechnic, for example, cost units might include a course, a refectory meal, or a library issue. In an advertising agency, examples of cost units might be a specific promotion or a market research survey. Finally, a cost unit in a manufacturing firm might be the end product or the cost of an internal service, for example a computer hour or a purchase order.

A 'cost centre' on the other hand is not a unit of output but a physical location within an organization, namely a department or a section, or even a piece of equipment. These locations are identified by having a unique number as part of the coding system described later.

Again in a polytechnic, examples of cost centres might be an academic department, an administrative department, a computer unit or a careers service. In a leisure complex, cost centres might include a pool, squash courts, gymnasium, hall or other separate activities. In a manufacturing firm, cost centres may include each functional department or service activity.

Cost centres and cost units eventually come together in that the costs in cost centres are somehow charged to cost units for control, pricing and decision-making purposes.

Direct and Indirect Costs

As the term implies, direct costs are those which can be specifically identified with the output of the firm, be that a product or a service. We might also use the term when relating costs to intermediate products or services within the firm, so we need to watch the context in which it is used. For the moment we will concentrate on the former definition.

All costs can be classified as labour, materials or expenses, so we can classify direct costs in this way:

• Direct labour is the cost of wages and/or salaries of those personnel specifically working on the provision of the product or service to the customer.

- Direct materials are materials, parts, components forming part of the product or provided in the service to the customer.
- Direct expenses include other bought-in services that are specific to a product or service provided to a customer. They embrace royalties, design fees, hire charges, contract labour and similar items.

The distinctive nature of direct costs, therefore, is that their whole cost can be charged to the end product sold to the customer, without having to be channelled through intermediate stages.

Indirect costs, however, are different. As their name implies they are the exact opposite to direct costs. The easy definition of indirect costs is to say they are all costs which cannot be identified as direct costs! Although true, this begs the question somewhat, so we shall define them as costs which cannot be immediately identified with the end product going to customers, but which first must go through some intermediate channelling process.

As with direct costs, we can classify indirect costs by their elements as follows:

- Indirect labour includes the wages/salaries of all supervisory, maintenance, cleaning, administrative, sales, distribution and management staff. In effect, it includes the pay of any employee not engaged on the product or service supplied to the customer.
- Indirect materials may often be relatively insignificant in total value, but will include stationery, cleaning materials and maintenance parts.
- Indirect expenses include power, insurance, depreciation, rent, rates and any other general expense that is neither labour nor material.

The name often given to the total cost of all the indirects is that of 'overheads' whilst the total of all direct costs is referred to as 'prime cost'. To summarize, so far we can say:

PRIME COST = DIRECT LABOUR + DIRECT MATERIALS + DIRECT EXPENSES

OVERHEADS = INDIRECT LABOUR + INDIRECT MATERIALS + INDIRECT EXPENSES

TOTAL COST = PRIME COST + OVERHEADS

As much of costing is concerned with the determination of profit or selling price, we can go a stage further and show the build-up of costs and profit to a final selling price as follows:

Build-up of costs

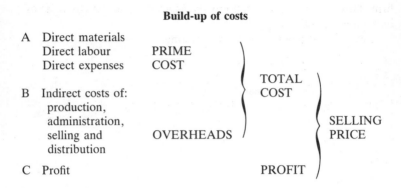

The ascertainment of the prime cost of any cost unit seldom causes any problem. This is because the very nature of direct costs specifically relates them to such units. Much more problematical is the ascertainment of the amount of the various overheads to charge to cost units. If these indirect costs are general in nature, rather than specific to one cost unit, then they need to be allocated or apportioned to cost units as best they can.

Cost Allocation and Apportionment

When a cost can be charged in whole to either a cost unit or a cost centre, without first being divided into smaller parts, we say it is allocated. One example would be the material components of a microcomputer being allocated to the cost unit for that particular model. Another example of cost allocation would be the purchase cost of invoice sets from a printing firm being allocated to the user cost centre, namely the sales department.

All direct costs can be allocated to cost units but some indirect costs may not be allocatable to cost centres without first being split into smaller parts and spread over a number of centres. This process is known as cost apportionment. A typical example is the rent paid for a building which can be apportioned to the different departments within it on a floor area basis.

There are a number of generally agreed guidelines, or bases, for overhead apportionment to user cost centres. Each individual firm, however, must determine what is appropriate in the light of its own circumstances.

Some typical examples of apportionment bases are:

Cost to be apportioned to centres	Basis
Establishment charges, e.g. rent, rates	Floor area
Stores handling and storage	Number or value of issues
Canteen subsidy	Number of employees
Depreciation	Value of assets
Administration	Number of employees

Overhead Recovery and Absorption

Whatever the output of a firm happens to be, the total cost of each product line needs ascertaining for both control purposes and pricing requirements. By definition, direct costs are easily

The costing process

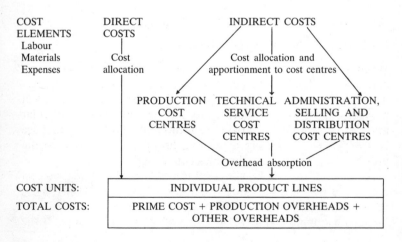

identifiable with individual products, but indirect costs, or overheads, have no such direct link. They are therefore allocated or apportioned to cost centres first, and from there are shared out among the different cost units/products.

Products are said to absorb overheads which are charged to them from cost centres by way of either one global or a number of individual overhead recovery rates. Typical overhead recovery rates occur when overheads are expressed as '£ per hour' or '£ per £ of prime cost'.

We can summarize our knowledge of the costing process so far in the diagram on the previous page.

Cost Classification

We have already seen that costs can be classified into the two broad categories of direct or indirect. In order to allocate and apportion costs in a logical way we need to group them in much more detail. The groupings, or classifications, to be used will vary from firm to firm as they are determined both by their origin and by their destination in the costing system.

Grouping costs by their origin is a subjective classification based on the nature of the cost concerned. For example, labour costs can be classed together according to the work carried out:

Direct labour	– Wages	– Forming
		– Wiring
		– Assembling
		– Testing
Indirect labour	– Wages	– Packing
		– Dispatch
		– Driving
		– Maintenance
	– Salaries	– Administration
		– Personnel
		– Sales
		– Accounting

The other main requirement is for an objective classification of costs so that we group costs according to the cost centre and/or cost unit to which they are to be charged. All these classifications will find expression in the cost coding system, but there are other classifications outside the coding system, as we shall see later.

Cost Coding

A cost code is like a system of shorthand consisting of a series of numbers and/or letters used to describe both the nature and destination of costs. It facilitates the input of financial data to computerized accounting systems which cannot sort information described in words.

The following characteristics are present in a well-designed cost code:

- Clarity — the structure of the coding system and the logic of the classifications used should be clear to all users. Codes should be grouped in short blocks of about three digits with only one code possible for any one item of cost. Letters like 'O' and 'I' which can be mistaken for numbers should be avoided.
- Brevity — the number of digits should be kept to a minimum, consistent with the need for information. Nothing can be retrieved that is not separately coded at the input stage.
- Flexibility — there should be enough spare capacity in the system to allow further codes to be allocated as the need arises, without destroying the original logic of the structure.

Most coding systems are composite systems where the codes are expressed in two or three blocks or sections. Typically, the first block will relate to the cost centre which initiated the cost, the second block will describe the nature of the expenditure and the third block will allow appropriate costs to be charged to cost units.

An example of this kind of structure would be 50–963–374 where the number 50 identified the originating department, the

number 963 described the work carried out and the number 374
identified the cost unit to which it was charged:

Example

Cost centre	Description	Cost unit
50	963	374
Location number of dept/section where cost incurred.	Nature of the expense.	Batch, job or customer order number.

Although cost codes have been described as a system that allows
the complete analysis of costs, it should not be thought that they
cater only for costs. Coding numbers are also allocated to sales
receipts, stocks and work-in-progress, capital receipts and capital
expenditure, all of which may be reserved for accountants' use
only.

The branch of accounting called financial accounting is
concerned solely with the subjective classification of costs denoted
by the describing number. The other main branch called management accounting, however, is concerned with all three classifications. Here, much use is made of the objective classification of
costs in terms of cost centres and cost units for overhead recovery,
pricing and cost control purposes.

Other Classifications

So far, we have grouped costs subjectively into direct and indirect
categories by the elements of labour, materials and expenses. We
have also grouped them objectively by cost centre and by cost
unit. All of these classifications are built into the cost coding
system.

There are, however, other classifications of cost which normally do not fit into the cost coding system, but nevertheless have very important applications in costing.

The first of these is the classification of costs by behaviour, aspects of which appear continuously throughout this book as it permeates all management decision making. By behaviour we mean the relationship of cost to the level of activity or output.

Costs can be classified according to whether they remain a constant total sum, irrespective of fluctuations in short-term activity levels, or whether they vary in a roughly pro rata manner. The former constant costs are called 'fixed', whilst the latter pro rata costs are called 'variable'. It is also possible to have an inbetween category of costs composed of both elements and suitably described as 'semi-fixed' or 'semi-variable'.

The reason why this classification is not built into the cost coding system is that it is not constant over time. In the very short term of a week or two, it is correct to describe direct labour as a fixed cost, although we normally regard it as a variable cost. Conversely, rent and rates which we regard as fixed costs in the short term become variable costs if we extend our time horizon enough. This is because in the long term, firms can reduce the size of premises from which they operate and hence reduce the fixed costs of rent and rates.

Other classifications of costs appearing elsewhere in the text include 'opportunity cost' which is the cost of a resource in its alternative use, 'sunk cost' which is a cost already incurred, and 'controllable' or 'non-controllable' cost which relates to the authority of the manager receiving such information.

Summary

This chapter has very much set the scene for this part of the book which deals with costing and pricing. We have introduced some of the key terms used in the costing process that allow costs to be charged to the end products/services.

Fundamental to this process is the classification of costs in both a subjective and an objective way. The subjective classification is based on the nature and description of the cost whilst the objective classification is concerned with the cost unit (product/service) or cost centre to which it is charged.

Direct costs can be allocated directly to cost units, whilst indirect costs have to be allocated or apportioned to cost centres and then absorbed by products in some suitable way.

Much of the classification of costs is designed into the cost coding system which is a kind of shorthand that allows cost information to be uniquely described and input to computer systems.

The next chapter examines the costing and pricing of labour, materials and overheads where these topics are pursued.

2. Costing labour, materials and overheads

The three main elements of cost are labour, materials and overheads, which in the final analysis are all charged to the end product or service sold to customers. The amount of direct costs to charge to any cost unit is easy to identify, but the amount of indirect costs is less certain.

This chapter looks at each of these cost elements in turn, as there are a number of issues that need clarifying before we can understand how total costs are built up.

Labour Costs and Remuneration Systems

All organizations need to keep records of employee attendance for holiday, sickness and other personnel functions. In addition, the remuneration of the employee is related to attendance and possibly to performance. Finally, the destination of the cost of labour to cost centres and cost units needs recording to enable the input of labour cost details into the accounting system.

For all these reasons there is a need for one or more documents to record employee attendance and performance. The attendance document takes the form of either a timecard or a timesheet. A timecard can be clocked into a time recording machine to record working hours for a week. Subject to security safeguards, it is a cheap and efficient system to operate.

Timesheets can be used simply to record working hours when they are certified by a supervisor. More often, they are used in conjunction with timecards to record details of work performed during each day. In this case, timecards are used to confirm attendance hours which should reconcile with those on the timesheet. This latter document, however, contains details of work done and the codes of cost units and cost centres to be charged.

Where remuneration is to be based on output, some kind of

piecework ticket will be required to record and certify the good production qualifying for payment. A further document which may be required is a job card. As the title suggests, this relates more to the job or batch being produced than to any one individual. Labour times for many workers over the whole length of the production cycle can be entered on such documents.

The costing section of a firm can use all of these documents, job cards, piecework tickets and timesheets, to charge labour costs to the appropriate cost centres and cost units. Direct labour, including bonuses and premiums, can readily be charged to the cost units involved. Indirect labour must first be channelled to a cost centre and absorbed into cost units by an overhead recovery rate.

The remuneration of employees can take two main forms. It can either be based on time attendance, or on output achieved, with many variations on the theme.

Time-based systems pay a basic rate per hour up to the normal weekly hours, say thirty-eight hours, and enhanced rates in excess of that. Bonuses can be paid in addition to basic time rates for shift work or other unsocial hours. Such systems are easy to administer and understand but do little to provide motivation and incentive.

'Measured day work' is a variety of time-based system where relatively high basic time rates are paid in return for high output/quality. Production line operation, as in car assembly, is a typical situation for this payment method, where group rather than individual performance is measured. The title derives from the use of industrial engineers in applying work study and work measurement techniques to set agreed output rates.

The other main payment system relates wages to output with some kind of incentive scheme. This can be of benefit to both parties, as employees earn more for their extra effort whilst the employer reduces his unit cost by spreading overheads over a greater output. Arguments against incentives are that they may be complex and costly to administer, leading to disputes and jealousy among workers. Most systems allow for a minimum guaranteed or fall-back wage should incentive earnings not suffice through no fault of the operative.

The simplest form of incentive is 'straight piecework' where operatives are paid a constant rate or amount of time for each unit produced. To increase incentive at higher levels of production a 'differential piecework' system may be used where higher and higher rates are paid for successive chunks of output.

A hybrid of a time base and an incentive base is the 'premium bonus system' which pays normal hourly or daily rates plus a bonus depending on the time taken relative to the time allowed.

It is also possible to provide incentives on a group rather than on an individual basis. This may be more appropriate where production is group based, as in coal-face working, or where a process cannot be identified with one individual. An extreme example of group incentives is where all employees are rewarded on a profit sharing or value added basis. This allows employees to share in the general prosperity of the company but has the disadvantages of being remote and capable of being affected by external influences.

Sometimes there is confusion between the terms production and productivity. Production is an absolute measure of the physical quantity or value of the amount produced. Productivity is a relative measure of the output for a resource input. We might talk of production as 1,000 units but we would describe productivity as, say, 100 units per direct labour hour. The following example demonstrates this difference:

Example

You are at present considering the following results from one of your production divisions for an accounting period:

Production costs:	£
Direct material	6,000
Direct labour (rate of £3 per hour)	3,000
Variable overheads	1,200
Fixed overheads	4,500
Cost of production	£14,700

The number of units that were produced in the period was 5,000

The cost per unit was £2.94

You have been asked to investigate a form of productivity bonus, and to

explain the difference between production and productivity with specific reference to:
(a) the effect on the above figures of a 15% increase in production without any increase in productivity.
(b) the effect of the same 15% increase in production with an increase in labour productivity of 15%.
(c) the other considerations, other than labour, that should be taken into account when considering productivity bonuses.

(Certified Diploma)

The production level is initially 5,000 units which would rise to 5,750 units if increased by 15%. Provided the rate of labour productivity remained constant then the labour, material and variable overhead costs will rise by 15% in line with the increase in production. Fixed overheads, by definition, remain constant.

Should labour productivity rise by 15% also, then there will be no increase in the total labour cost for the extra output. Material and variable overhead costs will still increase pro rata. The total and unit costs can be set out as follows:

	Existing situation	Increased production	
		Same rate of productivity	Increased rate of productivity
Production level (units)	5,000	5,750	5,750
Production Costs:			
direct material	6,000	6,900	6,900
direct labour	3,000	3,450	3,000
variable overheads	1,200	1,380	1,380
fixed overheads	4,500	4,500	4,500
Cost of production	£14,700	£16,230	£15,780
Cost per unit produced	£2.94	£2.83	£2.74
Cost reduction due to increased production		11p	11p
Cost reduction due to labour productivity		–	9p
		11p	20p

The 15% increase in the production level has brought about a reduction of 11p per unit in the cost because the fixed overheads are now spread over 5,750 units instead of the previous 5,000 units. When labour productivity increases by 15% in addition to the 15% increase in the production level, then the unit cost falls by a further 9p because the labour cost per unit is less.

Although we talk of labour productivity, it can be misleading in that it may result from the introduction of more equipment or new technology, in many instances making the job easier than before. In this case the gain in labour productivity needs to be offset by the running costs of the equipment to gauge the net overall benefit. This point should be borne in mind in any nego- tiations on remuneration systems that are output based. We now turn our attention to the costing of materials.

Material Costs and Stores Pricing

When firms hold materials or parts in stores for subsequent issue, the final profit or loss of the company can be very much influenced by the management of those stores and the cost assigned both to material issues and to stocks.

There are a number of sequential stages in the acquisition, issue and holding of stores which require their own documentation for use in the costing system:

- A 'purchase requisition' is raised internally specifying the quan- tity and quality of materials required as soon as the re-order level is reached.
- A 'purchase order' for an 'economic order quantity' is then sent to the selected supplier offering the best combination of price, quality and delivery.
- In some industries these stages may form part of a 'materials requirement planning' system based on computerized infor- mation on needs to meet future orders.
- Materials received are checked for quantity/quality and a 'goods received note' raised after matching with the purchase order. A 'goods returned note' is issued in respect of any materials returned to suppliers.

- The invoice from the supplier is matched with the goods received note before payment is made.
- Stores issues are only allowed when authorized by a 'stores requisition'.
- Annual stocktaking, or preferably continuous stocktaking on sequential items throughout the year, confirms stores values in the books.

All of this documentation plays a part in the bookkeeping and costing for materials. The former deals with the correct payment to suppliers for materials received, but it is the latter in which we are primarily interested.

If a material is purchased for a specific purpose and the specific invoice is chargeable in full immediately without the materials being held in store for some time, then the cost unit or cost centre can be charged accordingly. It is by no means so straightforward when materials are stored for future issue on a piecemeal basis.

There are two key and interlocking aspects when we price materials. We need to value those materials remaining in store at any moment in time and we need to value each issue of materials as it takes place. If the purchase cost of materials never varied this would cause no problems, but costs do vary and the value we place on issues from stores affects the value of the items remaining in store.

The choice of stores pricing method rests between four main contenders which we shall examine in turn:

- First in first out method (FIFO)
- Last in first out method (LIFO)
- Weighted average method
- Standard price method

The FIFO method prices stores issues in the strict order in which they were taken into stock. The oldest stock is issued first at its purchase price, then the next oldest and so on. This could result in one issue of stores being composed of more than one price. Although materials are priced in order of receipt, it is possible that they may not physically be issued in that same order, particularly if they are not identifiable in this way.

One effect of FIFO practice is that it will tend to understate product costs in times of rising material prices if they are held in stock for any great length of time. However, the materials remaining in stores reflect the more up-to-date prices of recent purchases and therefore stock values are more realistic.

FIFO is one of the methods approved by the accounting profession in its Statement of Standard Accounting Practice No.9 and is also allowed by the Inland Revenue in the computation of profit for tax purposes.

We will take a few sample transactions in one month to illustrate the principle of FIFO:

Example

A firm starts the month of July with 50kg of Material X in stock which it bought at £2 per kg, and has further receipts and issues during the next few weeks:

1 July	Opening stock 50kg at £2
6 July	Issued 10kg
17 July	Received 50 kg at £2.40
20 July	Issued 60kg
31 July	Closing stock 30kg

Using the FIFO system we can price the issues of materials and value the stock of Material X remaining at the month end as follows:

The first in first out (FIFO) method

Date	Receipts			Issues			Balance		
	Qty	Price	Value	Qty	Price	Value	Qty	Price	Value
1 Jul	50	£2.00	£100.00				50	£2.00	£100.00
6 Jul				10	£2.00	£20.00	40	£2.00	£ 80.00
17 Jul	50	£2.40	£120.00				(40	£2.00	£ 80.00
							(50	£2.40	£120.00
20 Jul				(40	£2.00	£80.00			
				(20	£2.40	£48.00	30	£2.40	£ 72.00
31 Jul							30	£2.40	£ 72.00

It can be seen that any issue or receipt relates the quantity concerned to the specific price at which it is held in stock with materials being issued in strict rotation. For example, the issue of 60kg that took place on 20 July uses up all the 40kg oldest stock at £2 before issuing the 20kg balance at the later price of £2.40 per kg. The stock in hand at the month end is valued at the most recent price at which Material X has been purchased.

The LIFO method prices stores issues in the reverse order to the FIFO system by saying that the last materials to be received are the first to be issued. This has the effect that materials are always issued at near current prices but the value of stock remaining in stores is always out of date.

LIFO is more popular in America and is not acceptable in the UK to either the Inland Revenue or as a basis for the preparation of statutory final accounts.

Using the same example as we did for FIFO we can price the issues and value the stock on a LIFO basis and draw conclusions:

The last in first out (LIFO) method

Date	Receipts			Issues			Balance		
	Qty	Price	Value	Qty	Price	Value	Qty	Price	Value
1 Jul	50	£2.00	£100.00				50	£2.00	£100.00
6 Jul				10	£2.00	£20.00	40	£2.00	£ 80.00
17 Jul	50	£2.40	£120.00				(40	£2.00	£ 80.00
							(50	£2.40	£120.00
20 Jul				(50	£2.40	£120.00			
				(10	£2.00	£ 20.00	30	£2.00	£ 60.00
31 Jul							30	£2.00	£ 60.00

The essential differences between LIFO and FIFO centre around the pricing of the issue of materials on 20 July and the valuation of the remaining stock at the month end. LIFO values the 60kg issued at £140 which is £12 more when compared with FIFO's £128, but this is compensated by LIFO valuing remaining stock at only £60 which is £12 less than FIFO's £72 value.

Without the use of computers, both FIFO and LIFO systems would be cumbersome as they entail the recording of the same stock item at various prices. One way round this problem is to value all items at a single price which can best be described as a weighted average. This method also has the effect of smoothing out material price changes rather than them being implemented in one jump. It also has the advantage of being accepted by both tax and accountancy authorities.

The weighted average price at any time is the total value of a material held divided by the number of units of that stock item. Issues of materials do not affect the weighted unit price, but every time the stock is replenished a new weighted average price must be calculated. This can be illustrated by using the same example above that was used to demonstrate the LIFO and FIFO methods:

The weighted average method

Date	Receipts			Issues			Balance		
	Qty	Price	Value	Qty	Price	Value	Qty	Price	Value
1 Jul	50	£2.00	£100.00				50	£2.00	£100.00
6 Jul				10	£2.00	£20.00	40	£2.00	£ 80.00
17 Jul	50	£2.40	£120.00				90	£2.22	£200.00
20 Jul				60	£2.22	£133.33	30	£2.22	£ 66.67
31 Jul							30	£2.22	£ 66.67

The only time the average price changes is when new materials are purchased on 17 July at a higher price than that reigning at the time. This purchase brings the previous average of £2 per unit up to approximately £2.22 per unit, which may need to be calculated to more decimal places in practice.

The final method of stores pricing occurs when a firm uses the standard costing system described in Chapter 6. In this case, all materials are given a standard price and all stock and any subsequent issues are priced at this rate. Any variation of purchase prices from standard are transferred to the profit and loss account at the time of purchase.

Referring back to the original example, let us now assume that the standard price of Material X was set at £2 per kg. In a standard costing system all receipts are put into stock at £2 and all issues priced at the same rate. The balance of stock will also be priced at £2 per kg at any time until the standard is revised. The purchase on 17 July, however, was executed at £2.40 per kg, so the excess £20 (i.e. 50kg × 40p) is written off as a loss to the profit and loss account immediately.

Four methods of stores pricing have now been discussed, each of which will give different values for the materials issued on 17 July and differing stock valuations at the month end. Over the whole life of a company there is no difference between the methods on the profit or loss made, as the cost of the materials will be allowed in full on each method.

When looking at the performance over a discrete period of one month or one year, then the method chosen will affect the profit or loss made. This is because the cost of materials used, and hence the residual stock value, varies from method to method when purchase prices change.

We have now examined the two principal direct costs of labour and materials. Any remaining direct expenses should never cause any pricing or costing problems, as the cost is chargeable immediately to a specific cost unit. Would that we could say the same about indirect costs or overheads, to which we turn our attention next!

Overhead Recovery and Apportionment

Overheads is the collective term for indirect costs which includes every cost other than direct labour, direct materials and direct expenses. Direct costs pose no problem in the costing process because of their specific link with the end product/service sold to customers. Unfortunately this is not the case with overheads as there is no such link with individual products for many general administrative costs.

We therefore need to examine the ways in which overheads are absorbed by products, recognizing that by their very nature this process may be somewhat arbitrary at times.

If we take a very small firm as an example first, such firms may decide to lump all overheads together and absorb them by reference to some element of the direct cost going into products:

Example

A television repair company has total overheads of £50,000 per annum. The direct labour bill for the year amounts to £40,000 and the company decides to recover its overheads by reference to the labour cost of each repair. We can therefore calculate the overhead recovery rate as:

$$\text{Overhead recovery rate} = \frac{\text{Total overheads p.a.}}{\text{Direct labour cost p.a.}} \%$$

$$= \frac{£50,000}{£40,000} \% = 125\%$$

This overhead recovery rate states, in effect, that £1.25 overheads will be added for every £1 of direct labour cost incurred on a repair. If a certain repair required £15 of new components and took one and a half hours to complete by an engineer paid £4 per hour, then the total cost of the repair would be:

Materials	15.00
Labour	6.00
Overheads	7.50
Total cost	£28.50

In this way the total overheads will be absorbed by all 'products' and recovered in the total cost charged to customers, together with an element of profit. The overhead recovery rate illustrated above should be based on forward estimates for the coming year for both overheads and labour costs.

Should either or both of these estimates turn out to be incorrect, as is likely to happen in practice, then an under- or over-recovery of overheads will occur. An under-recovery results in a lower profit than was anticipated, whilst an over-recovery results in more profit than expected.

Referring back to the previous example, let us assume the estimate of £50,000 overheads was more or less correct, but the direct labour cost amounted to only £35,000 for the year due to the loss of an engineer. If the 125% recovery rate remained unaltered then only £43,750 of the £50,000 overheads would have been recovered in customer charges during the year.

Although direct labour cost was chosen as a basis on which to illustrate how overheads are recovered in a small firm, there are a number of other suitable candidates. These include:

Basis	*Overhead recovery rate*
• Direct labour hours	£ overheads per labour hour
• Machine hours	£ overheads per machine hour
• Direct material cost	% of direct material cost
• Prime cost	% of prime cost
• Volume of products	£ per unit

The choice of an appropriate basis rests with an individual firm and depends on the nature of the product or service provided for customers. Where only one product is made, then overheads can be recovered at £x per unit, as when a number of similar products are made taking similar times and with similar direct costs. Should one product have double the direct cost of another, then it is patently unfair to charge them an equal amount of overheads, and another basis must be used.

Many overheads, such as rent, rates and salaries, relate to the passing of time, and many popular overhead recovery rates reflect this by charging £x overheads per labour or machine hour. The other main approach is to base overhead recovery on the direct costs of the product concerned using direct labour cost or direct material cost or prime cost. If either labour or material cost predominates then it will be chosen.

The above system of lumping all overheads into one pot and absorbing them into products by means of one global overhead recovery rate may work quite satisfactorily in small firms. It will be much less satisfactory the more diverse the products and processes become, when some products would be charged for services from which they had no benefit.

This necessitates that overheads are identified with specific cost centres and absorbed in the most appropriate way for that centre. It is worth repeating, at this stage, part of a diagram we met in the previous chapter when describing the costing process. In it, overheads are seen to be allocated and apportioned to individual cost centres and then absorbed into products by the most appropriate overhead absorption rate for each centre:

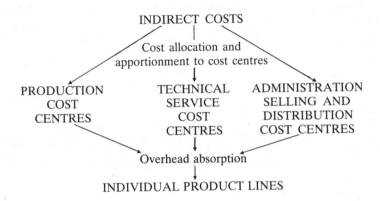

Overheads incurred in production cost centres will be absorbed into product costs using one of the overhead recovery rates mentioned above in the context of small firms. The cost of technical services, such as maintenance, storekeeping and purchasing, are all overhead costs and are apportioned to production or other cost centres on a suitable basis. For example:

Cost centre	*Suitable basis*
• Maintenance	Value of equipment
• Storekeeping	Number/value of issues
• Purchasing	Number of orders placed

Production overheads and technical service overheads can now be absorbed by individual product lines passing through each production cost centre. When these overhead costs are added to prime cost, we arrive at the 'production cost', but there are many general overheads remaining.

These other overheads include the cost of all administrative departments, research and development, selling and distribution. By their very nature most of these overheads have no identifiable link with individual product lines. They are therefore usually recovered by an overhead absorption rate based on production costs.

An example of overhead recovery and absorption leading up to the pricing of products is given in a section on full cost pricing contained in Chapter 4.

A problem sometimes arises in the apportionment of service cost centre overheads to production cost centres. One or more of these service cost centres may carry out work for other service or administrative cost centres in addition to servicing production needs. The maintenance and stores departments are typical cases in point, where requests for repairs and servicing or stores issues may be initiated from anywhere in the firm.

This leads to the situation where one service cost centre may be apportioning its costs partly to other service cost centres who in turn may be apportioning costs to the first cost centre. Such a process could be never-ending, but there are a number of ways to resolve this interlocking situation.

A manual method is to carry out the service cost centre apportionments in the way described and to keep repeating the process until the amounts become small enough to ignore. A variation on this theme is to place the service cost centres in some order of priority and not allow further apportionments in once the apportionment out has been completed.

Other methods of resolving the problem of interlocking service departments involve the use of mathematical formulae which are most easily performed by computer.

Summary

In this chapter we have examined the recording and costing of the three key costs: materials, direct labour and overheads. The aim is to charge the appropriate amounts to each product or service provided to customers, as a basis for pricing and control.

Methods of remuneration for direct labour fall into one of two camps. Workers are either rewarded on a time basis or on the volume of output they achieve, with a number of possible variations around these themes.

Materials to be held in stores for subsequent issue are not as straightforward to deal with as might be supposed. It is possible to price stores issues in four main ways, but whichever method is chosen affects the value of the remaining stock differently.

Overheads are certainly the most difficult costs to deal with due to their lack of identity with the end product sold to customers. Using suitable location coding numbers, we must allocate over-heads to cost centres directly wherever possible and apportion other overheads to cost centres.

Once all overheads are identified with cost centres we need to absorb them into product costs by using appropriate overhead absorption or recovery rates.

The next chapter continues the discussion with a look at the costing of various kinds of end products found in different industries.

3. Job and process costing

There are a number of costing methods which are specially designed so that they suit the way in which a particular product or service is made or provided. Basically, there are only two types of costing method – 'job costing' and 'process costing' – which are adapted to suit the requirements of any industry's output, whether it is a product or a service.

These adaptations of job or process costing go under the names of 'batch costing', 'contract costing', 'operation' or 'service costing', 'by-product' and 'joint product costing'. Whichever of these costing methods is selected as appropriate, the principles of cost allocation and apportionment described in the previous chapters still apply. We start with a look at job costing before tackling its many variants.

Job Costing

This system is employed where goods or services are provided on a one-off basis as opposed to being mass produced. Each product or service is distinguishable from others, being designed to the specific requirements of an individual customer. It is therefore the appropriate costing system for engineering firms fabricating to a blueprint, ship repairers, jobbing builders, printing firms, and architects.

Job costing is performed for three reasons. It informs managers, at any time, of the progress of a job in cost terms. It also gives a valuation of work-in-progress on that job which is needed to prepare final accounts at period ends. Finally, it identifies the profit or loss on the job at completion, which, if fed back to the manager concerned, can provide useful data for future price estimation and control.

In an uncomputerized system, a document called a 'job card'

will be used to accumulate all costs as the job progresses over its whole life, irrespective of accounting periods. In a computerized accounting system, the unique job number allocated as an integral part of the cost code structure will record all costs allocated to each job and overheads absorbed by it. A print-out can be obtained at any time to serve the same effect as the job card.

Any direct costs can be charged straight to the job number through the coding system when applied to timesheets, stores requisitions and invoices. The job will also attract production overheads at the predetermined departmental absorption rates. In this way the costs are built up as the job progresses and, at any moment in time, represents the value of work-in-progress.

In addition to being charged to individual jobs, production costs on all jobs are also charged to a 'Work-in-Progress Account'. This acts as a check, or control, on the value of all work-in-progress at any time. When a job is completed it is transferred from this 'Work-in-Progress Account' to the 'Cost of Sales Account' if sold immediately; alternatively it is transferred to the 'Finished Goods Stock Account' at production cost.

Batch Costing

Essentially, batch costing is a variant of job costing where a batch of homogeneous products is treated as an individual job for costing purposes. Costs are recorded against a batch number instead of a job number, and the final production cost is divided by the quantity of articles produced to get the production cost per article. It is ideally suited to the cost requirements of mass production industries such as car components, electrical goods and shoemaking.

Contract Costing

This again is another variant of job costing where costs are accumulated for an individual contract, and has obvious relevance for construction, civil engineering and shipbuilding. The 'product' is usually individually designed to the client's specification and may take months, if not years, to complete.

With the exception of shipbuilding, in most cases the work is carried out on clients' premises rather than at the contractor's own premises. When the work is performed 'on site', some indirect costs can be charged directly to the contract which would not normally be possible with factory work. Examples here include site power, site telephone, use of plant, site administration and site management salaries.

When contracts extend over a long period of time it is usual for progress payments to be allowed for in the legal document. This avoids the contractor having to provide enormous sums of working capital which he would otherwise be obliged to do. In the case of construction, the value of work completed is assessed on a monthly basis by a surveyor or architect.

The monthly certificate of the value of work certified in effect becomes an interim invoice, but is normally subject to a deduction of 5% or 10% which is called the 'retention'. These monthly retentions are a safeguard for the client that the contractor will complete the whole job satisfactorily, and are not released until some time after contract completion.

The final profit on any contract will not be known with great accuracy until the contract is actually completed and all adjustments agreed with the client. The company needs to report to its shareholders at least twice a year on the profit made in the period. It is usual, therefore, for companies to take some profit on the work as it progresses without waiting until the end of the contract, which may take years to complete. In this way companies avoid the violent fluctuations in yearly profits which would occur if they were solely dependent on contract completions.

There are two reasons why companies will tend to underestimate the amount of profit made to date. First, there is the accounting concept of conservatism which states that profits should not be anticipated before realization. Until a contract is completed, a company cannot be certain that it will not encounter difficulties with the job and possibly incur unanticipated costs. Second is the tax angle which, in effect, states that because profits are taxable, deferring the declaration also defers the payment of tax on those profits.

This interim profit-taking is a problematical field for construction companies, treading a path between the requirements of shareholders, tax authorities and accounting standards. Whatever they agree to do about taking profit on long-term work-in-progress, the policy must be followed consistently from year to year and not conflict with Statement of Standard Accounting Practice No. 9.

A typical practice might be to compare the contract sales value of the work certified to date with the cost of the work certified, and so identify the total profit. This is then reduced by the percentage retention and by a further conservative factor, say one third, to allow for unforeseen events to come:

Example

Suppose a contract for a new bridge was let at a value of £300,000 with monthly progress payments subject to a retention of 10%. The value of work certified to date is £100,000 and the cost of the work including overheads amounts to £90,000. The contractor restricts his profit on work-in-progress to two thirds. Profit to date is therefore:

	£
Value of work certified	100,000
Total cost of work certified	90,000
Total profit	£ 10,000

Profit to be taken = (£10,000 − 10%) × 2/3
        = £6,000

Process Costing

Unlike job and batch production where activity ceases when the individual or group of products is completed, process costing applies in industries where production is continuous. In this situation we cannot identify specific costs with individual products. We can say, however, that certain costs were incurred during a particular period of time and relate that to the number of units produced. In this way we arrive at an average unit cost.

In many industries there may be partially completed products at any one time, and these need to be converted into 'equivalent whole units' in order to calculate the average unit cost of one complete unit.

Example

A company started a process on 1 February and incurred the following production costs during the month:

	£
Direct materials	30,000
Direct labour	4,000
Production overheads	16,000
Total production cost	£50,000

Output for the month consisted of 2,000 complete products plus 200 partially completed products on which the stage of completion for each cost element was:

Direct materials	70%
Direct labour	40%
Production overheads	40%

We can combine this information in the following statement to calculate the average cost per complete unit as £23.63:

Cost element	Complete units	Equivalent part units	Total equivalent units	Total cost £	Average cost £
Direct materials	2,000	200 × 70%	2,140	30,000	14.02
Direct labour	2,000	200 × 40%	2,080	4,000	1.92
Production overheads	2,000	200 × 40%	2,080	16,000	7.69
Total				£50,000	£23.63

Process costing is applicable to industries not only where production is continuous, but also where production passes through sequential stages, with the output of one process being fed into the next process, and so on. If the above example related to the first of a number of sequential processes, then the completed work would be transferred to the second process at £23.63 per unit.

It is also possible that losses normally occur in a process, and accounting for these is necessary for control purposes. Such losses increase the cost of the good production:

Example

A firm introduces 1,000 gallons of chemicals into a process at a cost of £10,000, being an average cost of £10 per gallon input. It is normal for a 20% loss to occur through evaporation, so the average cost per gallon of good output is:

$$\text{Cost per gallon} = \frac{£10,000}{(1,000 - 20\%)} = £12.50$$

When a firm uses a 'standard costing system', the abnormal gain or loss compared to the norm level stipulated in the standard cost specification is quantified as a material yield variance. This topic is pursued in Chapter 7.

It is important to distinguish between 'waste' and 'scrap' as their costing treatment is necessarily different. Waste occurs when there are process losses with no recoverable value, the result of which is to enhance the cost of good production, as illustrated in the above example.

Scrap is a term used to describe losses which have a recoverable value, either by resale to another party or by being fed back into a similar process. In this case, any 'recovery value' goes to reduce the cost of the initial process.

A similar treatment is usually given to 'by-products' where the 'net realizable value' goes to reduce the process costs of the main product. A by-product is one which arises in the course of the process to produce the main product(s), and is of relatively insignificant value. The net realizable value is the resale or re-usable value of the by-product after taking account of any handling costs incurred after separation from the main product.

A further situation to examine is where more than one product is produced simultaneously in a process. Each product may have a significant value of its own, either as a final product or as a feed into separate new processes. Such products are called 'joint products', and are primarily distinguished from by-products by their significant value.

When joint products are produced we need to separate their common process costs at the point of separation of the joint products themselves. This can be done in one of two ways:

1 The common costs can be apportioned to individual products pro rata to a 'physical measure' of the quantity of each product produced

OR

2 The common costs can be apportioned on the basis of the 'market value' of each joint product at the time of separation.

Example

A particular process is used to manufacture Product A and Product B jointly. The joint process costs for last month amounted to £15,000 and the production, work-in-progress and sales data were as follows:

Product	Production quantity kg	Work-in-progress quantity kg	Sales quantity kg	Sales unit value £
A	6,000	1,000	5,000	£2.00
B	9,000	2,000	7,000	£3.00

We can use this data to apportion the costs between the two joint products, to value the work-in-progress and to calculate the profit per product, comparing the two possible bases:

Physical quantity method

This averages the total process cost over the combined quantity of production, namely:

$$\text{Cost per kg} = \frac{£15,000}{6,000 + 9,000} = \frac{£15,000}{15,000\text{kg}} = £1.00 \text{ per kg}$$

This unit cost of £1 per kg is now used to value work-in-progress and the cost of sales to arrive at profit:

Product	Work-in-progress		Cost of sales	
	kg	£	kg	£
A	1,000	1,000	5,000	5,000
B	2,000	2,000	7,000	7,000
	3,000	3,000	12,000	12,000

Product	Sales		Sales value	Cost of sales	Profit
	kg	£	£	£	£
A	5,000	2.00	10,000	5,000	5,000
B	7,000	3.00	21,000	7,000	14,000
			£31,000	£12,000	£19,000

Market value method

This method apportions joint process costs on the basis of the market or sales value of production at the point of separation:

Product	Production quantity	Selling price	Sales value of production	Apportionment of costs
	kg	£	£	£
A	6,000	2.00	12,000	4,615
B	9,000	3.00	27,000	10,385
			£39,000	£15,000

Now we need to apportion the costs of each product between work-in-progress and the cost of sales:

Product	Costs	Work-in-progress		Cost of sales	
	£	kg	£	kg	£
A	4,615	1,000	769	5,000	3,846
B	10,385	2,000	2,308	7,000	8,077
	£15,000		£3,077		£11,923

We can now calculate the profit on sales:

Product	Sales		Sales value	Cost of sales	Profit
	kg	£	£	£	£
A	5,000	2.00	10,000	3,846	6,154
B	7,000	3.00	21,000	8,077	12,923
			£31,000	£11,923	£19,077

Finally, we can summarize the two methods and compare them as follows:

Product	Physical quantity method			Market value method		
	Value of W.I.P.	Profit		Value of W.I.P.	Profit	
	£	£	%	£	£	%
A	1,000	5,000	50%	769	6,154	61%
B	2,000	14,000	67%	2,308	12,923	61%
	£3,000	£19,000		£3,077	£19,077	

With the physical quantity method, the relative profitability of the two products differs when profit is expressed as a percentage of the sales value. This is because the joint costs are apportioned on the basis of volume, giving an equal unit cost for both products. Products with higher sales prices therefore have higher profit margins.

Under the market value method, when joint costs are apportioned to products pro rata to their sales value then the profit margins must be identical for the products concerned.

A word of caution is appropriate here. Firms will choose whichever of the above two methods seems most relevant to their circumstances. The costing that results will allow them to value stocks and the cost of sales for the purpose of producing final accounts. However, neither method will provide a firm basis for pricing- or product-mix decisions based on product profitability. The reason for this is the arbitrary way in which joint costs are apportioned, as there is no such thing as the 'true' cost of a joint product.

Service Costing

This final method of costing is applicable when a uniform or standard service is provided to clients. Railways, bus companies and transport firms all cost in terms of passenger-miles and tonne-miles. Hospitals relate costs to patient-days, and electricity boards to kilowatt-hours.

Example

Suppose a lorry carried a load of 10 tonnes on a journey of 200 miles, and the total cost of wages, fuel and operating costs came to £250. The cost per tonne-mile can be ascertained in this way:

$$\text{Cost per tonne-mile} = \frac{\text{Cost incurred for journey}}{\text{No. of tonnes} \times \text{No. of miles}}$$

$$= \frac{£250}{10 \times 200} = \begin{array}{l} \text{12.5p per} \\ \text{tonne-mile} \end{array}$$

Such information is useful for overall cost control and general pricing policy, but care must be exercised in its use on individual pricing decisions. This is because some costs will not vary precisely with the size of the load or length of the journey, a topic pursued in the next chapter.

Summary

This chapter has examined two broad methods of costing called job costing and process costing, and a number of other related methods. It is possible to adapt costing methods to suit any industry's requirements, but the principles of cost allocation and apportionment are applied throughout.

Individual job costing, contract costing and batch costing provide few problems in the sense that specific items are being costed. This is not the case with process costing as costs are not specifically related to individual items but to the volume of 'throughput' during a period of time. This requires us to cost for incomplete production, process losses, and joint products produced by the same process. .

The next chapter takes costing on a stage further to its use in the pricing of products.

4. Pricing

Every firm needs to recover all its costs, and make a reasonable profit, to survive in the long run. Some firms live through loss-making periods of a year or two, but this partly depends on their liquid resources at the outset. Survival may also depend on their ability and willingness to sell off, or close down, loss-making activities, and on the generation of cash from the sale of surplus assets.

Critical to the health and survival of any firm is the decision of what price to charge its customers for the goods and services it supplies. Obviously the costs a firm incurs are relevant to this decision, but there is more than one way to look at these costs, and there are many other non-cost factors to take into account.

A common approach to pricing is that known as 'cost plus', where a predetermined profit element is added to the total cost of the product or service being sold. The amount of profit to aim for can be determined from a 'full-cost pricing' approach or a 'rate of return pricing' approach, which are now discussed.

Full-Cost Pricing

This system of pricing gets its name from the fact that all costs are charged to products. It is also known as 'absorption cost pricing' because products absorb indirect costs in addition to the direct costs. A profit margin is added as a mark-up on the combined total of direct and indirect costs to obtain the selling price. Therefore we can say:

Selling price = Direct costs +   Share of   + Profit margin
indirect costs

Example

The following data are extracted from the current year's budget of GHI Limited:

	Machine shop	Assembly shop	Finishing shop
Direct labour hours	20,000	18,000	10,000
Hourly wage rate	£3.25	£3.10	£3.00
Production overheads	£70,000	£45,000	£20,000

A customer has requested a quotation for supplying a special piece of equipment, and the estimator has worked out the following details:

Components to be purchased	£216
Materials from store	£270
Direct labour times:	
machining	80 hours
assembling	40 hours
finishing	30 hours
Delivery cost to customer	£ 60

Administration and marketing costs are covered by adding 10% to the cost of manufacture. A further 12.5% is then added to the total (delivered) cost for profit. A calculation of the price to be quoted is required. (LCCI)

From the information supplied, it would appear that GHI Limited use separate hourly recovery rates for the production overheads. These can be calculated as follows:

Machine shop $\dfrac{£70,000}{20,000 \text{ hours}} = £3.50$ per hour

Assembly shop $\dfrac{£45,000}{18,000 \text{ hours}} = £2.50$ per hour

Finishing shop $\dfrac{£20,000}{10,000 \text{ hours}} = £2.00$ per hour

Having determined the overhead recovery rates, the cost data can now be tabulated into a price quotation:

Direct costs:			
materials	– purchased components	216	
	– stores issues	270	486
labour	– machining 80 hrs @ £3.25	260	
	– assembling 40 hrs @ £3.10	124	
	– finishing 30 hrs @ £3.00	90	474
Total direct costs			960
Production overheads:			
machine shop	80 hrs @ £3.50	280	
assembly shop	40 hrs @ £2.50	100	
finishing shop	30 hrs @ £2.00	60	440
Cost of manufacture			1,400
Administration and marketing costs (10%)			140
			1,540
Delivery cost			60
Total cost			1,600
Profit (12.5%)			200
Selling price to be quoted			£1,800

One advantage of this approach is its apparent simplicity, enabling senior management to delegate price fixing to a lower level once recovery rates and profit margins have been set. However, a few words of warning are in order. Both the production and administrative overhead recovery rates are based on budgeted figures for the coming period. By their very nature many of these overheads will be fixed rather than variable. Should the budgeted volume of activity, or the budgeted cost of these overheads change in reality, then the overhead recovery rates cease to be appropriate because the fixed cost per hour will have changed.

Margins and Mark-ups

A further question to address is the size of the profit mark-up to be used. The above example begs the question by stating the mark-up to be applied to total costs for this purpose. It is perhaps appropriate that we digress for a moment to examine the difference between a profit margin based on selling price and a profit mark-up based on total cost. A simple illustration should suffice:

Total cost   80
                        25% profit mark-up on cost
Profit   20
                        20% profit margin on selling price
Selling price   100

Although the money value of profit is the same £20 in both cases, the percentage profit varies because it is calculated on different bases. We now need to consider how this profit is assessed.

Many industries have a normal mark-up peculiar to that particular trade. In retail trade, mark-ups are normally applied to the cost of the goods being resold which, in effect, is at the gross profit level. In the engineering industry, mark-ups may be applied to total costs which relate more to the net profit level.

Whichever way profit is expressed, we cannot assume that firms can charge either the profit mark-up they want, or what is the norm for their industry. If one firm's costs are high it may have to trim its mark-up to remain competitive. If general market conditions are poor then all participating firms in that industry may have to trim prices and profit margins.

In conditions of low demand a firm needs to have a flexible pricing policy and not stick to a rigid profit mark-up on total costs. It is better to make sales at a lower than normal profit, or even at a small loss, than not to make any sales at all. This approach is explained later under marginal cost pricing, and we return to it again in Chapter 12.

The size of the target profit margin is really determined by the required rate of return on capital. Capital comes from the two main sources of shareholders' funds and borrowed capital. Each of these sources has its own cost which can be amalgamated into a weighted average cost of capital. This encapsulates the return required by owners and the interest needed to service any loans.

The required return on capital is therefore the weighted average cost of capital, which varies from firm to firm and industry to industry. Factors influencing the required rate of return are the track record of the company, the perceived risk of its industry, and its future prospects.

Even when two firms have the same required rate of return it does not mean that it will be achieved in an identical way. Some industries are capital intensive and others not. Some industries have a rapid stock turnover rate whilst others have a very long operating cycle from the start of work to eventual payment by the customer.

Contrast in your mind a food supermarket turning over its stocks every two weeks and receiving immediate cash settlement, with a heavy engineering firm taking months to assemble products and then waiting a further two months for settlement. These factors all find expression in a trio of key performance ratios which are more fully discussed in a later chapter. Meanwhile we can say:

Rate of return on = Profit margin × Rate of turnover of
capital p.a.   capital p.a.

  e.g. 20%   = 10%   × 2 times

We can now turn this relationship round to identify the required profit margin:

$$\text{Profit margin} = \frac{\text{Rate of return on capital required}}{\text{Rate of turnover of capital per annum}}$$

using the illustrative figures above:

$$\text{Profit margin} = \frac{20\%}{2} = 10\%$$

This 10% profit margin can therefore be achieved by a mark-up of just over 11% on total costs. On average, should all work be done for their budgeted costs, then an 11% addition to total costs will broadly achieve a 10% profit margin on selling prices.

Rate of Return Pricing

Essentially, rate of return pricing is just another variation on full-cost pricing with the emphasis being transferred from the profit margin to the return on capital. As mentioned earlier, the target return on capital is determined primarily by the weighted average cost of capital which incorporates the cost of loan interest and the return expected by shareholders on all their funds. This target return on capital can be used for long-term price-fixing in the following way:

Example

Haphi Ltd have a target rate of return on capital of 20%. Their total costs are £5m, and capital employed amounts to £2.5m. The percentage mark-up needed to earn a 20% return on capital can be found from the following formula:

$$\text{Target mark-up on total costs} = \text{Target return on capital} \times \frac{\text{Capital employed}}{\text{Total annual costs}}$$

$$= 20\% \times \frac{2.5m}{5.0m}$$

$$= 10\%$$

This can be verified for a 10% mark-up on £5m total costs yields a profit of £0.5m which represents a 20% return on the £2.5m capital employed. A 10% mark-up on total cost is consistent with a 9% profit margin on the £5.5m sales value as follows:

$$\text{Return on capital} = \text{Profit margin} \times \text{Turnover of capital}$$

$$= \frac{£0.5m}{£5.5m}\% \times \frac{£5.5m}{£2.5m}$$

$$20\% = 9\% \times 2.2 \text{ times}$$

When using the rate of return pricing approach, two points should be borne in mind. In a multi-product firm it will be necessary to apportion the capital employed to individual product lines which may inevitably be arbitrary at times. It should also be remembered that the capital employed, and not just total costs, relates to a specific level of output. The amount of working capital included in capital employed will vary roughly pro rata with the volume of production and sales. The capital employed on fixed assets, however, may not vary very much whatever the level of output, provided it is within present capacity limits.

With both full-cost pricing and rate of return pricing, some further points should be remembered. It will also be necessary to apportion fixed costs to individual products irrespective of the general nature of some overheads and the arbitrary way this will be done.

Both pricing methods represent a static rather than a dynamic picture, as they relate to long-term objectives. Prices may have to be discounted to cope with short-term demand conditions. Also, it is not easy to see the effects of changing volumes on prices or profit, hence the marginal costing approach is more useful for firms facing rapidly changing demand conditions.

Marginal Cost Pricing

Marginal costing is the term applied to the separation of total costs into their fixed and variable categories, as described in detail in the following chapter. With marginal costing, fixed costs are not apportioned to individual products but are left as a total sum for the firm. This overcomes the arbitrariness of overhead apportionment inherent in full-cost pricing. When the variable costs of one product are deducted from its sales revenue we get what is termed its 'contribution':

$$\text{Sales revenue} - \text{Variable costs} = \text{Contribution}$$

The contributions of all products go to pay for total fixed costs and provide the profit. The aim of marginal cost pricing is to maximize the contribution towards fixed costs and profit. This approach allows firms to charge different prices in different markets or in changing market conditions. An example of marginal cost pricing is found on the railways when the same journey can have varying prices depending on the time of day, or the season of the year, or the competition from other forms of transport.

It is very easy to say that firms should maximize their contribution, but sales people will find it reassuring to have some target contribution in mind. We can supply the answer by reference to the budgeted plans that firms make to achieve their objectives. Consider the following case:

Example

A firm sets its sales budget at £10m for the coming year, composed of a number of different products. Its fixed costs in various departments come to £2m in total for the year, and a satisfactory return on the capital employed would be £1m. The total contribution required by this firm is therefore £3m, which represents 30% of the total sales value. This 30% figure is often referred to as the 'contribution ratio' or 'profit/volume ratio'. Provided that the sales force are well informed of the contribution earned by each individual product, they can attempt to maximize contribution in the prices they obtain whilst bearing in mind the overall contribution ratio required.

Should the budgeted sales value be subject to some uncertainty, then the contribution ratio could be calculated for varying levels of sales in this way:

Contribution target	£3m	£3m	£3m	£3m
Sales	£8m	£9m	£10m	£11m
Contribution ratio	37.5%	33.3%	30.0%	27.3%

These falling contribution ratio requirements do not mean that the firm should necessarily reduce its prices at higher overall sales levels. Profit-maximizing firms would certainly not do so and it should be borne in mind that a higher profit element is required at higher levels of sales to provide a return on the extra working capital. In reality, therefore, the £3m contribution target will not remain static. The fixed cost element in contribution will, however, remain constant.

Examples of marginal costing applied to pricing in special situations can be found in Chapter 12, dealing with short-term decision making.

Summary

In this chapter we have seen that there are two broad cost-based approaches to pricing. Full-cost pricing says that all costs are charged to individual product lines; direct costs directly so but indirect costs being apportioned in as relevant a manner as possible. To this total of direct and indirect costs is then added a profit element to arrive at the selling price. This profit element is related to the long-term return on capital objective. In the short term, such prices may not necessarily be obtainable due to demand conditions, and few firms stick rigidly to full-cost prices.

The other broad cost-based approach is based on marginal costing principles. This takes the view that fixed costs for the firm should be left as a total sum and not apportioned to individual product lines at all. In this way, the somewhat arbitrary nature of overhead apportionment inherent in full-cost pricing is avoided.

Each product line is said to make a contribution towards the firm's total fixed costs and profit target, as only variable costs are charged against sales. A firm's objective should be to maximize contributions from its sales and not to adhere to rigid full-cost selling prices. Sales personnel are therefore given more flexibility to respond to short-term demand conditions but may be given an overall contribution ratio at which to aim.

Part II
Planning and control

Overview

One description of management views it as a cycle of three key activities, namely:

- Planning   – deciding what to do, who is to do it and when to do it.
- Implementing   – putting the plan into operation.
- Controlling   – monitoring whether the plan is working and taking corrective action when necessary.

This definition of management has obvious relevance to management accounting, and to the second part of this book in particular. The following chapters go on to explain the planning and control techniques of profit/volume planning, standard costing and budgetary control.

Once plans are made, however, they need constant monitoring to highlight any problem areas at an early stage and so allow corrective action to be taken in good time. Much of this book is concerned with financial performance measurements that are used to compare actual results with planned activities.

Some of these measurements may be absolute, as with budgets or standards, when we calculate the variance – the difference between actual and planned values – in money terms. Other financial measurements are relative measures using ratios such as the return on capital employed or the more sophisticated idea of residual income used in decentralized organizations.

First, we turn to profit/volume planning to examine more

closely the link between costs and levels of activity, and so determine how profit varies with fluctuations in the level of output.

5. Profit/volume planning

The basic separation of costs into only two categories – 'fixed' or 'variable' – was briefly mentioned in two previous chapters. This classification of costs by behaviour is at the heart of an accounting technique called 'marginal costing' which has many applications in planning, control and decision making.

We have, of course, already met one application of the technique in the previous chapter dealing with marginal cost pricing. Examples of its use will also be found in later chapters dealing with standard marginal costing, flexible budgeting, short-term decision making and long-term investment. In this particular chapter we will examine the role of marginal costing in profit/volume planning.

The simplistic view of cost behaviour is that fixed costs remain a constant total sum over a range of output levels and that total variable costs increase in linear fashion with output. Both these costs can be combined to show total costs. These start at the level of fixed costs and increase from that point as more and more variable costs are required for the increased output. This situation is shown below:

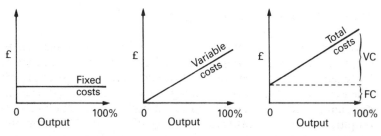

Figure 1: Cost behaviour (simplistic view)

It is clearly not realistic to assume that costs will behave in this fashion over a wide range of output levels. Some fixed costs, such as rent and rates, will be constant from zero output through to maximum capacity. Other fixed costs, like administrative salaries, may increase in a series of stepped rises as staff become unable to cope.

The assumption of linear variable costs is also suspect. Firms expect greater discounts for bulk purchase of goods or materials, which would reduce the slope of the variable cost curve as output increases. Other economies of scale may result from the division of labour but, eventually, diseconomies of scale may set in near maximum capacity with, for example, the use of overtime working.

These two more realistic pictures of fixed and variable costs are now shown below:

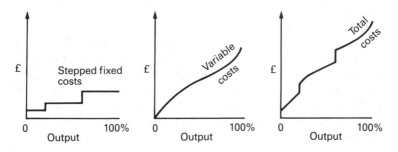

Figure 2: Cost behaviour (realistic view)

Having looked at the non-linearity of costs in real life it may seem surprising that the assumption of linearity still exists, and even more surprising that we are about to make the same assumption! The reason for this is that although cost linearity, as shown in diagram A below, is patently untrue at both low or high levels of output, it could be realistic for the range of output levels normally concerning a particular firm.

The range of output levels of practical significance to a firm is referred to as the 'relevant range'. The total cost is shown in diagram B below to be linear within that range.

Figure 3: (A) Linear costs   *(B) Non-linear costs*

A similar assumption of linearity is also made for sales revenue. It would be quite feasible to draw the sales revenue curve with a decreasing slope at higher output depicting the possible need to reduce unit price to achieve greater volume sales. Within the relevant range of output for a firm, it could be that the unit sales price is constant and hence the total revenue curve is assumed to be linear throughout. This is illustrated as follows:

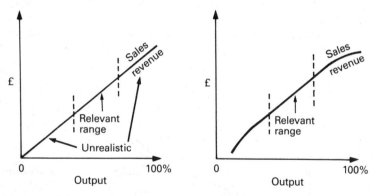

Figure 4: Sales revenue curves

Break-Even Analysis

The study of the relationship of costs and sales revenue to various levels of sales volume is often referred to as 'cost/profit/volume analysis' or 'break-even analysis'. With the proviso that it is looking at a short-term situation where fixed costs and unit variable cost are unlikely to change within the relevant range, break-even analysis can be a useful planning technique for managers.

Break-Even Chart

We start our look at break-even analysis with a single product break-even chart. This will allow us to see at a glance how profit or loss varies with the change in volume. It is also useful in depicting the approximate effects of a change in the cost structure, say, a switch from manual labour to automatic machinery which reduces variable costs but increases fixed costs.

Example

A firm makes only one product which sells for £10. The variable cost per unit is £5 and fixed costs total £75,000 per annum. Maximum capacity would be about 25,000 units per annum but the firm normally operates around the 80% capacity level.

The following diagram shows the break-even chart drawn from this information:

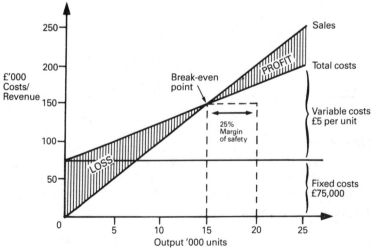

Figure 5: Break-even chart

Break-even is reached at 15,000 units when sales revenue exactly equals the total costs of £150,000. Output of less than this amount results in a loss, whilst greater output makes a profit. The size of the profit or loss at any output can be read off the graph at a glance. To do this we use the scale on the vertical axis to evaluate the gap between the total cost line and the sales line.

Margin of Safety

Also represented on the break-even chart is the 'margin of safety' which represents the amount by which output can fall from its present level back to the break-even point. This cushion, or safety margin, is usually expressed as a percentage and gives management an idea of how far they are away from a loss-making situation.

In the example illustrated, the present level of output of 20,000 units can fall by 25% (5,000 units) before a loss would result.

Calculation of Break-Even Point

If our firm happened to be operating below the break-even level at the present time, then we could use the graph to calculate the percentage increase in sales needed to return to a profit-making situation. If sales were, say, only 10,000 units at present, then an increase of 5,000 units, equivalent to a 50% increase, would be needed to get back to the break-even point. Alternatively, we can calculate the break-even point.

If we assume that selling prices and variable costs are linear, then we can also assume that total sales revenue and total variable costs will move pro rata with sales volume. This means that every sale will yield a constant surplus of revenue over its variable cost. The special name we give to this surplus is that of 'contribution', and it is of fundamental importance in marginal costing.

Contribution = Sales − Variable costs

The notion of contribution applies both to an individual unit sale and also to total sales. In the above break-even example a selling price of £10 was assumed, together with a unit variable cost of £5 and fixed costs of £75,000 per annum. If we sell a product for £10 that has a variable cost of only £5, then we are gaining a contribution of £5 from each unit sale. The number of sales we need to pay for our fixed costs equals the number of £5's needed to make up £75,000, being 15,000 units. We can therefore say:

$$\text{Break-even point} = \frac{\text{Fixed costs}}{\text{Contribution per unit}}$$

$$= \frac{£75,000}{£5}$$

$$= 15,000 \text{ units.}$$

Calculation of Target Volume

If we need to know what volume of sales will yield a certain target profit, then we extend the above break-even analysis by adding profit to the fixed costs, and so find the total contribution required.

Using the same example but now also assuming that the firm wants to make a profit of £30,000 per annum, the total contribution required will equal £105,000. As each unit sale contributes £5, then 21,000 unit sales will be needed to achieve the target profit of £30,000 as follows:

$$\text{Target volume} = \frac{\text{Fixed costs} + \text{Required profit}}{\text{Contribution per unit}}$$

$$= \frac{£75,000 + £30,000}{£5}$$

$$= 21,000 \text{ units.}$$

Contribution Ratio

Instead of expressing the break-even point or target volume in numbers of units, it is equally possible to express them in sales revenue terms. This uses the concept of 'contribution ratio' which measures the proportion of contribution to sales as either a percentage or as a decimal.

Taking the same example of a £5 contribution on a £10 selling price this gives a contribution ratio of 50% (or 0.5 when expressed in decimal terms) as follows:

$$\text{Contribution ratio} \quad = \quad \frac{\text{Contribution}}{\text{Sales price}} \%$$

$$= \quad \frac{£5}{£10} \%$$

$$= \quad 50 \%$$

Target Sales Value

The sales value necessary to earn any required contribution is found by dividing that contribution by the contribution ratio when expressed as a decimal. Continuing with the same example, when a target profit of £30,000 is required in addition to recovering the £75,000 fixed costs we find:

$$\text{Target sales value} \quad = \quad \frac{\text{Total contribution required}}{\text{Contribution ratio}}$$

$$= \quad \frac{£105,000}{0.5}$$

$$= \quad £210,000$$

Operating Gearing

The angle at which the total cost line crosses the sales line on a break-even chart is called the 'angle of incidence'. Large fixed costs relative to sales value will result in a wide angle, whilst a low level of fixed costs to sales value will result in a narrow angle.

The significance of this angle is in the speed with which losses or profits accumulate when output changes. A large angle of incidence depletes profit more rapidly than a small angle, when sales volume falls. Conversely, profits are made more quickly with a large angle when sales volume rises.

These relationships are also expressed in what is termed 'operating gearing' which quantifies how much effect a given change in sales will have on profit. To find the operating gearing we divide the contribution by the net profit:

Example

Assume that a firm makes a contribution of £80,000 and a net profit of £20,000. What is the operating gearing ratio?

$$\text{Operating gearing} = \frac{\text{Contribution}}{\text{Profit}}$$

$$= \frac{£80,000}{£20,000}$$

$$= 4 \text{ times}$$

The application of this gearing figure is a fourfold change in profit for any given change in sales. If, for instance, sales were to fall by 10% then there would be a 40% (10% × 4 gearing ratio) drop in profit as a consequence.

We can now look at an example which applies many of the above techniques:

Example

The following standard cost statement relates to a product which sells for £100 per tonne:

	per tonne £	
Direct materials	30.00	
Direct wages	20.00	
Variable overhead	10.00	
	60.00	
Fixed overhead	20.00	(based on output of
Total cost	80.00	3,000 tonnes)

You are required to calculate:

    (i)   the break-even point (a graph is not required)
    (ii)   the contribution to sales ratio
    (iii) the margin of safety
    (iv) the percentage increase in profit if sales volume is increased by 10 per cent
    (v)   the extra tonnes to be sold in order to maintain the existing profit level if the selling price is reduced by 10 per cent.

(LCCI)

(i)   Unit contribution = selling price − variable cost
$$= £100 - £60$$
$$= £40 \text{ per unit.}$$

Break-even point $= \dfrac{\text{fixed costs}}{\text{contribution per unit}}$

$$= \frac{£60,000}{£40} = 1,500 \text{ tonnes}$$

(ii)   Contribution to sales ratio $= \dfrac{\text{contribution per unit}}{\text{selling price per unit}} \%$

$$= \frac{£40}{£100} \% = 40\%$$

(iii) Margin of safety $= \dfrac{\text{present output} - \text{break-even point}}{\text{present output}} \%$

$$= \frac{(3,000 - 1,500)}{3,000} \% = 50\%$$

(iv) % profit increase = % increase in sales × operating gearing ratio

$$= 10\% \times \frac{\text{contribution}}{\text{profit}}$$

$$= 10\% \times \frac{£40}{£20} = 20\%$$

(v)   Existing profit level =   £20 × 3,000 tonnes = £60,000

$$\text{Target sales} = \frac{\text{total contribution required}}{\text{new contribution per unit}}$$

$$= \frac{£60,000 + £60,000}{£30} = 4,000 \text{ tonnes}$$

Contribution Break-Even Chart

The original break-even chart made no mention of contribution. It is possible to redraw the same information in a slightly modified form to show the contribution made at all levels of activity. The following diagram presents the original break-even example in the form of a contribution break-even chart:

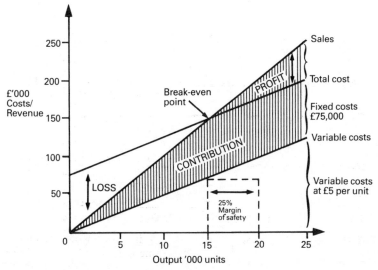

Figure 6: Contribution break-even chart

This chart shows contribution increasing with volume sales but also shows the identical profit, loss, break-even point and safety margin, as the original break-even chart.

Planning for Change

One of the uses of break-even charts is to examine the possible effects of a change in any of the data, be it a different selling price or a change in cost structure. Take, for example, the original situation of a selling price of £10 with a unit variable cost of £5 and fixed costs of £75,000 per annum. This information is now amended to show the effects of an increase in selling price to £12 per unit.

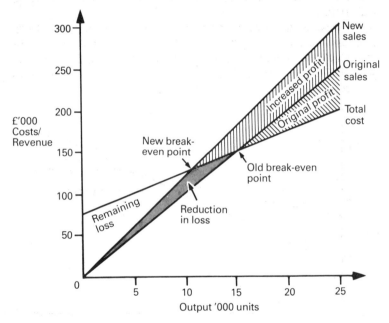

Figure 7: Effect of changed selling price

The shaded area between the original sales line and the new sales line shows the reduced loss/increased profit that would result from such a move. It also shows the reduction in the break-even point brought about by the higher unit sales price. What it does not predict, of course, is the number of sales that would be achieved at a higher price. To answer that question would require some market research and an estimate of the so-called 'price elasticity of demand'. The concept of price elasticity examines the relationship of sales volume to different selling prices and thus helps marketing people decide on pricing policy.

Break-even charts can also show the effects on profits of any change in the cost structure. The example of a switch from manual labour (variable cost) to automated production (fixed cost) is a case in point. This situation would show as an increase in fixed costs coupled with a reduction in variable costs, so that the total cost line would start at a higher point but rise at a less steep slope than before.

The before and after situations are shown in figure 8 below. It gives an indication of whether such a change would be worthwhile and what sales volume is needed for savings in variable costs to cover the increase in fixed costs. In this case, sales volume needs to exceed 12,000 before it would be worthwhile.

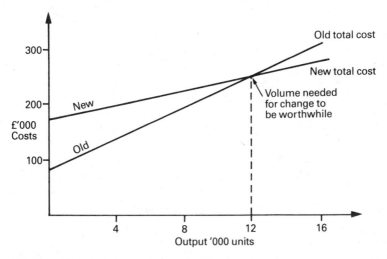

Figure 8: Changed cost structure

Multi-Product Chart

Previous examples and discussion of break-even charts have been limited to single-product situations which, in practice, are hard to find. Very few firms supply only one product and, although a break-even chart can be drawn for one product in a multi-product firm, the problem of fixed cost apportionment inherent in the system of absorption costing remains.

It is perfectly feasible to draw a break-even chart for the whole product range, the only difference in the layout of the chart being that the horizontal axis needs to be scaled in terms of total sales revenue rather than units of products. This is because the products may be very dissimilar, and adding them together in unit terms may be likened to mixing chalk and cheese!

Example

Let us take the case of a two-product firm where the following information applies:

		Product A	Product B	Total
	Sales quantity	10,000	2,000	
	Sales price	£10	£50	
	Variable cost per unit	£5	£35	
	Sales revenue	£100,000	£100,000	£200,000
Less:	Variable costs	£50,000	£70,000	£120,000
	Contribution	£50,000	£30,000	£80,000
Less:	Fixed costs			£60,000
	Profit			£20,000

This information is laid out in the following break-even chart, showing that break-even is achieved when sales revenue equals £150,000 for the two products combined.

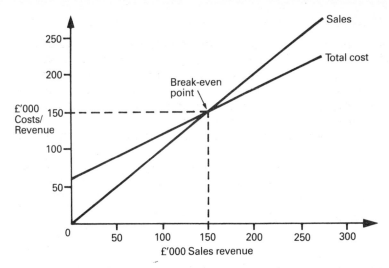

Figure 9: Multi-product break-even chart

The weakness of this presentation is that the chart shows the profit or loss at various levels of sales but it assumes the same proportionate mix throughout. Should those proportions change, then a new break-even chart is required.

Profit/Volume Chart

We have looked at two alternative forms of break-even chart and it is possible to simplify them by drawing a chart showing either the profit or loss at various levels of output. It is therefore similar to a break-even chart without the sales and cost lines.

To draw such a chart we plot the value of profits and losses on the vertical axis and the level of activity along the horizontal axis. If we take the same information as used in the original break-even chart then the profit/volume chart shown below is the result:

This shows break-even to be achieved at exactly the same level of sales, i.e. 15,000 units, as on the break-even chart. At zero sales the loss will amount to the £75,000 fixed costs whilst the profit at maximum output will be £50,000.

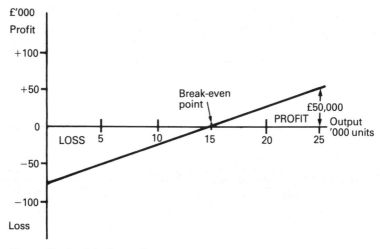

Figure 10: Profit/volume chart

Summary

When relating costs or profit to volume we need to identify which costs are fixed and which are variable with output. We can then express this information on charts to readily show the profit or loss at any particular output level, in addition to the break-even point.

The classification of costs into these fixed and variable categories also allows us to identify the contribution a product makes towards fixed costs and profit. Contribution is a key concept in accounting and comprises the sales value less variable costs only.

The break-even point and the volume required to make a target profit can both be calculated by dividing the total contribution required by the contribution per unit.

When contribution is expressed as a percentage of sales value, we get the 'contribution ratio' or 'profit/volume ratio' as it is sometimes called. This is used as a measure of product profitability in other chapters, but here it is used to calculate target sales value and the operating gearing ratio.

We return to this analysis of costs by behaviour and the concept of contribution numerous times in later chapters. Standard marginal costing, flexible budgeting and short-term decision making are all based on these ideas, as we shall see.

6. Standard costing I

Standard costing is the name given to a detailed accounting technique, the aim of which is to plan and control both costs and revenue, and hence profit. It is centred on the products of mass-production industries where a repetitive manufacturing or processing activity is carried out. The list of industries where it can be applied is endless, but includes brewing, food, paper, textiles, electrical goods, furniture, clothing, chemicals, pharmaceuticals, car components and building materials, to name but a few.

The standard cost of a product is the total cost of direct labour and materials plus a share of overheads that should be incurred in the production process. Standard costing is the continuous comparison of the standard costs with the actual costs of the products. This comparison may take place daily, weekly or even monthly. Inevitably, differences will occur between the standard and actual results, so these are examined for their causes in order to improve future performance.

There are a number of advantages claimed for standard costing:

- Setting up standards requires a thorough review of materials used and methods of operation.
- Continuous monitoring engenders cost consciousness and increases motivation if standards are realistic.
- It frees senior management from day-to-day routine when 'management by exception' is practised.
- It provides a firm basis for price fixing and stock valuation.

The Control Cycle

Control is one of a small number of key management functions and is often described as a cycle of five sequential stages. Standard costing is an excellent example of one such control cycle and we go on to examine its five stages. These can be expressed in the following diagrammatic way:

Standard costing control cycle

1 SETTING STANDARDS OF PERFORMANCE	→	2 DEFINING PERFORMANCE MEASUREMENTS	→	3 MEASURING ACTUAL PERFORMANCE	→	4 COMPARING ACTUAL WITH STANDARDS

5 TAKING CORRECTIVE ACTION IF NECESSARY

The conclusions we draw from these five stages are that:

1 Setting standards of performance means the preparation of a standard cost specification for each and every product to be included in the standard costing system.
2 Defining performance measurements is the identification of the detailed variances to be used for this purpose.
3 Measuring actual performance is the recording of actual costs and revenue for each product.
4 Comparing actual with standards identifies any significant variances to draw to management's attention.
5 Taking corrective action, if and when necessary, completes the control cycle.

Standard Cost Specification

The setting of direct labour and material standards involves determining the best layout, methods of operation and most suitable materials for the job. This is where management science plays a role in the person of an industrial engineer bringing techniques like method study, work measurement and value analysis into play.

When first applying standard costing to any product the starting point is to specify quantities and grades of the labour and material elements, and to include an apportionment of budgeted overheads to arrive at the total standard cost. This standard cost specification will nowadays usually be set out on a standard cost card or sheet, and stored in a computer system.

The setting-up process may yield economies over existing costs due to the painstaking investigation of all aspects of operations. Such economies may also occur when standards are occasionally revised in the light of changed working conditions.

When setting standards, it is important that they are realistic. There is no point in setting 'ideal' standards that are only capable of achievement under perfect conditions, without waste, breakdowns, disputes or other disruptions. The more realistic standards are called 'expected standards' as they reflect what can reasonably be expected to be achieved within the timescale of the budget year.

Example

The following standard cost data refer to one unit of Product GR 49:

Direct material costs:	
material M77	9.0 kilos at £2.67 per kilo
M210	12 units at £6.90 per unit
material reclamation allowed	1.8 kilos at £0.90 per kilo
Direct labour:	
machining	10.5 hours at £4 per hour
assembly	3.6 hours at £3.50 per hour
Variable overhead:	
machining	£1.40 per direct labour hour
assembly	70% of direct labour cost
Fixed overhead:	
machining normal capacity	40,000 labour hours per year
annual budget	£100,000
assembly normal capacity	200,000 labour hours per year
annual budget	£60,000

The standard cost sheet is required for Product GR49 to show the total standard cost of one unit and the profit when the unit selling price is £200.   (Certified Diploma)

It is helpful to set out the standard cost sheet in a similar order quoting quantities, unit cost and value for each element of cost.

Fixed overhead absorption rates need to be calculated from the annual budget information of the two departments if the standard cost is based on absorption costing. An alternative marginal costing approach will be discussed in a later chapter. If the unit sales price is also included, the profit or loss is simply the difference between the total standard cost and the standard selling price.

Standard cost sheet for product GR49 (one unit)

	Quantity	Rate	Value	Total
Direct material costs:				
material M77	9.0 kilos	£2.67	£24.03	
M210	12 units	£6.90	£82.80	
material reclamation	1.8 kilos	£0.90	(£1.62)	£105.21
Direct labour:				
machining	10.5 hrs	£4.00	£42.00	
assembly	3.6 hrs	£3.50	£12.60	£54.60
Variable overhead:				
machining	10.5 hrs	£1.40	£14.70	
assembly	70% × 3.6 hrs	£3.50	£ 8.82	£23.52
Fixed overhead:				
machining	10.5 hrs	£2.50	£26.25	
assembly	3.6 hrs	£0.30	£ 1.08	£27.33
Total standard cost				£210.66
Loss per unit				(£10.66)
Standard selling price				£200.00

The total standard cost is seen to be £210.66, which is more than the selling price of £200 per unit. The resulting loss is therefore £10.66 per unit, which demands immediate management action.

Variances

Periodically, the actual costs of labour, materials and overheads are compared with the predetermined standards laid down in the specification. Differences are almost bound to occur, and the accounting term for them is variances, which is given the symbol letter (F) when favourable or (A) when adverse. Favourable variances are so called because they increase the expected profit, whilst adverse variances reduce profits.

These variances arise because either the quantity and/or cost of the resources used differs from what should have been consumed for that amount of production. Management have to decide which variances are relevant to their situation, and those selected become performance measurements for that firm.

Basically, there are only two main types of variance: those relating to the unit price of labour, material and overhead resources, and those relating to the quantity or volume of resources consumed. We now examine both these types by reference to material M77 in the standard cost specification above:

Example

Suppose the firm made 100 products last week using 920 kilos of material M77 which it purchased at £2.50 per kilo. We want to compare this actual cost of material with the standard cost specified to identify any variance, as follows:

Standard cost of M77   =   900 (i.e. 100 × 9)   kilos × £2.67 = £2,403
Actual cost of M77   =   920   kilos × £2.50 = £2,300

Total material M77 cost variance   = £103(F)

This variance of £103 results from two causes and not just one. On one hand, extra costs are incurred by using 20 kilos of material more than specified for that level of production. When these 20 kilos are priced at the standard price, the excess cost amounts to £53.40(A) which is called the material usage variance. On the other hand, the firm bought the material more cheaply than it expected, and saved 17p on each of the 920 kilos used. This resulted in what is called a material price variance of £156.40(F).

In summary, therefore, we can say that the firm saved £156.40 on the buying-in price of material M77 but that it used £53.40 too much in quantity. These two separate variances net off against each other, as one is favourable and the other adverse, to comprise the total material cost variance as follows:

Material price variance	=	£156.40(F)
Material usage variance	=	£53.40(A)
Total material cost variance	=	£103.00(F)

Variances for other costs and for sales can be similarly divided into two main types relating to price and volume, although they are given different names. A full list of these basic variances is given in the box below based on an absorption costing approach.

Types of basic variances

Element	Price variance	Volume variance
Direct materials	Material price	Material usage
Direct labour	Labour rate	Labour efficiency
Variable overheads	Variable overhead expenditure	Variable overhead efficiency
Fixed overheads	Fixed overhead expenditure	Fixed overhead volume
Sales	Sales price	Sales margin volume

Before we look at a more comprehensive example we need to define each variance carefully and explain the reasons why they occur in more general terms. Various symbols are used in the formula and these are based on the following key:

A = Actual S = Standard P = Price Q = Quantity

C = Cost B = Budgeted SAR = Standard Absorption Rate

O/H = Overhead

( ) = difference between, irrespective of whether (+) or (−).

Materials

The 'material price variance' represents the difference between the actual and the standard purchase prices of material for the total quantity purchased. Unlike other variances, which are calculated at the time production takes place, this variance is normally calculated at the time of purchase.

$$\text{Formula: } (AP - SP)\ AQ$$

Example

When the 920 kilos of material M77 were actually bought in at £2.50 as opposed to the standard price of £2.67, the calculation is:

$$
\begin{aligned}
\text{Material price variance} \quad &= \quad (AP - SP) \quad \times \quad AQ \\
&= \quad (£2.50 - £2.67) \quad \times \quad 920 = £156.40(F)
\end{aligned}
$$

This material price variance is the responsibility of the buyer or purchasing officer. Reasons why the variance occurred could include a switch to a new supplier, a fall in market price, extra discount received or a lower quality of material purchased.

If the material price variance is calculated at the time of purchase, it is because the materials are put into stock at their standard cost. When they are subsequently issued to production, there will be no price variance at that point of time.

The 'material usage variance' represents the difference in the cost of material used that is caused by its more, or less, efficient use compared to that specified. It is important to note that the principle of flexible budgeting is applied to materials and all other variable costs in standard costing. This means that whatever the level of actual production turns out to be, we compare the actual cost of any variable cost with its flexed budgeted cost.

The material usage variance is calculated from the difference between the actual quantity of material used and the standard quantity specified for that level of production. This quantity difference is evaluated at the standard price because any difference in the actual price is subsumed in the material price variance.

$$\text{Formula: } (AQ - SQ)\ SP$$

Example

The above firm used 920 kilos of material M77 instead of the 900 kilos specified for the 100 products made. The calculation is:

Material usage variance =   (AQ − SQ)   ×   SP
$\qquad\qquad\qquad\qquad$ =   (920 − 900)   ×   £2.67 = £53.40(A)

This material usage variance could be the responsibility of the buyer if sub-standard material were to blame, but normally the responsibility lies with the production supervisor or manager. Other possible reasons for the variance include machine faults, unskilled labour, poor supervision and mishandling.

Where a number of materials are combined in a mix, as, say, with chemicals, then it is useful to analyse the material usage variance into two further parts called mix and yield variances. We examine this situation in the next chapter.

Labour

The 'labour rate variance' represents the difference in direct labour cost caused by any variations from the standard rates of pay, and is akin to the material price variance, using the same formula. It is calculated from the difference between the actual and standard rate per hour multiplied by the actual number of hours paid. Where more than one grade of labour is employed then a labour rate variance will be calculated for each one.

Formula: (AP − SP) AQ

Example

The standard machining time allowed for one unit of Product GR49 is 10.5 hours at a standard rate of pay of £4 per hour. When 100 units were made last week they took 1,120 hours to complete and were paid at £3.60 per hour. The calculation is:

Labour rate variance = (AP − SP) × AQ
= (£3.60 − £4.00) × 1,120 = £448.00(F)

Responsibility for this variance would lie with the production supervisor if he had switched to a lower grade of labour. It is unlikely that the reduced rate is the result of collective bargaining, but in any new permanent situation the standard cost specification should be revised.

The 'labour efficiency variance' represents the difference in labour cost caused by the degree of efficiency in the use of labour compared with the standard specified. Again, it is akin to the material usage variance and is calculated the same way.

Formula: (AQ − SQ) SP

This firm should have used 1,050 hours to produce the 100 units, taking 10.5 hours for each one. It actually took 1,120 hours to complete production. The calculation is:

Labour efficiency variance = (AQ − SQ) × SP
= (1,120 − 1,050) × £4.00
= £280.00(A)

In summary, therefore, the firm has saved £168 on the cost of labour overall. The £448 saved by paying a lower than normal rate per hour has been partially offset by paying £280 for the excess hours worked. The total labour cost variance can be summarized as follows:

Labour rate variance	£448 (F)
Labour efficiency variance	£280 (A)
Total labour cost variance	£168 (F)

Variable Overheads

These are overheads whose total cost should vary pro rata with the level of production, as opposed to fixed overheads whose total cost remains constant irrespective of fluctuations in production levels.

The 'variable overhead expenditure variance' represents the difference between the actual cost of the variable overheads and the total amount recovered on the actual level of production at the standard absorption rate. It is calculated from the difference between the actual variable overheads and the quantity of output multiplied by the standard absorption rate per unit:

$$\text{Formula: AC} - (\text{AQ} \times \text{SAR})$$

Assuming for the moment that variable overheads are recovered at the rate of £14.70 per unit of product, then the total recovery amounts to £1,470 for the 100 products. If the actual variable overheads cost £1,555 then we get the following calculation:

Variable overhead expenditure variance =	AC −	(AQ × SAR)
=	£1,555 −	(100 × £14.70)
=	£85(A)	

Because variable overheads are supposed to vary with the level of production, this variance represents the difference in spending between actual cost and the standard cost allowed for that level of production. However, where variable overheads are absorbed on a direct labour-hour basis, it is possible that there are two reasons for the variation in variable overhead costs. One reason is the above, namely that the actual overheads cost more or less than expected. The other reason is that the direct labour carried out its work with a greater or lesser degree of efficiency than allowed in the standard cost specification. This results in a 'variable overhead efficiency variance'.

Example

We will again assume that the actual variable overheads cost £1,555 in total, but this time the variable overhead standard absorption rate was set at £1.40 per labour hour for machining. Each product was allowed

10.5 hours for completion. The variable overhead expenditure variance now becomes:

$$\text{Actual cost} - (\text{Actual hours} \times \text{Standard absorption rate})$$
$$£1,555 - (1,120 \times £1.40) = £13.00(F)$$

The variable overhead efficiency variance represents:

$$(\text{Actual labour hours} - \text{Standard labour hours}) \quad \times \text{SAR}$$
$$(1,120 - 1,050) \quad \times £1.40$$
$$= £98.00(A)$$

The total variable overhead variance is now seen to be composed of two elements:

Variable overhead expenditure variance	= £13(F)
Variable overhead efficiency variance	= £98(A)
Total variable overhead variance	= £85(A)

The £13 favourable variance represents a saving in the actual cost of the overheads incurred whilst the adverse efficiency variance of £98 represents the extra cost of spending too long on the work and mirrors the direct labour efficiency variance.

Fixed Overheads

There are also two reasons why fixed overheads can vary from the standard cost allowed. On the one hand, the actual cost of the fixed overheads can turn out to be more than that budgeted, say, when a higher rate bill than expected is received from the local authority. On the other hand, fixed overheads are recovered on the basis of a standard absorption rate of £x per product or per hour. When the level of production exceeds that budgeted, then more overheads will be recovered than are actually incurred. This leads to a favourable fixed overhead volume variance. The converse is also possible when a shortfall in production leads to an under-recovery of overheads because the standard absorption rate anticipated overheads being spread over more units of production.

The 'fixed overhead expenditure variance' represents the difference between the actual cost and the budgeted cost:

Formula: $(\text{AC} - \text{BC})$

Example

Suppose the actual fixed overheads for the machining department were £2,800 whilst the budgeted cost was £2,887, then the fixed overhead expenditure variance is £87(F).

The 'fixed overhead volume variance' represents the under- or over-recovery of fixed overheads caused by the actual volume of production varying from the budgeted volume used to set the standard absorption rate. When this standard absorption rate is based on a unit of production (as opposed to an hourly rate), the volume variance is calculated from the difference between actual and budgeted volume multiplied by the standard absorption rate per unit.

$$\text{Formula: } (AQ - BQ)\ SAR$$

Example

Assume the standard absorption rate for machining fixed overheads was £26.25 per unit of product irrespective of hours taken to produce it. The budgeted level of production last month was 110 products but only 100 were actually produced.

The fixed overhead volume variance is therefore:

$$
\begin{aligned}
(AQ - SQ) &\times SAR \\
(100 - 110) &\times £26.25 = £262.50(A)
\end{aligned}
$$

When fixed overheads are absorbed on the basis of an hourly rate then the above volume variance is composed of two separate elements which can be independently evaluated. On the one hand, the under- or over-recovery is affected by the actual level of production compared to that budgeted. This is known as the capacity variance. On the other hand, the overhead recovery is also affected by the actual number of hours taken to produce the goods compared to the standard hours allowed. This part is known as the efficiency variance. Together, the capacity and efficiency variances make up the volume variance.

Sales

Variances occur when sales are made at non-standard prices and/ or when the actual volume of sales differs from the budgeted level. In this latter case it is the profit margin which is gained or lost on the extra or lost sales.

The 'sales price variance' represents the profit lost or gained by selling at a non-standard price. It is calculated from the difference between the actual and standard selling price multiplied by the actual sales quantity.

$$\text{Formula: } (AP - SP)\, AQ$$

Example

The standard selling price of Product GR49 is £200 but £205 was achieved because smaller than normal discounts were allowed. During the month, 100 products were sold. The sales price variance is:

$$
\begin{array}{ll}
(AP - SP) & \times\ \ AQ \\
(£205 - £200) & \times\ \ 100 = £500(F)
\end{array}
$$

The 'sales volume variance' represents the profit margins gained or lost on the variation in sales from the budgeted level. It is calculated from the standard profit margin multiplied by the difference between actual sales volume and budgeted sales volume.

$$\text{Formula: } (AQ - BQ) \times \text{Standard profit margin}$$

Example

The sales volume was budgeted at 110 but turned out to be only 100 last month. The standard profit margin is £13.26. The sales volume variance is:

$$
\begin{array}{lll}
(AQ - BQ) & \times & \text{Standard profit margin} \\
(100 - 110) & \times & £13.26 = £132.60(A)
\end{array}
$$

The total of these two sales variances does not measure the difference in sales value between budgeted sales and actual sales. It does measure the difference in the profit earned that is brought about through sales effort, either by selling at a non-standard price, or by selling a different quantity to that budgeted.

Summary

This chapter introduced the idea of yardsticks being set, needed against which future performance can be measured. Standard costing can thus be seen as an example of the control cycle which applies in other areas of management.

Standards can be set for each cost element, and for sales, for both prices and volume. When actual results are compared to these standards, we get both price and volume variances. Favourable variances explain how extra profit was gained, whilst adverse variances show how profit was lost. This aspect is taken further in the following chapter when we look at management control statements.

The variances we have encountered so far provide a good grounding for most standard costing systems. However, it should not be assumed that all standard costing systems will use the exact same basis. Firms use the system that suits their industry, their costing methods and their management requirements best.

As mentioned earlier, the variable overhead variances depend on the way that overheads are absorbed by products. Fixed overhead volume variances are capable of sub-division into capacity and efficiency variances. In certain industries, the material volume variance is capable of further analysis into mix and yield variances, as explained in the next chapter. Labour efficiency is also capable of more breakdown into the root causes.

In this chapter, variance analysis was based on the assumption of an absorption costing system being used. An alternative approach is to base the standards on a marginal costing approach, which is also examined in the next chapter.

7. Standard costing II

In the previous chapter we have seen how standard costing sets yardsticks, or standards of performance, in money terms. Actual results are compared with these predetermined yardsticks and variances identified which, if significant, lead to managerial action. In this way the control cycle is completed.

Management do not always have time to sift through large quantities of detailed cost variances, and want information in a global or summarized form. One way to satisfy this need is to calculate standard costing ratios which measure aspects of overall efficiency and activity. Another way is to produce a management control statement on profit and loss account lines. We now look at these ideas in turn before returning to variances of a more distinct nature.

Standard Costing Ratios

A later chapter examines the use of accounting ratios to measure aspects of company performance and liquidity. At this point we are restricting our discussion to measures of company performance associated with the standard costing technique, additional to the variances already discussed.

Central to these other measures is the concept of the 'standard hour' which represents the amount of work which can be done in one hour under standard conditions. This standard hour is a useful common denominator with which to aggregate different operations and different products.

With this definition we can measure the operating efficiency of a firm by relating the 'standard hours equivalent of the work produced' to the actual hours taken:

$$\text{Efficiency ratio} \quad = \quad \frac{\text{standard hours produced}}{\text{actual hours worked}} \times \frac{100}{1}\%$$

Example

Suppose last week a firm took 500 actual hours to produce goods equivalent to 450 standard hours. The efficiency ratio is:

$$\frac{450}{500} \times \frac{100}{1} \% = 90\%$$

It is theoretically possible for the efficiency ratio to reach 100% or even exceed it. Much will depend on the realism of the standards and the motivation (including payment incentives) of the labour force. Like many other ratios it is a comparison with previous performance that may inform most.

Another ratio is used to measure the 'level of activity' as opposed to the level of efficiency with which that activity was carried out. The 'activity ratio' relates the actual work produced to the budgeted work for that period, both being expressed in standard hours.

$$\text{Activity ratio} = \frac{\text{standard hours produced}}{\text{budgeted standard hours}} \times \frac{100}{1} \%$$

Example

Taking the same example where the actual standard hours produced were 450, let us now assume that there were 475 budgeted standard hours. The calculation is:

$$\frac{450}{475} \times \frac{100}{1} \% = 94.7\%$$

The activity ratio of 94.7% measures the shortfall from the budgeted level of activity, i.e. 100%.

A third ratio measures 'capacity usage' by relating the actual hours worked to the budgeted standard hours.

$$\text{Capacity ratio} = \frac{\text{actual hours worked}}{\text{budgeted standard hours}} \times \frac{100}{1}\%$$

Example

Using the same figures from the previous illustrations, when 500 actual hours were worked but the firm had budgeted for 475 standard hours, the calculation is:

$$\frac{500}{475} \times \frac{100}{1}\% = 105.3\%$$

This capacity ratio indicates that more hours were worked than planned whereas the activity ratio states that less production was achieved than planned. This apparent anomaly is explained by the efficiency ratio which states that more time was taken on production than should have been taken.

We now turn our attention to another way of measuring overall performance which combines budgeted profit, variances and actual profit in one explanatory statement to management.

Management Control Statement

The variances we examined in the previous chapter all rely on the preparation of budgets and standards which detail costs, income and output. This means that a firm operating budgetary control and standard costing systems should be able to predict the future profit from its trading operations.

If the sales and cost variances are negligible then the actual profit made will more or less equate with the budgeted profit. Any significant variances will radically affect the profit actually achieved, but the nature of the particular variance will give a good guide to its possible causes. Adverse variances reduce the actual profit from the budgeted level, whilst favourable variances enhance it.

A common practice is to incorporate standard costing variances into a management control statement. This takes the form of a standard costing profit and loss account, reconciling the budgeted profit with the actual profit achieved. The reasons why the actual profit varies from the budgeted level are contained in the cost and sales variances which replace the absolute values of costs and sales found in a conventional profit and loss account. A comprehensive example based on a 'standard absorption costing system' now illustrates this approach.

Example

Carr Chemicals Ltd are a one-product firm. The company uses a standard absorption costing system and prepared the following budget for last month which was expected to result in a profit of £7,000.

Budget for last month

	£	units	£
Sales at £6 per unit		10,000	60,000
Direct materials			
10,000 kilos at £1 per kilo	10,000		
Direct labour			
5,000 hours at £4.80 per hour	24,000		
Variable overheads			
10,000 units at 50p each unit	5,000		
Fixed overheads			
£7,000 per week (70p per unit)	7,000		
Total cost of sales		10,000	46,000
Budgeted profit at standard profit margin of £1.40			£14,000

Unfortunately, Carr Chemicals did not produce and sell as many products as they had planned, yet made a greater profit. The actual results were:

Actual results for last month

	£	units	£
Sales at £6.20 per unit		9,000	55,800
Direct materials			
9,500 kilos at 90p per kilo	8,550		
Direct labour			
4,500 hours at £4.90 per hour	22,050		
Variable overheads	4,000		

Fixed overheads	6,500		
Total cost of sales		9,000	41,100
Actual profit			£14,700

We can now draw up a statement reconciling the actual profit of £14,700 with the £14,000 budgeted profit by detailing the adverse or favourable variances for the month. These variances explain how the extra profit was achieved. Management examining this statement are not asked to look at absolute cost and sales values, but are pinpointed to the deviations from planned activities. If they consider any variance to be significant it can be discussed and/or further examined to see if anything can be learned to improve future performance.

Standard costing profit and loss account

	(F)	(A)	£
Budgeted profit for the month			14,000
Variances:			
Sales price variance (£6.00–£6.20) 9,000	1,800		
Sales margin volume variance (9,000–10,000) £1.40		1,400	
Material price variance (£1.00–£0.90) 9,500	950		
Material usage variance (9,500–9,000) £1.00		500	
Labour rate variance (£4.90–£4.80) 4,500		450	
Labour efficiency variance (4,500–4,500) £4.80	–	–	
Variable overhead expenditure variance £4,000–(9,000 × 50p)	500		
Fixed overhead expenditure variance (£6,500–£7,000)	500		
Fixed overhead volume variance (9,000–10,000) 70p		700	
	3,750	3,050	700(F)
Actual profit for the month			£14,700

(Note that the standard quantity of material and labour used in the material usage and labour efficiency variances respectively are based on the quantities that should have been used for the actual level of production i.e. 9,000 products. In other words, a flexed budget approach is used to quantify the standards for labour, materials and also variable overheads.)

This example, and all discussion on variances in the previous chapter, were based on an absorption costing basis as opposed to a marginal cost basis. It is equally possible to base standards on this latter approach.

Standard Marginal Costing

Referring back to the original budget for Carr Chemicals, we find that the standard profit amounted to £1.40 per product and the fixed overheads were budgeted at 70p per product. The actual output turned out to be 1,000 products less than the quantity expected and, therefore, the firm would lose £2.10 on each of the 1,000 sales shortfall, making £2,100 in total.

Standard absorption costing separates the effects of this shortfall into two variances which quantify the lost profit and the under-recovery of overheads as:

		£
Sales margin volume variance	=	1,400(A)
Fixed overhead volume variance	=	700(A)
Total	=	£2,100(A)

These two separate variances were included in the standard costing profit and loss account illustrated above, but it would have been equally valid to combine them in a marginal costing approach.

Marginal costing, you may recall, does not apportion fixed overheads to products but takes the view that products make a contribution towards fixed costs and profit. In brief we can say:

Sales − Variable costs = Contribution

and   Contribution = Fixed costs + Profit

Standard marginal costing combines the lost profit and under-recovery of overheads on the 1,000 units in the one contribution volume variance. Using the same example from Carr Chemicals above, we find:

Contribution volume variance   =   (AQ − BQ) × Unit contribution
                                     =   (9,000 − 10,000) × £2.10
                                     =   £2,100(A)

The final effect is the same for both standard marginal and standard absorption costing, because each shows that the 1,000 lost sales resulted in a reduction in profit of £2,100.

A third and final approach to standard costing systems is to restrict the calculation of standards to direct costs only. Variances would therefore be limited to those pertaining to direct materials, direct labour and direct expenses. This would leave overheads to be controlled by a system of fixed departmental budgets with the option of flexible budgets should the situation demand it.

We now return to look at variances of a more detailed nature than those encountered in the previous chapter. These will apply to some firms only, but give an indication of the further analysis which can be obtained.

Material Mix and Yield Variances

In certain processes a number of different materials are combined together to make a particular product. Where the materials include chemicals and/or liquids it may be perfectly normal for some wastage or evaporation to occur. This scenario gives rise to two further reasons why the actual costs of products may differ from their standard costs.

When different chemicals are combined together in a mix, they will not be combined on an *ad hoc* basis, but in specific ratios one to another. It will be very unlikely that all ingredients have identical costs and therefore any variation from the proportions laid down as standard will affect the total cost of materials. This is referred to as a 'mix variance' and is a sub-variance of the material usage variance.

Example

Suppose two liquids A and B are normally combined together in the standard proportions of 50:50 with no loss in process. Their prices are £1 and £2 per litre respectively. Last week they were combined in the non-standard proportion of 45:55, and 1,000 litres of acceptable product were made.

We now want to compare the actual cost of the inputs with the standard cost to identify the difference in cost attributable to the change in mix proportions. Both sets of quantities are priced at the standard prices per litre, because any variations from standard would be disclosed in the material price variances.

Material	Standard input	Actual input	Difference	Standard price	Cost
	litres	litres	litres	£	£
A	500	450	−50	1.00	50(F)
B	500	550	+50	2.00	100(A)
Total	1,000	1,000	Nil	–	£50(A)

The material mix variance amounts to £50 adverse, being the extra cost of materials due to using more of the dearer material B and less of the cheaper material A, compared to the standard proportions.

Returning to our original scenario, the other possible reason why the material cost of processes may differ from standard is when evaporation or wastage occur in process. Although a standard loss is allowed in standard cost specifications, there is every likelihood that the actual loss will be different. The 'material yield variance' quantifies this abnormal gain or loss in money terms.

Example

Returning to the example above let us now assume that a 20% loss in process is regarded as normal, so that inputs of 1,000 litres are expected to yield only 800 litres of final product. Last week's input of 1,000 litres resulted in, say, 780 litres of saleable product.

There is a shortfall of 20 litres of product which needs to be valued at the standard cost per input litre:

Standard cost per litre of standard mix

				£
Material A	500	litres at £1	=	500
Material B	500	litres at £2	=	1,000
Total input	1,000			£1,500
Standard loss	200			
Standard yield	800	litres at cost of		£1,500

Therefore cost per input litre $= \dfrac{£1,500}{1,000} = £1.50$ per litre

The material yield variance amounts to 20 litres at a standard cost of £1.50 per litre which equals £30.00 adverse. Like the mix variance, this yield variance is also a sub-variance of the material usage variance.

We can summarize the material cost variances with the aid of a simple diagram. Basically there is a material price variance and a material usage variance, with the latter breaking down further into a material mix variance and a material yield variance.

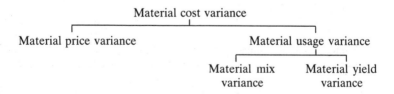

Now we can combine all these variances in one illustration:

Example

An adhesives firm makes one of its products, 'Tac', from a mixture of three chemicals T, A and C which are combined together in the specified ratio of 1:2:3. Each mix comprises 1,200kg of materials and is expected to yield 1,080kg of 'Tac' after the standard loss of 10% is allowed.

The standard mix is:

		kg			£
Chemical:	T	200	at £2.00 =		400
	A	400	at £1.00 =		400
	C	600	at £0.50 =		300
Standard input		1,200			£1,100
Standard loss 10%		120			
Standard production of 'Tac'		1,080			

The actual results for last week were:

		kg			£
Chemical:	T	1,600	at £1.90 =		3,040
	A	4,800	at £1.10 =		5,280
	C	6,800	at £0.60 =		4,080
Actual input		13,200			£12,400
Actual loss		2,400			
Actual production of 'Tac'		10,800			

The total material cost variance compares the actual cost of £12,400 with the standard cost of the actual output. As one mix comprises one tenth of the actual production then the standard cost amounts to £11,000 (i.e. £1,100 × 10).

Total material cost = variance	Standard cost of production	−	Actual cost of production
=	£11,000	−	£12,400
=	£1,400(A)		

This total material cost variance can now be broken down into a material price variance and a material usage variance, which can itself be divided into mix and yield sub-variances.

The material price variance compares the actual unit price of each chemical with its standard unit price for the actual quantity of material used as follows:

Material price variance	=	(Standard price −	Actual) price	×	Actual quantity		£
T	=	(£2.00 − £1.90)		×	1,600 kg	=	160(F)
A	=	(£1.00 − £1.10)		×	4,800 kg	=	480(A)
C	=	(£0.50 − £0.60)		×	6,800 kg	=	680(A)
Total material price variance						=	£1,000(A)

This firm has paid £1,000 more for the ingredients used in making Tac than the standard cost specification allowed. If these materials have been held in store for some time it may be that the material price variance was taken into account at the time of purchase. In this case materials are held in store at their standard price, and when issued to production there will be no further price variance.

The material usage variance compares the actual quantities of materials used with the standard quantities that should have been used to get the actual output. Any differences are then priced at the standard price of each material as follows:

Material	Actual input kg	Standard input kg	Difference kg	Standard price £	Variance £
T	1,600	2,000	400(F)	2.00	800(F)
A	4,800	4,000	800(A)	1.00	800(A)
C	6,800	6,000	800(A)	0.50	400(A)
	13,200	12,000			£400(A)
Loss	2,400	1,200			
Output	10,800	10,800			

The material usage variance is £400 adverse overall for the three ingredients. This is partly caused by using the chemicals in a non-standard ratio and also by having an abnormally high loss in process. We now want to evaluate these two causes separately by calculating the mix and yield variances.

The material mix variance follows a somewhat similar approach to the usage variance with one important difference. Now the actual inputs of chemicals are compared with the same total input in their standard proportions. Any variations are evaluated at the standard price as follows:

Material	Actual input	Standard input	Difference	Standard price	Variance
	kg	kg	kg	£	£
T	1,600	2,200	−600	2.00	1,200(F)
A	4,800	4,400	+400	1.00	400(A)
C	6,800	6,600	+200	0.50	100(A)
Total input	13,200	13,200			£700(F)

The material mix variance therefore amounts to £700 favourable. We can now conclude that because the three materials were used in a different ratio to standard, this firm saved £700. But this is not the full story. Possibly because the materials were combined in a non-standard way, the actual output was well below that expected. We now want to quantify the cost of this abnormal loss in process, in the form of the material yield variance:

In the original information about the standard mix of Tac we were told that 1,200kg of standard mix input cost £1,100 so that:

$$\text{Standard cost of 1kg input} = \frac{£1,100}{1,200 \text{ kg}} = £0.917 \text{ per kg}$$

$$
\begin{aligned}
\text{Yield variance} &= (\text{Actual} - \text{Standard}) \times \text{Standard cost} \\
&\quad\ \ \text{loss} \quad\ \ \text{loss} \qquad\quad \text{per kg input} \\
&= (2,400 - 1,200) \times £0.917 \\
&= £1,100(A)
\end{aligned}
$$

Summarizing all the variances in the simple diagram described earlier we find:

Total material cost variance £1,400(A)

Material price variance		Material usage variance
£1,000(A)	+	£400(A)
Material mix		Material yield
variance £700(F)	+	variance £1,100(A)

Summary

The previous chapter introduced basic variance analysis as a way of explaining and controlling variations in costs and revenues from budgeted levels. This chapter has continued the discussion on standard costing in a few more ways.

First we examined the use by management of standard cost information as a monitoring and control device. This can be done in a global way by using ratios based on the concept of the standard hour and also by the preparation of standard costing profit and loss accounts.

Next we looked at the basis of the costing system underlying the standard cost system and found that standard costs can be based on absorption, marginal, or direct cost principles. Obviously there are differences in the types of variance that can be extracted from these different systems. Their basic purpose to control performance, however, remains the same.

Finally, we looked at materials as an example of how more detailed variances can be calculated than those initially described in the previous chapter. Here the material mix and yield variances were used to illustrate how material usage can be further analysed. It is also possible to analyse labour and overheads in further detail in many situations, but this is outside the scope of this book.

Standard costing is primarily a planning and control system based on product lines. We now go on to discuss budgetary control, which is a complementary planning and control system based on functions and departments.

8. Budgetary control I

There are many similarities between a system of budgetary control and the standard costing technique described in the previous two chapters. Both are concerned with the planning and control of operations by a continuous monitoring of actual results against those budgeted. Any significant variances arising from this comparison are then subject to further investigation and management action as appropriate.

Much detailed preparatory work is common to both budgetary control and standard costing as they are both concerned with detailed costs and revenues. Where the two systems differ is in the unit of application. Standard costing is product based, where the standard costs, particularly for overheads, are not confined to one single department but straddle a number of departments. Budgets, on the other hand, are prepared for differing functions, each of which is likely to mirror the departmentally based structure of the firm.

Corporate strategy and strategic planning are concerned with the broad objectives of the firm over a future time scale of a few years. Budgetary control, however, is often described as the expression of detailed financial plans to meet corporate objectives. These plans are essentially short term for the coming months up to one year ahead. They are based on short-term objectives such as a target return on capital, a sales value or a certain percentage share of the market. These short-term plans must, of course, be compatible with the longer term corporate objectives.

By the use of budgeting systems, senior management can carry out their roles of delegating, co-ordinating, controlling and motivating. Responsibility is delegated to departmental managers who can see how their function fits into the global plan and who should be motivated to achieve targets, provided they have not been imposed without consultation. Using this system, senior management can delegate responsibility and concentrate on deviations from plans without getting bogged down in day-to-day activities that are running smoothly. They are therefore practising the principle of 'management by exception'.

Organizing for Budgetary Control

It is the responsibility of top management, personified in the board of directors in a private sector company, to specify the broad objectives for the coming year. These are communicated to a budget committee comprising representatives of both the board and key functional managers. This committee then interprets these objectives into outline plans for each departmental head who, in turn, submits his/her detailed proposals.

This process may have to be repeated a number of times to get the necessary integration and co-ordination of the individual budget proposals into a viable state. The detailed procedures to be followed, coding numbers, inflation policy and similar matters should all find expression in a budget manual which is issued to each manager involved.

Budget preparation

When finally accepted by the budget committee, the functional budgets are aggregated into a master budget consisting of monthly profit and loss accounts, a balance sheet at the year end and a statement of sources and applications of funds for the year. If approved by the board, this becomes the policy to be pursued for the coming year.

In many firms this procedure outlined in the figure below is assisted by an accountant or budget officer who provides information and advice to all concerned. Regrettably, in some firms the complete system of budgetary control is run by accountants for accountants and imposed on other managers without proper consultation. Consequently the technique loses much of its motivating appeal as it is very important for it to be seen and implemented as a management tool.

Identification of the Key Factor

The starting point with budgeting is to identify the key or limiting factor which restricts the firm's growth at this moment in time. In most firms this key factor will be sales volume, but it could equally be a shortage of space, skilled labour, raw materials, machinery or even working capital. Assuming sales is the key or limiting factor for a firm, this places the major responsibility for budgeting on the shoulders of the sales manager or director, as all other functions will be geared to this level of activity.

The sequential budgeting process can be shown in the diagram on page 110.

We now examine each of these budget statements in turn to see the principles on which they are prepared and the most suitable layout with which to express them.

Sales Budget

This budget is not just one total sales figure for the coming year, but must be broken down and classified by:

```
┌─────────────────────────────┐
│        SALES BUDGET         │
│  Analysed by products, areas, │
│    customers and months.     │
└─────────────────────────────┘
              │
              ▼
┌─────────────────────────────┐
│      OPERATIONS BUDGET      │
│    Analysed by products,    │
│    departments and months.   │
└─────────────────────────────┘
```

| MATERIALS PURCHASE BUDGET | MANPOWER BUDGET | MACHINERY UTILIZATION BUDGET |

```
┌─────────────────────────────┐
│         DEPARTMENTAL         │
│     PRODUCTION COST         │
│           BUDGETS            │
└─────────────────────────────┘
              │
              ▼
┌─────────────────────────────┐
│         DEPARTMENTAL         │
│   ADMINISTRATION COST       │
│           BUDGETS            │
└─────────────────────────────┘
              │
              ▼
┌─────────────────────────────┐
│         DEPARTMENTAL         │
│  SELLING AND DISTRIBUTION   │
│        COST BUDGETS          │
└─────────────────────────────┘
              │
              ▼
┌─────────────────────────────┐
│  RESEARCH AND DEVELOPMENT    │
│           BUDGET             │
└─────────────────────────────┘
              │
              ▼
┌─────────────────────────────┐
│        MASTER BUDGETS       │
│   Profit and loss account,   │
│       balance sheet and      │
│ sources and applications of funds. │
└─────────────────────────────┘
              │
              ▼
┌─────────────────────────────┐
│   SPECIAL FINANCIAL BUDGETS  │
│        Cash budget,          │
│   capital expenditure budget. │
└─────────────────────────────┘
```

- individual product lines
- differing distribution channels e.g. wholesale, retail
- sales areas or regions
- months in which sales will occur

An extract from such a budget, with random figures, could be set out in the following matrix manner which is a layout applicable to many other budgets:

Sales budget for 198–

Product:		*Jan*	*Feb*	*Mar*	*Apr*	*May*	*Jun*	*etc.*	*Total*
P1 units '000		10	10	10	11	12	11		132
value £000		20	20	20	22	24	22		264
wholesale	£000	12	13	13	12	14	12		150
retail	£000	8	7	7	10	10	10		114
area 1	£000	6	5	6	7	8	7		84
area 2	£000	9	9	8	10	9	8		114
area 3	£000	5	6	6	5	7	7		66

P2 repeat as above

Information to compile a sales budget for an existing business will be drawn from many sources, including:

- current sales level
- past seasonal trends
- sales representatives' reports
- market research, economic trends
- price/demand relationships

Production Budget

On the assumption that sales is the key or limiting factor, then the production/operations level is determined by the sales budget quantities. When production capacity is insufficient then resort may be made to subcontracting. Assuming capacity is sufficient, then the production levels are determined by the length of the production/operations cycle, target stock levels and the month in which the sale is budgeted to occur.

Example

Using the sales volumes for product P1 in the sales budget above, let us assume that the product takes one month to complete and the firm carries sufficient finished goods stock at any month end to satisfy all the budgeted sales in the following month. Assuming stock on 1 January was 8,000 units, the production budget can now be set out in the following way:

Production budget for 198– ('000 units)

	Jan	Feb	Mar	Apr	May	Jun	etc.	Total
Closing stock	10	10	11	12	11			
Sales during month	10	10	10	11	12			
	20	20	21	23	23			
Less: Opening stock	8	10	10	11	12			
Completed production required	12	10	11	12	11			

Once the production/operations budget is determined, the resources of materials, manpower and machinery needed to carry out such production can be determined.

Materials Purchase Budget

There are two main purposes of this particular budget. Advance warning of global requirements for the coming year enables the buying department to arrange supplies on the best possible terms to ensure delivery, quality and the most competitive price. It also provides essential information to feed into the cash budget at a later stage.

A purchase budget follows a very similar pattern to a production budget when both opening and closing stocks, in addition to the materials consumed in the production process, are taken into account.

Example

The formula for a chemical product 'Zedell' is:
  50% of 'Zed' costing £2.50 per kilogram
  25% of 'Ell' costing £2.00 per kilogram
  25% of water by weight (no loss of weight in process)
The ingredients required for production in a particular month are bought in the preceding month and the month's output is sold in the following month. The sales forecast is as follows:

Month	kg
June	6,500
July	7,000
August	8,000
September	6,500
October	6,000

The separate quantities and cost values of Zed and Ell are required for purchases in each of the three months, May, June and July.   (LCCI)

The material content of the sales quantities can be derived as follows:

Sales Forecast	Zedell kg	50% Zed	25% Ell
June	6,500	3,250	1,625
July	7,000	3,500	1,750
August	8,000	4,000	2,000
September	6,500	3,250	1,625
October	6,000	3,000	1,500

Taking into account that materials are purchased two months before the sale of the finished product takes place, then the material purchase quantities and values are:

Material purchase budget

	Zed		Ell	
	kg	£	kg	£
May	3,500	8,750	1,750	3,500
June	4,000	10,000	2,000	4,000
July	3,250	8,125	1,625	3,250

Manpower Budget

This aims to tell the personnel department the manpower requirements for the coming year so that adequate recruitment, training or retraining can take place. It also feeds information into the production cost and cash budgets.

Example

The members of the budget committee of BCD (Engineers) Limited are working on the preparation of budgets for the year commencing 1 January 198–. As management accountant, you are assisting the personnel manager in the preparation of that section of his budget which relates to direct operatives, based on the production budget which has already been approved by the committee. The following details are available:

Machine budget centre

Component	Quantity (units)	Standard labour hours per unit
A1	53,000	2
A2	52,500	2
B1	39,000	2
B2	39,500	4

Assembly budget centre

Product		
A	52,000	3
B	39,000	4

Relaxation has been allowed for in the establishment of standard hours.

A 40-hour week will be worked throughout the 52 weeks of the year and no overtime is envisaged. Each employee is entitled to 20 days holiday (including 5 days public holidays) and is expected to average 5 days absence through sickness. The 40-hour week consists of 5 days of 8 hours.

A calculation of the number of direct operatives to be employed, to the nearest whole number, is required for each of the two budget centres.

(LCCI)

In this example the number of effective working hours per man year is 47 weeks × 40 hours = 1,880 hours per annum, excluding the odd extra day in each year. We can therefore multiply the units produced by the hours taken per unit to get the total hours required. These total hours are divided by the effective working hours per annum for one man. The computations are as follows:

Machine budget centre

Component	Quantity (units)		Hours per unit		Total hours
A1	53,000	×	2	=	106,000
A2	52,500	×	2	=	105,000
B1	39,000	×	2	=	78,000
B2	39,500	×	4	=	158,000
					447,000

$$\text{Manpower required} = \frac{447,000}{1,880} = 238 \text{ persons}$$

Assembly budget centre

Product	Quantity (units)		Hours per unit		Total hours
A	52,000	×	3	=	156,000
B	39,000	×	4	=	156,000
					312,000

$$\text{Manpower required} = \frac{312,000}{1,880} = 166 \text{ persons}$$

Machinery Utilization Budget

The procedure for calculating machine time requirements follows an identical pattern to that of the above manpower budget. The resultant information is used to determine if any new asset purchases are required after allowance has been made for down-time due to routine maintenance and breakdowns. This mirrors the allowances built into the manpower budget for sickness and holidays.

Production Cost Budget

This summarizes the cost of resources consumed by each separate production department and includes direct costs and indirect costs. The complete budget feeds into both the budgeted profit and loss account (after allowing for stock changes) and the cash budget.

A suitable layout for a departmental production cost budget is:

Departmental production cost budget

£000	Jan	Feb	Mar	Apr	May	Jun	etc.	Total
Direct costs:								
labour								
materials								
expenses								
Total direct costs								
Indirect costs:								
labour								
salaries								
materials								
expenses								
depreciation								
Total indirect costs								
Total departmental costs								

Departmental Administration, Selling and Distribution Cost Budgets

These all comprise indirect costs for the firm and can be displayed in the same manner as the indirect costs in the production cost budgets above. The level of each budget should not just be an inflated figure from the previous year but a genuine attempt to measure the resources needed to give the level of service demanded from the department.

In the case of administrative costs this may be achieved by a zero-based budgeting approach. This literally starts from scratch with no prior assumptions, and lists the resources required to perform various functional tasks. These tasks can then be placed in order of priority and the budget prepared on the basis of what is deemed essential, or how far the money allocated will stretch.

The selling and distribution departments' budgets are directly linked to the level of activity contained in the sales budget. Some selling and distribution costs may be fixed in nature irrespective of the exact level of activity, whilst other costs may vary directly with the level of sales. The following example illustrates this approach and includes some sample figures:

Selling and distribution cost budget

	Jan	Feb	Mar	Apr	May	etc.
Sales quantity '000 units	20	20	25	30	30	
Variable costs: £000						
sales commission at 10%	2.0	2.0	2.5	3.0	3.0	
vehicle fuel and servicing	0.4	0.4	0.5	0.6	0.6	
Fixed costs:						
basic salesmen's salaries	9.0	9.0	9.0	9.0	9.0	
advertising	6.0	6.0	6.0	6.0	6.0	
office salaries	8.0	8.0	8.0	8.0	8.0	
drivers' wages	9.0	9.0	9.0	9.0	9.0	
vehicle standing charges	5.0	5.0	5.0	5.0	5.0	
Total budget	39.4	39.4	40.0	40.6	40.6	

Budget Reports

The accounting year is the natural choice for the budgeting process, although it is broken down into months for regular comparison with budgeted figures. These months may be of calendar or lunar variety, or some other constant working period. This avoids distorted comparisons due to the incidence of works and statutory holidays. Some firms also work on a rolling year, adding a new month's budget as each month passes.

The comparison of actual results with budget takes place on two different time planes. Each departmental manager is fed information about the costs (and income) under his control on a regular basis, normally every month. This monthly report compares actual costs/income with budgeted costs/income for the month under review and for the cumulative months of the accounting year so far elapsed. The following pro forma illustrates this approach:

Month:		Typical Monthly Budget Report					Dept.
Cost code	Description	Current month			Cumulative		
		Budget £	Actual £	Variance £	Budget £	Actual £	Variance £
612	Salaries	5,200	5,400	+ 200	15,600	16,100	+ 500

Controllable Costs

A problem often arises in budgeting which is somewhat similar to the problem met in a subsequent chapter on responsibility accounting for decentralized organizations. Reduced to its basics, the problem amounts to how far to go in recharging costs to cost centres for budgeting and monitoring purposes.

When costs actually incurred by a departmental manager are charged against that same department, there is a strong motivating element at work. However, when the cost centre is charged with apportioned establishment charges over which the departmental manager has little control, if any, then the practice may have a demotivating effect. On the other hand, if all costs are not charged or apportioned to departments then the cost of functional activities are understated and a manager may be unaware of the true cost of his function's existence.

A compromise might seem to be to report back at two levels. The first stage of the budget-monitoring report should include controllable fixed and variable costs which are agreed to be the direct responsibility of the departmental manager. The second stage of the report can include apportioned general overheads which are not seen as the direct responsibility of the departmental manager. In this way, both purposes are served. The departmental manager can concentrate on the controllable costs which are his prime responsibility, and at the same time be aware of the remaining costs incurred on behalf of his department.

Research and Development Budget

Normal accountancy policy, as expressed in Statement of Standard

Accounting Practice No. 13, is that revenue expenditure on research and development activities is charged to the profit and loss account as and when incurred. This would include depreciation on fixed assets, which are themselves shown in the balance sheet statement.

Many firms think of research and development as just another overhead and allocate a small percentage of income to cater for its costs. It is perfectly feasible to think of research and development as just another department, to budget for it in the same way as administrative, selling and distribution expenses and to subject it to the same kind of monthly report back.

Such practice will provide useful global feedback on the elements of costs, but misses the distinguishing feature of this kind of expense. From a control and report-back point of view, research and development has much in common with capital expenditure. In both cases, money is committed to individual projects which may take years rather than weeks to complete.

What is useful in both cases is additional information on the nature of expenditure on each individual project, together with an estimate, where possible, of the further expenditure required until completion. The former provides valuable information to each project manager and department head on the state of each project, whilst the latter allows top management to exercise judgement on the continued viability of particular projects.

Summary

Up to this point we have seen how budgets are set for individual departments or functions, all integrated towards common objectives set by top management. In the next chapter we see how these detailed budgets are drawn together in master plans for the firm as a whole, and how such global plans can be tested for their viability.

9. Budgetary control II

The previous chapter examined the organization of budgetary control and showed how functional budgets are developed and integrated, starting with the key or limiting factor. Such functional budgets are used to monitor progress and feed information back to the manager concerned by a regular comparison with actual results.

We now want to look at the way top management and accountants draw all the detailed budgets together to obtain an overall view of both viability and performance.

Master Budgets

These are so called because they summarize the detailed transactions contained in the various functional budgets and look at them from different points of view. The budgeted profit and loss account summarizes the planned income and expenditure month by month to arrive at the budgeted profit for the year. A typical example would look like the table opposite.

A number of tests for viability can now be carried out on the budgeted profit figures to see if the projected trading results are acceptable. These would include an examination of the absolute monthly and yearly profit figures with the same period in the previous year. Comparisons can also be made with profit objectives laid down by top management. Use is also likely to be made of ratio analysis to quantify profit margins, return on capital, and rate of turnover of capital. These ideas are explored in the following chapter.

Just as departmental budgets are subject to constant monitoring as the budgeted year progresses, so will the budgeted profit and loss account be compared with the actual result for the same month and with the cumulative total to date. Where a manufac-

Budgeted profit and loss account

		Jan	*Feb*	*Mar*	*Apr*	*May*	*Jun*	*etc.*	*Total*
Sales	£000	100	100	100	110	115	110		
Less:									
direct labour		12	12	12	13	13	13		
direct materials		20	20	20	22	23	22		
direct expenses		2	2	2	2	2	2		
production overheads		15	15	15	15	16	15		
administration costs		10	10	10	10	10	10		
selling costs		12	12	12	13	14	13		
distribution costs		15	15	15	17	19	17		
Total costs		86	86	86	92	97	92		
Profit/(Loss)		14	14	14	18	18	18		

turing or processing firm uses standard costing, then a different type of profit and loss account can be prepared showing the reasons why the actual profit differs from that budgeted. This was explained in the previous chapter on standard costing.

A budgeted balance sheet will also be projected for the end of the budget year showing the assets owned and the sources of finance with which they were acquired. This statement is required to calculate the projected profitability of operations and also to do various tests on the liquidity and capital structure resulting from a further year's trading. A typical balance sheet in vertical 1981 Companies Act format would look like the table on page 122.

The final statement making up the trio of master budgets is the budgeted statement of sources and applications of funds. This could be projected monthly, but even the yearly statement will provide valuable information for management. In essence, this is a statement about cash flow, summarizing the different ways cash has been received during the period and the ways in which it has been used.

The balancing figure between total inflows and outflows of cash represents the change in the liquidity position. Identification of the main causes of liquidity problems and the size of the potential problem are both obtainable from this statement. It is therefore of great use to management in pinpointing candidates for remedial treatment.

Budgeted balance sheet

	£000	£000
Fixed assets		2,000
Current assets:		
stocks and work-in-progress	3,000	
debtors	1,500	
bank balance and cash	500	
	5,000	
Less: creditors due within one year	2,000	
Net current assets (working capital)		3,000
Total net assets (capital employed)		5,000
Less: creditors due after one year		1,000
Share capital and reserves		4,000

The format of the statement as laid down in Standard Statement of Accounting Practice No. 10 is as follows:

Statement of sources and application of funds

	£000	£000
Sources of funds:		
profit before tax		105
add back depreciation		15
Total cash generated from trading operations:		120
Other sources:		
issue of new shares		45
new loan		15
Total sources of funds:		180
Less: Applications of funds:		
payment of tax	40	
payment of dividend	35	
purchase of fixed assets	50	
		125
Increase in working capital		55

Comprising:

increase in stocks	47
increase in debtors	30
increase in creditors	(2)
increase in liquid funds	5
	55

Special Financial Budgets

These comprise the cash budget and the capital expenditure budget and are primarily working tools for the accountant, although summarized information from both may be fed to top management.

Taking the cash budget first, this is a very detailed statement showing all the planned receipts and payments of cash for the coming year broken down into monthly intervals. It therefore quantifies any potential surpluses or deficits of cash, and their expected duration, in time for any necessary action to be implemented.

Unlike the statement of sources and applications of funds, it does not summarize the reasons for the monthly surplus or deficit. For example, purchases are shown as a cash payment in the month when actually paid without distinguishing between materials consumed and those remaining in stock. The sources and application of funds statement separates this one transaction and charges materials consumed against profit whilst showing any change in stocks as a movement of working capital.

A cash budget includes all revenue and capital transactions with one exception. Purchases of fixed assets are included in the cash budget whereas depreciation on them is not. To do otherwise would be to 'doublecount' the same transaction, but, even more important, it would ignore the fact that depreciation is not a cash expense but a notional expense designed to spread the initial cost over a number of years' profit and loss accounts.

The two important things to remember when compiling a cash budget are to ignore depreciation and to allow the necessary time lags on credit transactions. The following example will illustrate:

Example

You have been presented with the following information relating to Midas Ltd.

Forecast trading and profit and loss account

	Jul £	Aug £	Sept £	Oct £	Nov £	Dec £	Total £
Sales	30,000	25,000	26,000	28,000	30,000	40,000	179,000
Less purchases	15,000	12,500	13,000	14,000	15,000	20,000	89,500
Gross profit	15,000	12,500	13,000	14,000	15,000	20,000	89,500
Wages	9,000	9,200	8,500	9,500	9,600	12,000	
Expenses	3,000	3,600	7,000	4,000	3,000	3,100	
Depreciation	1,500	1,500	1,500	1,500	1,500	1,500	
	13,500	14,300	17,000	15,000	14,100	16,600	90,500
Net profit (loss)	1,500	(1,800)	(4,000)	(1,000)	900	3,400	(1,000)

No account has been taken of cash discounts allowable or receivable in the above figures.

As the company's future is uncertain, you have been asked by the Sales Director to prepare a cash forecast for the six months to 31 December given the following additional information:

(i)	Sales	– 50% of sales are made for cash; 30% are settled in the month following the month of sale and are subject to a 2% prompt settlement discount; the remaining 20% is received the following month.
(ii)	Purchases	– the company's policy is to pay suppliers in the month of delivery, claiming a 5% discount.
(iii)	Wages and expenses	– are paid in the month to which they relate.
(iv)	It is anticipated that, during the six months, the following receipts and payments will occur:	
	August	– sale proceeds from the disposal of freehold property £40,000.
	September	– sale proceeds from disposal of investments £6,100

– rent on leaseback of premises sold in August now payable at £6,000 per annum, payable half-yearly in advance.

November   – purchase of machinery £7,500.

(v)   The company's bank balance at 1 July is £7,500 overdrawn.

(vi)   Sales for May and June amount to £18,000 and £21,000 respectively.

(IOM)

The cash forecast/budget can be laid out in a matrix format similar to the profit and loss account. However, the individual items are not the same. Each month the cumulative cash position can be determined and the continued viability, or otherwise, of the company ascertained:

Cash forecast/budget

	Jul £	*Aug* £	*Sept* £	*Oct* £	*Nov* £	*Dec* £
Cash in:						
Cash sales	15,000	12,500	13,000	14,000	15,000	20,000
Credit sales						
net of discount	6,174	8,820	7,350	7,644	8,232	8,820
	3,600	4,200	6,000	5,000	5,200	5,600
Asset sales		40,000	6,100			
Total cash in	24,774	65,520	32,450	26,644	28,432	34,420
Cash out:						
purchases (net)	14,250	11,875	12,350	13,300	14,250	19,000
wages	9,000	9,200	8,500	9,500	9,600	12,000
expenses	3,000	3,600	7,000	4,000	3,000	3,100
rent			3,000			
machinery					7,500	
Total cash out	26,250	24,675	30,850	26,800	34,350	34,100
Monthly +/(−)	(1,476)	40,845	1,600	(156)	(5,918)	320
Cumulative balance	(8,976)	31,869	33,469	33,313	27,395	27,715

Our interpretation of the cumulative cash balance is that the initial bank overdraft of £7,500 ceases to be a problem in August when the once-and-for-all sale and leaseback is expected to take place. Thereafter, the cash balance remains strongly positive despite the increasing working capital requirement brought on by rising sales. In the event of the property sale not taking place, however, this would have serious consequences for the level of overdraft required.

The trading and profit and loss account paints a gloomier picture. There is a net loss in three months out of six and a marginal loss of £1,000 in total for the period. Although Midas Ltd can survive this scale of loss for a number of years it would find it difficult to attract new capital and hence its long-term survival is open to question.

Capital Expenditure Budget

As mentioned earlier in the chapter, this budget has a close affinity with the budgeting of research and development activities. The total spend requires monitoring, and individual project spending projected to completion also needs watching carefully to avoid any serious overspends.

The techniques of individual project appraisal are discussed in the final chapters dealing with investment appraisal. There it is explained how the profitability of investments is assessed using discounted cash flow techniques, which also assist us in choosing between competing projects.

Before any selection can take place, top management have to decide how much capital to make available for the coming year. Because of the long-term nature of many investments, they will also have to give serious thought to more than one year ahead so that projects, once started, are not starved of funds before completion in a subsequent year.

Sources of funds for capital expenditure include:

- Depreciation provision for the year on existing fixed assets
- Sales of scrap and surplus/redundant assets
- Grants
- New loans or share issues

To some extent a chicken-and-egg situation can exist, with top management not knowing how much capital to put into the pool without knowing the investment requirements of line management. This is partly answered by their own corporate strategy. If, say, they want to pursue growth by expansion or acquisition, then they must allocate sufficient funds for that purpose.

When compiling the total capital budget for the coming year, a useful way forward is to categorize various types of investment and allocate funds to programme areas before selecting the individual projects that can proceed:

Investment category	Amount requested £	Amount allocated £	%
Legal/safety requirements	20,000	20,000	100.0
Replacement vehicles	100,000	80,000	80.0
Cost saving/efficiency	250,000	170,000	68.0
New products	500,000	500,000	100.0
Totals	870,000	770,000	88.5%

The implication of the above budget is that top management agree that the company must meet its legal and safety obligations in full. They are also fully committed to implementing the new products which are probably part of their corporate strategy. This means that the other two categories must be cut back as the total amount requested exceeds by £100,000 the £770,000 capital that is available for investment.

Notwithstanding that regular replacement of vehicles is company policy, they are prepared to trim this category back in the light of other demands for capital this year. The same observation applies to cost-saving investments where there is insufficient capital being made available to allow all viable projects to proceed. Selection will be based on those which offer the maximum benefit for each pound invested, which forms the basis of the 'profitability index' calculation mentioned in the next chapter.

Once projects have been authorized, their progress needs careful monitoring, and each project manager should receive monthly reports on the costs incurred to date, analysed by element of cost and by stages of the project. A suitably designed job number, as an integral part of the cost code structure mentioned in the first chapter, will facilitate this process.

Top management also need updating on the state of the capital budget as a whole. They need to know how the total spend compares with the total budgeted for the year and, more particularly, how each individual project spend relates to the amount allocated. A suitable form of presentation for this purpose is:

Capital Budget Report						
		Actual/projected costs				
Project number	*Title*	*Last year* £	*This year* £	*Total to date* £	*Projected to complete* £	*Authorized amount* £

We have now completed our examination of functional budgets, but there remains the discussion of two somewhat opposing types of budgeting systems.

Flexible Budgeting

The system of budgeting described throughout these two chapters is based on 'fixed' budgets which remain unchanged irrespective of the actual level of activity achieved. If this actual level is significantly different from the budgeted level, there will be significant 'volume' variances.

When standard costing systems are used, the difference in profit attributable to the variation in activity level from that budgeted is quantified in specific volume variances. In the absence of a standard costing system, the solution to the problem of variable levels of activity lies in the use of a 'flexible budget'.

This is defined by the Institute of Cost and Management

Accountants as a 'budget which is designed to change in accordance with the level of activity attained'. Essentially, the flexible budget consists of not one budget, but a series of budgets, each being based on a different level of activity within the expected range.

For example, if a firm never expects activity to fall below 70% it can prepare four budgets of income and expenditure at 70%, 80%, 90%, and 100% levels of the maximum capacity. Should the actual level turn out to be, say 85%, then the budget for that level can be derived by interpolating the 80% and 90% budgets. Comparison of actual results can then be made with the budget for the same level of activity. Any resulting variances are of a controllable nature as the change in volume has been eliminated.

Flexible budgeting obviously entails the separation of costs into fixed and variable categories to forecast expenditure at different levels of activity. This is not the same analysis as that for indirect and direct costs because some indirects (power, for example) vary with the level of activity, and some directs (possibly wages) are fixed.

We can compare the variances arising under a fixed budget system with those obtaining under a flexible budget system in the example on page 130.

Firms may use a mixture of fixed and flexible budgets for different departments; for example, fixed budgets in administrative and sales administration departments, and flexible budgets in production, operations and distribution departments. Alternatively, a system of fixed budgets only may be used, coupled with a standard costing system to disclose relevant volume variances. In environments where standard costing is inapplicable, then flexible budgeting is most appropriate where the level of activity is very uncertain.

Comparison of fixed and flexible budget systems

1 Illustration of a fixed budget report

	Fixed budget for month	Actual results for month	Variances
Activity level	100%	85%	15%(A)
	£	£	£
Direct labour	33,000	31,000	2,000(F)
Direct materials	27,000	23,700	3,300(F)
Overheads	36,000	34,100	1,900(F)
Total	£96,000	£88,800	£7,200(F)

2 Flexible budget for the same month

Activity level	70%	80%	90%	100%
	£	£	£	£
Direct labour	27,000	29,000	31,000	33,000
Direct materials	18,900	21,600	24,300	27,000
Variable overheads	10,500	12,000	13,500	15,000
Fixed overheads	21,000	21,000	21,000	21,000
Total	£77,400	£83,600	£89,800	£96,000

3 Flexible budget report for the same month

	Flexed budget	Actual results	Variances
Activity level	85%	85%	0%
	£	£	£
Direct labour	30,000	31,000	1,000(A)
Direct materials	22,950	23,700	750(A)
Variable overheads	12,750	12,600	150(F)
Fixed overheads	21,000	21,500	500(A)
Total	£86,700	£88,800	£2,100(A)

Summary

Just as we in our private lives need to budget and monitor our finances to achieve objectives, say to buy a new car, so firms need to plan and control their activities to achieve corporate objectives.

The planning and control mechanism used by firms is known as budgetary control and consists of monthly plans for all functions covering all departments within the firm. All plans are interlinked because no one function acts independently and the level of activity in each function must be linked to the key or limiting factor at that point in time.

Plans need to be consistent with the corporate objectives laid down by top management and their viability will be tested in this light, perhaps by a return on capital criterion. Once those plans have been accepted for the coming year, then regular monitoring on a monthly basis will ensure that management's attention is directed to any significant deviations.

The way in which budgeting systems are implemented is very important from the behavioural point of view. Systems should not be imposed by accountants but implemented by a management committee seeking the co-operation of all managers. If responsibility for plans is to be vested in managers, and their success or otherwise judged by such performance, then they should be involved in the detailed planning process.

10. Ratio analysis

We saw in the previous chapter that detailed financial plans are summarized in a master budget consisting of a budgeted profit and loss account and a budgeted balance sheet. Control can be exercised by a comparison of actual figures with the budgeted figures, but extensive use is likely to be made of accounting ratios. These can be used in the setting of targets or budgets and also in the subsequent control process, to ensure that company objectives are being achieved.

A 'ratio' is a pair of figures taken from a profit and loss account and a balance sheet to examine the particular relationship between them. A typical example is the 'return on capital' which relates the profit earned in a year to the amount of capital employed by the business to earn it. In this case one figure is taken from each of the two statements, but some ratios use both figures from the same statement.

When two figures are brought together in this way it is called a ratio, even though it may be expressed as a percentage, or one figure as a factor of the other. The absolute size of a ratio rarely has any meaning as they are usually used in the context of comparisons with target ratios, or with previously achieved ratios, or with other firms' ratios.

Ratios can be used to measure and/or control the following:

- Profitability
- Cost efficiency
- Use of fixed assets
- Working capital requirements
- Liquidity
- Gearing
- Debt level
- Investment performance

Throughout this chapter, examples of ratios will be drawn from the following typical profit and loss account and balance sheet drawn up in the style of the Companies Act 1981:

Profit and loss account

		£000
Sales		10,000
Less: cost of goods sold	6,000	
administrative expenses	1,500	
selling and distribution expenses	1,000	
research and development	500	9,000
Operating profit		1,000
Interest payable		140
Profit before tax		860
Corporation tax		260
Profit after tax (earnings)		600
Dividends paid and proposed		200
Retained profit		400
Earnings per share		10p

Balance sheet

		£000
Fixed assets		2,000
Current assets:		
stocks	3,000	
debtors	1,500	
bank balance	500	
	5,000	
Less: creditors due within one year	2,000	
Net current assets (working capital)		3,000
Total net assets (capital employed)		5,000
Less: creditors due after one year		1,000
Ordinary share capital and reserves		4,000

Profitability

We have already met the key ratio for any profit-seeking organization, which is its return on capital. This expresses the annual profit as a percentage of the capital employed in the business. This is influenced by two further ratios, namely, the 'profit margin' (net profit as a percentage of sales) and the 'rate of turnover of capital' (sales divided by capital).

Example

Assuming profit is £1m, sales are £10m and capital is £5m then:

return on capital   =   profit margin   ×   turnover of capital rate
     20%   10%   2 times

which are calculated in the following way:

$$\frac{\text{profit £1m}}{\text{capital employed £5m}}\% = \frac{\text{profit £1m}}{\text{sales £10m}}\% \times \frac{\text{sales £10m}}{\text{capital employed £5m}}$$

The return on capital varies from firm to firm, industry to industry, and from year to year. However, many industries produce a return on capital within the range of 15%–25% before charging interest and tax, but wider variations may be found in their profit margins and rates of capital turnover. The table below shows how a 20% return on capital could be achieved in different industries:

Industry	return on capital		profit margin		rate of capital turnover
Heavy engineering (capital intensive)	20%	=	10%	×	2 times
Food retailing (material intensive)	20%	=	2%	×	10 times
Construction (labour + material intensive)	20%	=	4%	×	5 times

Profit margins in food retailing may be only of the order of 2–3% but this is offset by a very high rate of turnover of capital. In more capital intensive industries with a long production cycle, the low rate of capital turnover is compensated by a relatively high profit margin.

These three key ratios are only the starting point from which a number of subsidiary ratios can be calculated, relating operating costs or assets to sales. The following diagram illustrates this approach and then precise definitions and an example are given for each ratio:

Diagram of performance ratios

$$\frac{\text{Profit}}{\text{Capital employed}} \quad 20\%$$

$$\frac{\text{Profit}}{\text{Sales}} \quad 10\% \qquad \times \qquad \frac{\text{Sales}}{\text{Capital employed}} \quad 2 \text{ times}$$

| Profit and loss account analysis | Balance sheet analysis |

$$\frac{\text{Direct labour}}{\text{Sales}} \% \qquad \frac{\text{Sales}}{\text{Fixed assets}} \text{ No. of times}$$

$$\frac{\text{Direct material}}{\text{Sales}} \% \qquad \frac{\text{Sales}}{\text{Working capital}} \text{ No. of times}$$

$$\frac{\text{Administrative costs}}{\text{Sales}} \% \qquad \frac{\text{Sales}}{\text{Stocks}} \text{ No. of times}$$

$$\frac{\text{R \& D costs}}{\text{Sales}} \% \qquad \frac{\text{Sales}}{\text{Debtors}} \text{ No. of times}$$

Return on Capital

This ratio is always expressed as a percentage in the way we might personally think about our financial investments in, say, a building society. When applied to firms, we need to consider which profit and whose capital is used in the ratio as the choice depends on the use to which the ratio is put.

Looked at from the owners' viewpoint, the concern is with the profit earned for them relative to the amount of funds they have invested in the business. The relevant profit here is after interest, tax and any preference dividends have been deducted. This leaves the profit solely attributable to the ordinary shareholders, and is often referred to as the earnings. The capital to which earnings relate is the share capital plus accumulated reserves which make up the total shareholders' funds invested in the business. Therefore:

$$\text{Return on shareholders' funds or equity} = \frac{\text{profit after interest, tax \& pref. divds}}{\text{ordinary shareholders' funds}} \%$$

$$= \frac{£0.6m}{£4m} \% = 15\%$$

This ratio will be influenced not only by the trading performance of the company but also by tax allowances on investment and the mix of owners' capital relative to borrowed capital.

A wider view of company performance that ignores these latter influences and concentrates just on company performance is the ratio normally referred to as the return on capital or return on investment. Often this ratio is abbreviated to the initial letters ROC or ROI. It is calculated by taking the profit before interest, tax and any dividends, and expressing it as a percentage of the total capital employed, irrespective of whether it is owners' capital or borrowed capital. Therefore:

$$\text{Return on capital} = \frac{\text{profit before interest, tax and dividends}}{\text{total capital employed}} \%$$

$$= \frac{£1m}{£5m} \% = 20\%$$

When calculating either the return on equity or return on capital employed, it may be necessary to take account of the change in the capital figure during the year. This recognizes the fact that retained profit has not been available in full for a whole year and to take the year-end capital, as is normally done, ignores this fact. If a new loan was introduced part-way through a year, then the year-end figure is again not representative. The average of year-start capital with year-end capital can be used to overcome this problem, but if this is still not accurate enough then one can resort to a monthly average figure for capital employed.

Profit Margin

There are two levels at which profit margins can be calculated. The gross profit is obtained by deducting the cost of sales from the sales value before all the general expenses are taken into account. The 'gross profit margin' is this gross profit expressed as a percentage of sales in the same time period:

$$\text{Gross profit margin} = \frac{\text{Gross profit}}{\text{Sales}} \%$$

$$= \frac{\text{£4m}}{\text{£10m}} \% = 40\%$$

In retail trade, the gross profit represents the profit on sales when only the buying-in cost of the goods sold is taken into account. In the construction industry, the gross profit is after site costs have been deducted from sales turnover. In manufacturing, the gross profit is struck only after the manufacturing costs of goods sold are deducted from sales.

The second and more important ratio relates the final net profit to the sales value, again as a percentage. It is usual to take the net profit before interest, tax and dividends have been allowed. This is because all three of these factors can vary over time, for reasons which have nothing to do with the actual trading performance being monitored by the ratio. What we are really saying is that profit margins are determined by operating costs and selling prices rather than the capital mix or effective tax rate at any point in time.

$$\text{Net profit margin} = \frac{\text{net profit before interest, tax \& dividends}}{\text{sales}} \%$$

$$= \frac{\text{£1m}}{\text{£10m}} \% = 10\%$$

Turnover of Capital

This ratio is usually expressed as the number of times £1 of capital generates £1 of sales in the year. For example, if capital is £5m when sales are £10m, we say capital employed was turned over twice during the year, which is the same as saying that each £1 of capital generated £2 worth of sales.

$$\text{Turnover of capital} = \frac{\text{sales}}{\text{capital employed}}$$

$$= \frac{£10m}{£5m} = 2 \text{ times}$$

Cost Efficiency

An extension of the profit margin is to express every profit and loss account expense separately as a percentage of sales. Here is an example from the same profit and loss account used earlier:

Profit and loss account analysis

Cost of goods sold/sales	£6.0m/£10m =	60%
Administration/sales	£1.5m/£10m =	15%
Selling & distribution/sales	£1.0m/£10m =	10%
Research & development/sales	£0.5m/£10m =	5%
Net profit/sales	£1.0m/£10m =	10%
		100%

In a manufacturing context it would be advisable to break down the cost of goods sold into direct labour cost, direct material cost and production overheads, all expressed as percentages of sales value.

Again, it must be stressed that the absolute sizes of the above ratios have little value. Each one should be compared with what it was in previous time periods, with a budgeted or target figure, or with other firms' ratios in the same industrial segment.

Use of Fixed Assets

The intensity of use of any asset, fixed or current, is measured by its relationship to sales value. Fixed assets may be examined in this way as a total group, or in suitable sub-categories of buildings, plant and equipment, vehicles, fixtures and fittings.

Example

When sales are £10m and fixed assets are £2m then:

$$\text{Fixed asset turnover} \quad = \quad \frac{\text{sales}}{\text{fixed assets}} \quad = \quad \frac{£10m}{£2m} \quad = 5 \text{ times}$$

If, for example, the 'fixed asset turnover' ratio had been averaging about seven times in recent years, then the above performance is a marked deterioration warranting further investigation. An alternative explanation could be that a relatively large replacement programme has just been completed.

When comparing this ratio with previous time periods, we need to ensure that the fixed assets are at up-to-date values and not at outdated historic costs. Sales are less of a problem – they will always be relatively up-to-date as they refer to the last twelve months.

Working Capital Level

A somewhat similar calculation can be performed on working capital to identify the velocity of circulation of the same money being used over and over again in the same year. To illustrate this, let us take sales of £10m and working capital of £3m:

$$\text{Rate of turnover of working capital} \quad = \quad \frac{\text{sales}}{\text{working capital}}$$

$$= \quad \frac{£10m}{£3m} \quad = 3.33 \text{ times}$$

In effect, £1 of working capital generated £3.33 of sales within a one year period. The faster this velocity then the smaller will be the working capital required. As a result, the company will be more profitable as less interest will be payable on the reduced amount of capital.

Working capital is primarily composed of stocks, debtors and creditors, so each of these three items can be related to some appropriate measure of the level of activity. The resulting ratio finds expression as a number of times per annum or as a period of time. These approaches are now explored.

Stocks and work-in-progress are always valued at their purchase cost or manufactured cost for their present state. It would be invalid to relate such stocks to sales as this compares a cost price with a selling price. A more valid approach is to relate stocks to the cost of goods sold during the year.

Example

Assume stocks were valued at £3m at the year end, whilst the cost of goods sold was £6m for the year with little seasonal variation in sales.

$$\text{Stock turnover rate} = \frac{\text{cost of goods sold}}{\text{stocks}}$$

$$= \frac{£6m}{£3m} = 2 \text{ times per annum}$$

Ratios based on asset values in a balance sheet are snapshots at a moment in time. If there are seasonal fluctuations in sales then stock levels may also fluctuate in anticipation of demand, or to smooth out production in the case of manufacturing companies. Care must be taken to compare like with like when using such ratios to compare with other time periods or with other companies' ratios.

An alternative way of looking at the stock turnover rate is to express the stockholding as being equivalent to the cost of goods sold for a period of time. In the above example, a stock turnover rate of 2 times per annum equates to a stock level sufficient for 26 weeks' sales. This is calculated from:

$$\text{Stockholding period} = \frac{\text{stocks}}{\text{cost of goods sold}}$$

$$= \frac{£3m}{£6m} \times 52$$

$$= 26 \text{ weeks}$$

Debtors can be looked at in a similar way to the stockholding period. We are familiar with credit customers taking such and such a number of weeks to pay their invoice in line with the credit period allowed in the normal course of business. Some customers take longer, and very few pay early unless motivated by a cash discount. The average time taken to pay, again assuming no marked seasonal bias in yearly sales, can be found by relating the debtors at a moment in time with the sales for the previous twelve months. When sales are £10m for the year and debtors £1.5m we get:

$$\text{Credit period taken} = \frac{\text{debtors}}{\text{sales}} \times 52 = \frac{£1.5m}{£10m} \times 52$$

$$= 7.8 \text{ weeks}$$

The credit control department can be assessed for its efficiency by a comparison of this 7.8 weeks with the time previously taken by customers, or by an interfirm comparison, or with the average time allowed.

When examining other companies' annual accounts we may be interested in how long they take to pay their suppliers. If we are able to identify both trade creditors at the year-end and total purchases for the year, then the calculation is identical with the above credit period for debtors.

Liquidity

Previous ratios have examined the performance of a company from a viewpoint of profitability encompassing the control of operating costs and the capital tied up in assets. In order to survive, companies must also watch their liquidity position, by which is meant keeping enough short-term assets to pay short-term debts. Companies fail when they cannot pay monies due to employees, bankers, suppliers or the tax man. There are two main ratios used to examine the liquidity position of a company: the liquidity ratio and the current ratio.

The 'liquidity ratio' is sometimes referred to as the 'quick ratio' or the 'acid test ratio' because this is the one that really matters. It examines the ratio of liquid assets to current liabilities where a 1:1 ratio means a company has sufficient cash or near cash to pay its immediate debts.

Liquid assets are defined here as all the current assets excluding stocks and work-in-progress on the basis that these latter items cannot normally be converted quickly into cash. In effect, liquid assets are debtors, cash, bank balances and any other short-term investments.

Example

Using the balance sheet information at the start of this chapter we find that:

	£'000
Current assets:	
stocks and work-in-progress	3,000
debtors	1,500
bank balance	500
	5,000
Current liabilities:	
creditors due within a year	2,000

$$\text{Liquidity ratio} = \frac{\text{liquid assets}}{\text{current liabilities}} = \frac{£2.0m}{£2.0m} = 1:1$$

The above ratio is obviously satisfactory, but this precise figure will rarely be hit for most firms. When slightly in excess of 1:1 this is also satisfactory, but if it significantly exceeds parity then thought should be given to alternative uses of any cash balances.

Where a bank overdraft is included in current liabilities, a liquidity ratio of less than 1:1 may be quite satisfactory but only on the premise that the borrowing facility will not be withdrawn. In some industries, work-in-progress is turned into cash as quickly as trade creditors are due for payment. A case in point here is the construction and civil engineering industry where liquidity ratios of, say, 0.7:1 can be found in company published accounts.

The other test of a company's liquidity includes stocks and work-in-progress on the grounds that stocks eventually turn into debtors and later into cash itself. This 'current ratio' is calculated by relating all current assets to current liabilities when a norm of 2:1 is regarded as satisfactory in most industries. This norm is somewhat arbitrary and a better guide may be to look for the norm for a particular industry, as published by a trade association or magazine, or by one of the commercial firms collating such statistics. Using the above balance sheet data we get:

$$\text{Current ratio} = \frac{\text{current assets}}{\text{current liabilities}} = \frac{£5m}{£2m} = 2.5:1$$

Although above the quoted norm, this current ratio of 2.5:1 may be satisfactory for its particular industry. Even if the ratio is less than 2:1 it may also be quite satisfactory, as in the case of the construction industry for the same reasons quoted for the liquidity ratio.

Gearing

The distinguishing features of borrowed capital, as opposed to owners' capital, are that borrowings must be serviced by interest payments and the capital sum repaid at the agreed time(s). There is no such legal obligation to pay dividends to owners, nor is the share capital normally repayable before the liquidation of the company.

From a liquidity point of view, too much borrowing is risky, as the higher the proportion of capital raised by loans (or permanent overdrafts) the higher will be the proportion of profit going as interest. A measure of this proportion can be gained by expressing the annual interest payment as a percentage of the annual profit before interest, tax and dividend payments.

This ratio is known as 'income gearing'. The smaller the percentage then the less vulnerable the company will be to any setback in profits or rise in interest rates on variable rate loans. The larger the percentage then the more risk that level of borrowing represents to the company. A company risks liquidation should it be unable to meet its interest or repayment obligations.

Example

If we take the figures from the earlier profit and loss account we find that interest is £140,000 and the operating profit is £1m so that:

$$\text{Income gearing} = \frac{\text{annual interest charge}}{\text{annual operating profit}}$$

$$= \frac{£0.14m}{£1m} \% = 14\%$$

At this level the company does not appear very vulnerable to anything but a total collapse in profits. If, however, income gearing exceeds, say, 50%, then this leaves the company very vulnerable to any profits setback. Bank managers and other lenders certainly keep an eye on this ratio.

An alternative way to calculate income gearing is to divide the operating profit by the annual interest charge to find the interest cover:

$$\text{Interest cover} = \frac{\text{annual operating profit}}{\text{annual interest charge}}$$

$$= \frac{£1m}{£0.14m} = 7.1 \text{ times}$$

The other aspect of borrowed capital is the ratio of the amount of capital put in by the owners to that provided by financial institutions as loans. This relationship is known as 'gearing' because the profit earned for shareholders can be levered up by getting surplus profit on borrowed capital after the interest has been paid. Normally, bank managers and other lenders will not let this ratio get too high, but circumstances can arise which were not originally envisaged.

Example

Using the balance sheet information previously provided when share-holders' funds were £4m and long-term loans were £1m then:

$$\text{Gearing ratio} = \frac{\text{borrowed capital}}{\text{shareholders' funds}} \%$$

$$= \frac{£1m}{£4m} = 25\%$$

Another common way to express the gearing ratio is to find the proportion which borrowed capital bears to the total capital employed. Using the same figures as above this total capital must equal £5m, being the combination of owners' capital (£4m) and borrowed capital (£1m).

$$\text{Gearing level} = \frac{\text{borrowed capital}}{\text{total capital employed}} \%$$

$$= \frac{£1m}{£5m} \% = 20\%$$

Care must be exercised when considering gearing ratios in order to know precisely which definition is being discussed. The suggestion is sometimes made that not only have accountants invented a language of their own to confuse other managers, but that they have more than one term to mean the same thing!

There is no one level of gearing one can point to for all companies. Whether a company has borrowed too much or too little capital depends very much on its past record and future prospects. It should also be borne in mind that some industries are more cyclical than others and subject to a higher degree of commercial risk. This should not be compounded by exposing the company to too high a degree of financial risk by being overgeared.

A wider view of money owed to any party, as opposed to just lenders, is contained in the 'debt ratio'. This looks at the total amount of debt and relates it to the total assets of the company to identify what proportion of total assets is financed by money owed to third parties. Total debt includes loans and overdrafts but also includes future tax payments and all current liabilities. Total assets comprise all fixed and current assets. From our previous balance sheet we can identify total assets as £7m and total debt as £3m so that:

$$\text{Debt ratio} \quad = \quad \frac{\text{total debt}}{\text{total assets}} \% \quad = \quad \frac{£3m}{£7m} \% = 43\%$$

Investment Performance

An avid reader of the city pages of our serious newspapers may already be familiar with some of the financial ratios used to evaluate shares. Typical of such ratios are the 'gross dividend yield', the 'dividend cover' and the 'price/earnings ratio'.

The term 'earnings' is often found in the published profit and loss accounts of companies. It is a short way of describing the profit attributable to the ordinary shareholders after interest, tax and any preference dividends have been deducted. This does not mean that ordinary shareholders will receive all this profit by way of dividends, as some is usually retained in the company to provide further capital.

If we divide the earnings for the year by the number of shares in existence, we get what is known as the 'earnings per share'. If we then divide the current market price of one share by the earnings per share we find the 'price/earnings ratio'.

Example

Suppose a company had earnings of £600,000 for the last year and had three million shares in issue currently trading at £2.40 each.

$$\text{Earnings per share} = \frac{\text{earnings}}{\text{number of issued shares}}$$

$$= \frac{£0.6m}{3m} = 20p$$

$$\text{Price/earnings ratio} = \frac{\text{market price per share}}{\text{earnings per share}}$$

$$= \frac{£2.40}{20p} = 12$$

The earnings per share is used to compare performance from one year to the next when both the profit and the number of shares in issue may have changed. The price/earnings ratio, however, is used to compare the market rating of one company against that of similar companies in the same industry. If, say, one brewery had a price/earnings ratio of ten whilst other brewers were rated at about thirteen, then the performance expected of this company is below average.

As a generalization, high price/earnings ratios denote good management in growth industries, whilst low price/earnings ratios could signify poor management, risk or cyclical activities. An exceptional profit or loss in the previous year or a rumoured takeover bid may lead to unusual price/earnings ratios, but by and large this ratio can be used as an independent assessment of a company's performance.

As previously mentioned, all profit is not distributed as dividends in most companies. The proportion of profit so distributed can be found from the 'dividend cover'. If half the profit is distributed then the dividend is covered twice. If all the profit is paid out then the cover is a bare once and would be in danger should profits fall.

The dividend yield measures the money income per annum that a shareholder receives on his investment. Although dividends are paid net of income tax at the standard rate, the dividend yield is expressed gross of income tax so that it can be compared with the yield from alternative investments.

Example

Assume that the earnings per share are 20p and that the net dividend paid is 7p. The standard rate of income tax is 30% and the present market price is £2.40 per share.

$$\text{Dividend cover} = \frac{\text{earnings per share}}{\text{dividend per share}}$$

$$= \frac{20p}{7p} = 2.8 \text{ times}$$

$$\text{Dividend yield} = \frac{\text{gross dividend per share}}{\text{market price per share}} \%$$

$$= \frac{10p}{£2.40} \% = 4.2\%$$

Interfirm Comparisons

Mention was made earlier that ratios can be used to compare aspects of one company's performance with its competitors. It is quite possible to conduct such an exercise oneself in a rather crude fashion. Published annual accounts for selected competitors can be requested from the company secretary. Information can also be found more discreetly by reference to a database like Extel located in large public or college libraries. Alternatively, reference can be made to Companies House in Cardiff for photocopies of relevant information. A number of agencies offer to perform this kind of service.

Sometimes a particular trade association conducts a survey of firms in its industry. Alternatively, an organization called the 'Centre for Interfirm Comparisons' invites companies in a specified industry to participate in such a study from time to time. A participating firm submits its detailed profit and loss account and balance sheet in confidence, as the published results never disclose the names of the firms involved. The data is then adjusted to a common basis for all firms so that ratio comparisons are as valid as possible.

Uniform Cost Comparisons

You will be relieved to hear that uniform costing is not yet another system of costing! All the term refers to is that a number of different organizations use the same costing systems so that cost comparisons may be made between them. Imagine central government trying to collate information from all the local authorities if they had differing descriptions and code numbers for all their income and expenditure.

Here are some typical organizations where uniform costing can be applied, and two sample cost comparisons that can be made:

Local authority	– refuse collection cost per house
	– social service cost per '000 people
General hospital	– cost per bed/day
	– cost per hernia operation/recovery
Electricity board	– generation cost per kw
	– cost per meter reading
Polytechnic	– cost per engineering student
	– income per lecturer hour
Pig farm	– cost per lb carcass meat
	– income per lb carcass meat
Food supermarket	– staffing cost per £ sales
	– establishment costs per £ sales

Uniform costing can be based on either absorption or marginal costing principles, provided all member units use the same coding and classification system. Accounting policies regarding stock valuation, depreciation, fixed asset revaluation, length of accounting periods and the like, must also be uniform.

Cost comparisons by themselves are insufficient to justify the rigidities imposed on members by operating their costing system in a uniform way. The publication of cost comparisons will, it is hoped, lead to the adoption of best practice and the elimination of waste.

Summary

Ratios are pairs of figures related to each other, either as a percentage or the size of one figure relative to another. Most ratios use information from the profit and loss account and/or balance sheet, but yardsticks can also be constructed by relating a selected cost to some unit of output. They are mainly used as a tool to measure a company's profitability, efficiency, liquidity and gearing.

The absolute size of ratios often has little meaning and they are mainly used in a relative way by making comparisons with the previous period, with budgeted ratios or with competitors' ratios. We can liken ratios to clues in detective work. They do not tell us the answers directly but are useful in pointing management to areas that require further investigation.

11. Responsibility accounting

As firms grow in size, either organically or by amalgamation, top management find it impossible to control everyday events and make all the decisions. They get swamped by the minutiae and lose sight of the longer term objectives and strategy. This leads them to delegate responsibility for day-to-day decision making and operational control to lower levels of management. Such a process is described as decentralization, but the degree to which it is exercised can vary widely.

The main purposes of decentralization are therefore to allow central management to concentrate on corporate strategy and allow local management to make local operational decisions that they alone should have the knowledge to do best. Motivation of local management should also be enhanced and communication problems with head office removed by this increase in local autonomy.

However, it should not be assumed that decentralization can be carried out without giving rise to any problems. Much thought may need to be given to the degree of autonomy to allow local management, which finds expression in the types of responsibility centre used. Care must be taken to avoid situations which allow sub-optimal decisions to be taken by one centre which increases its benefits at the expense of another centre within the group, or to the detriment of the group overall.

Thought must also be given to which services are to be provided centrally, if any, to avoid possible wasteful duplication within each decentralized unit. A particularly thorny problem occurs where one unit sells goods or services to another unit within the same ownership. The performance of each of these two units will be influenced by the price at which these transfers are effected. We return to a fuller discussion of so-called 'transfer pricing' later.

It is appropriate that we now examine the various types of responsibility centre and see the context in which they may be used. Reference has already been made in earlier chapters to one type of financial responsibility centre, namely the cost centre. This was defined as any section or department of a business over which one person has the responsibility and authority for expenditure. Later again, this theme was referred to as being part of the rationale behind systems of budgetary control.

In addition to cost centres, there are also a number of other types of financial responsibility centres which may be appropriate to autonomous or semi-autonomous parts of large organizations which are decentralized or divisionalized. We start by examining the typical features of the main types of responsibility centres and suggest examples where each can be applied in a decentralized organization:

- Managed cost centre – where the manager is responsible for giving the best level of service whilst keeping within his/her budget. This type of centre is appropriate to administrative departments, but both inputs and outputs can be hard to measure. Other management techniques like work measurement, zero-based budgeting and management by objectives could play a useful role in either the budget setting or monitoring processes.
- Standard cost centre – this is relevant for production and operations departments where the manager is responsible for achieving the standard costs set for products. Standards will normally incorporate controllable costs to include direct labour, direct materials and variable overheads. Performance will be measured by reference to the size of favourable or adverse cost variances.
- Revenue centre – where the manager has the responsibility for maximizing sales revenue whilst keeping within his/her agreed cost budget. Normally, managers have no discretion to incur extra costs on additional resources nor to vary selling prices in a bid to maximize sales revenue in this type of responsibility centre. A typical application of revenue centres might be found in the retail trade of small branch outlets of a large chain. As the size of the branch increases it is likely that the manager's discretion increases, and we move into the next category.
- Profit centre – this removes the limitations of a revenue centre

by allowing a manager complete discretion over both costs and revenues. A new car showroom or a leisure centre are appropriate examples. The prime objective here is the maximization of profit, with local managers being free to make their own decisions regarding the costs they incur and the prices they charge and any trade-offs between them. No charge for interest on capital employed is included in costs, which distinguishes this type of responsibility centre from the next one.

- Investment centre – this takes the profit centre on a stage further by relating the profit objective to the capital employed in making it. The financial objective is likely to be expressed either as a percentage return on capital or as a profit target after deducting a charge for the amount of capital employed. This latter kind of profit target is usually referred to as 'residual income' or 'residual profit'. Investment centres are often seen as the most appropriate form of responsibility centre for relatively autonomous divisions of a large organization. A holding company with a number of separate trading divisions can regard each as an investment centre, responsible for costs, revenue and the amount of capital employed. This does not necessarily mean that each division has control over new capital expenditure, but that it will be charged with the cost of servicing the divisional capital employed in the business.

Divisional Reporting

When one small homogeneous firm wishes to decentralize, a judicious mixture of managed cost centres, standard cost centres and revenue centres may suffice. Large organizations and conglomerates with disparate activities are almost certain to divisionalize their organization structure and so create a number of near autonomous units. Performance of these divisions is most likely to be judged by reference to the profit they achieve, but there are a number of ways in which profit can be used for this purpose.

Profit targets can be expressed either as an absolute sum of money, say £5m, or as a percentage return on capital invested in the division, say 20%. Before we look at the pros and cons of these two basic approaches, we need to define what we mean by profit in the context of divisionalization. The following example lists sequentially the possible items that can be included in a divisionalized profit and loss account. It puts labels on the different kinds of profit and gives some idea of the factors that need to be considered:

A divisional profit and loss account

Sales revenue

Less:	direct costs
	divisional overheads incurred locally
=	**Controllable profit**
Less:	depreciation on divisional fixed assets
	charges for central services
	apportionment of central administration costs
=	**Divisional profit**
Less:	interest charges on divisional capital employed
=	**Residual profit/income**

There are three levels of profit described in this statement, any one of which could be used as an absolute profit target for a division. The 'controllable profit' is the least contentious as only the local costs under the control of the divisional management are taken into account. Where the division also controls its own investment in new fixed assets, then depreciation should also be included as a controllable cost.

The 'divisional profit' takes the controllable profit one stage further by including costs incurred on behalf of the division but not under its direct control. Depreciation comes into this category if fixed asset investment is controlled by central management. Also deducted are charges for any services provided by central units to the division for which it would otherwise have to pay an outside supplier. Included in the central apportionment is a charge for general administration and top management salaries.

To the extent that divisions see these charges as reasonably fair and equitable, then a divisional profit is a good yardstick to judge performance by as it incorporates all the costs controlled by or incurred on behalf of the division. When central apportionments for depreciation, services or administration are seen as unfair, the

use of divisional profit may have adverse behavioural consequences. In this case, the exclusion of the contentious item, or
reversion to controllable profit, may be preferable.

The last level of profit which can be used to measure performance is the 'residual profit' (or income), so called because it is the
profit remaining after interest has been charged on the capital
invested in the division. This interest is calculated at the firm's
cost of capital, the calculation of which is contained in the later
chapter on investment appraisal.

It should be appreciated that other definitions of profit are
possible. Interest and depreciation charges can be deducted from
controllable profit to get a 'residual controllable profit'. Tax may
or may not be imputed as a charge against a division's profit.
Because many of the factors leading up to the ascertainment of a
pre-tax profit are somewhat arbitrary – central administration,
capital allowances, interest, for example – then a tax charge may
be inappropriate.

At this stage we should attempt to line up the differing types
of absolute profit targets with appropriate profit-orientated
responsibility centres.

Profit centre	*Investment centre*
Controllable profit	Controllable residual profit
or	or
Divisional profit	Residual profit

There remains one important performance measure to discuss,
namely the divisional 'return on capital'. In the previous chapter
on ratios, this was described as the key performance ratio for any
profit-seeking organization. If this relative measure is used to
assess overall performance for a group, then it appears on the
face of it to be equally reasonable to apply the measure to any
component part, like a division.

This brings us back to a problem faced in the discussion on
depreciation, whether or not it should be deducted before calculating controllable profit. If divisional management do not control
their own investment then they may react against a performance
measure, such as return on capital, when one of the factors in the
ratio is outside their control.

Even when investment is totally within divisional control, a decision has to be made as to the value of fixed assets to be used. A choice lies between historic cost, which can be either gross or net of depreciation, or current replacement cost which similarly can be either gross or net. The historic cost convention overstates profit by allowing insufficient depreciation and it also understates capital employed by retaining fixed assets in the balance sheet at their original cost. The combination of these two factors overstates the return on capital earned in real terms. A valuation of fixed assets and therefore capital employed in current (real) terms has more attraction, particularly if the group assesses its own performance this way. Unfortunately, at the time of writing, interest in inflation accounting adjustments appears to be on the wane and historic cost asset values are therefore likely to be the norm.

The choice between gross and net for either historic or current cost assets is easier to understand. As each year's depreciation is cumulatively deducted in the balance sheet, then the capital employed is reduced, so increasing the return on capital. The use of gross asset values is therefore recommended regardless of whether they are historic or current cost based.

The profit figure to be used in a return on capital calculation for a division could be either the controllable profit or the divisional profit or some slight variant of the two. It will never be appropriate to use a residual profit figure, as interest would then be counted twice, once in the residual profit and again in the target return on capital. For the reasons outlined earlier, a pre-tax profit is preferred to a post-tax profit. We now turn our attention to a comparison of these two alternative profit measures.

Return on Capital (ROC) v Residual Profit

Without doubt, these two performance measurements are the most appropriate ways of appraising divisions as fully fledged investment centres. However, they are not identical in approach and the residual income is generally maintained to be the superior of the two. One reason for this is that the ROC measure can persuade divisional management to forego new investments that earn less than their current ROC. Their reasoning is that the new project will reduce their overall ROC in the future and will be counted against them. Even when the new project is expected to earn more than the group's cost of capital, it will be rejected. This may be a valid decision from the division's viewpoint, but for the overall group it is definitely a sub-optimal one.

Example

Division X currently earns an ROC of 30% and is considering whether to invest in a new project which is expected to earn an ROC of about 25%. After the new project is implemented the average ROC for Division X will be 28%. The cost of capital for the group is 20% and capital is freely available for projects earning in excess of this rate.

Group management would be happy for this investment to go ahead as it is expected to yield in excess of its cost of capital. The division is likely to reject this project, however, as the ROC yardstick on which they are to be judged will show a worse performance of 28% against their current 30%.

A solution would be for the group to set a divisional target in residual profit terms. If this were done in the above example then the division would happily go ahead with the project, as it would earn an additional profit of 8% on the capital invested after the 20% cost of capital had been allowed for in the residual profit target. We now look at a more comprehensive example showing this residual profit approach:

Example

The following information applies to the budgeted operations of the Goodman division of the Telling Company.

	£
Sales (50,000 units at £8)	400,000
Variable costs at £6 per unit	300,000
Contribution (Margin)	100,000
Fixed costs	75,000
Divisional profit	25,000
Divisional investment	150,000

The minimum Desired Return on Investment is the Cost of Capital of 20%.

Required:

    (a)   (i) Calculate the divisional expected ROI (Return on Investment)

            (ii) Calculate the division's expected RI (Residual Income)

            (iii) Comment on the results of (i) and (ii)

    (b)   The Manager has the opportunity to sell 10,000 units at £7.50. Variable cost per unit would be the same as budgeted, but fixed costs would increase by £5,000. Additional investment of £20,000 would also be required. If the Manager accepted the special order, by how much and in what direction would his Residual Income change?

    (c)   Goodman expects to sell 10,000 units of its budgeted volume of 50,000 units to Sharp, another division of the Telling Company. An outside firm has promised to supply the 10,000 units to Sharp at £7.20. If Goodman does not meet the £7.20 price, Sharp will buy from the outside firm. Goodman will not save any fixed costs if the work goes outside, but variable costs will be avoided.

        (i) Calculate the effect on the total profit of the Telling Company if Goodman meets the £7.20 price.

        (ii) Calculate the effect on the total profit of the Telling Company if Goodman does *not* meet the price and the work goes outside.

                                       (Certified Diploma)

The expected divisional ROC/ROI is the divisional profit expressed as a percentage of the divisional investment, namely:

$$\text{Return on Investment} \ = \ \frac{£25,000}{£150,000} \ \% \ = \ 16.7\%$$

The expected residual income (profit) is the divisional profit less the minimum desired return on the divisional investment which, in this instance, results in a negative balance as follows:

Residual income	=	Divisional profit	£25,000
		Minimum desired return	
		£150,000 × 20%	£30,000
			(£5,000)

Although the minimum desired return on investment is given as 20%, the Goodman division is only expecting to achieve an ROI of 16.7%. This also shows up in the calculation of the target residual income, as the expected profit of £25,000 is less than the £30,000 minimum return required, resulting in the negative £5,000 residual income.

When the new opportunity to sell a further 10,000 units is taken into account we can show the change in the original budget and the target residual income as follows:

	Original budget £	Additional budget £	Combined budget £
Sales	400,000	75,000	475,000
Variable costs	300,000	60,000	360,000
Contribution	100,000	15,000	115,000
Fixed costs	75,000	5,000	80,000
Divisional profit	25,000	10,000	35,000
20% cost of capital	30,000	4,000	34,000
Residual income target	(5,000)	6,000	1,000

The target residual income changes from a negative balance of £5,000 to a positive one of £1,000 as a result of the new opportunity. This occurs because the £10,000 expected profit from the additional order is offset by a further £4,000 cost of capital, thereby increasing residual income by £6,000.

Any transfer price for the sale of 10,000 units by Goodman division to Sharp division will have no effect on the total profit for the Telling Company. It will, however, affect the profit performance of each separate division as discussed in the next section. Were the order to be placed with another company, the total profit of Telling Company would suffer as follows:

Goodman loses contribution of 10,000 × £2 per unit	=	20,000
Sharp gains 10,000 × 80p per unit on buying-in	=	8,000
Overall effect on Telling Company is a loss of		£12,000

Transfer Pricing

Transfer pricing as a problem area only arises when there are internal transfers of goods or services and the performances of the individual centres are monitored. The practice of transfer pricing will be most prevalent in vertically integrated companies when, say, raw materials are passed to a related company to further process or manufacture.

From the global company point of view, overall profitability is not affected one iota by transfer prices between constituent centres. If the centres are treated as revenue, profit or investment centres, however, then the value of the transfer price will have a direct bearing on their individual performances. For example, if a transfer price is set too low then the selling centre's profitability is reduced and the buying centre's profitability is overstated. This may lead to the misallocation of new resources and will certainly dismotivate the management of the selling centre. Should the transfer price have been set too high, then an autonomous buying centre may shop elsewhere to the detriment of the combined group.

When setting transfer prices a number of criteria should be borne in mind. The whole purpose of decentralization is to allow local autonomy and to measure the overall results achieved on a profit centre or investment centre basis. Transfer prices should not distort the decisions made by local management nor the performance appraisals carried out by central management. Above all, transfer prices should allow "goal congruence" to take place, which in effect means that the objectives of divisional managers must be compatible with the objectives of the parent company.

In practice it may be hard to fix transfer prices that satisfy all these criteria. Wherever possible, reference should be made to the value of identical products or services in a competitive market environment. This values the transaction at arm's length as though it were conducted with a third party.

In many instances, particularly with intermediate products, market-based transfer pricing may not be feasible, so reference must be made to the costs of provision. Only a full-cost transfer with a profit mark-up is likely to satisfy the selling division, but this may have built-in inefficiences and lead to too high prices when fixed costs are apportioned to a low level of activity. In this case it would be preferable to set the transfer price on a standard cost basis.

One final approach is to allow the two divisions to negotiate the price between them. If the divisions were of equal bargaining power this may be possible without the unwanted intervention of central management. In many cases it is likely that either buyer or seller, or both, are in a monopoly situation where they are forced to deal with each other because of the absence of alternative sources of supply.

Summary

When firms decentralize, they need to appraise the performance of the separate units which then become financial responsibility centres. These range from simple cost centres through revenue centres to fully fledged profit or investment centres. The choice of appropriate responsibility centres largely depends on the degree of autonomy allowed by central management.

The performance of divisions is measured in profit terms but there are a number of definitions possible. The profit measure can be an absolute or a relative one. Relative measures, like return on capital, can lead to sub-optimal decision making, and an absolute measure like residual profit is preferred.

A particular problem arises when there are inter-company sales and purchases of goods and services. These demand the fixing of a transfer price, which, if set at the wrong level, distorts the performance measurement of the divisions concerned.

Part III
Decision making

Overview

The major part of the book so far has been concerned with the important management functions of planning and control, where the costing information generated in Part I has been used to design the planning and control systems discussed in Part II. Inevitably, this has involved some decision making, for example on the normal price to charge, and in this final part we are going to concentrate on the use of costing information for decision making in a wide variety of contexts.

Some decisions are concerned with making the best use of existing resources and can therefore be described as short term in nature. Examples of short-term decisions are:

• The price to charge for a special order
• Closure of an unprofitable product/department
• The most profitable product mix
• The best use of limited resources
• Whether to make or buy in

All of these short-term decisions are based on the technique of marginal costing, and require us to examine how costs and/or revenue will change as a result of any decision we make. Essentially, we choose the course of action which will increase our present profit (or minimize a loss), either by reducing operating costs or by selecting more profitable business.

Other decisions are concerned more with the acquisition of new resources, and lead to an examination of the costs and benefits that will accrue from such investments. These are decisions with long-term consequences because the resources may be used for many years to come. What they have in common with short-term decisions is that both are based on the same marginal costing technique.

The appraisal of a long-term investment again requires us to identify the costs and revenue resulting solely from that action. Examples of long-term investments are:

- New products requiring additional fixed/current assets
- Cost-saving investments in new equipment
- Lease or buy decisions

All investment situations demand the identification of yearly cash flows which lend themselves both to the application of discounting techniques and to further financial modelling to take account of risk. We start, however, with a look at short-term decision making.

12. Short-term decisions

The basis for all short-term decision making is the technique of marginal costing. This is the name given to a method of costing which looks at costs in terms of whether they change in sympathy with the level of output, or remain a constant total sum. In other words, whether they are variable costs or fixed costs respectively. We are going to concentrate on the financial aspects of decision making, but very often human and qualitative factors also come into play.

Decision making is about the future and involves a choice between alternative courses of action, of which one choice may simply be the status quo. To reach a decision we must concentrate on relevant information about costs and revenue, rather than past data, unless this is used as a guide to the future. Any sunk costs are ignored as irrelevant.

When making decisions within existing capacity limits we are trying to ensure that resources are used to the best advantage. The assumption is usually made that only variable costs need to be taken into account because, by definition, fixed costs will remain constant whatever action is taken. Situations where fixed costs may also change are examined later in the chapter when segment margins and differential costing are introduced.

We start by looking at the not uncommon situation of being asked to price a one-off order below the normal rate charged.

Pricing Special Orders

If we can make the assumption that fixed costs will remain unchanged when we use spare capacity for a special order, then we need only consider the effects of such an order on sales revenue and variable costs. These two items make up what has previously been referred to as 'contribution'. Therefore, we look at the change in contribution that results from accepting a special order to decide if it is worthwhile.

Example

A manufacturer has been offered a special contract to make equipment for which a valued customer is willing to pay £25,000 providing certain delivery requirements can be met.

The following provisional costing has been made:

	£
Material	3,000
Labour (1,600 hours)	8,000
Variable overhead	4,000
Allocated fixed overhead	8,000
Estimated cost	£23,000

(Certified Diploma)

Comparing the estimated cost of £23,000 with the offered price of £25,000 yields a profit figure of £2,000, but it is incorrect to think that total profits will increase by only this amount. The existing fixed costs will not change if this order is accepted, as the allocation of £8,000 to the new order will be offset by a reduction of £8,000 in the fixed costs being allocated to existing work. The correct way to examine the situation is to present the data in a marginal costing format as follows:

		£
Sales value		25,000
Less: variable costs		
material	3,000	
labour	8,000	
variable overhead	4,000	15,000
Contribution		£10,000

The conclusion we draw is that the firm will increase profit by £10,000 as the extra costs of this contract amounts to £15,000 and the price offered was £25,000.

If the firm had sufficient spare capacity to undertake the contract, then our advice would be to go ahead as this will increase profits by £10,000. It would also need to be sure that taking a one-off order at a specially low price does not harm existing customers, nor lead to requests for permanently low prices on regular work.

The situation is somewhat different when spare capacity does not exist and resources have to be switched from other work.

Consider the above example again if we are now told that it will be necessary to divert labour from casual work which takes 1,600 hours and yields a contribution of £6.50 per hour. Instead of charging labour to this contract at a cost price of £8,000, we need to charge it at the cost of the alternative foregone. The casual work would yield 1,600 × £6.50 = £10,400 and this is the 'opportunity cost' of labour for this special contract. The situation now looks like this:

		£
Sales value		25,000
Less: variable cost		
material	3,000	
labour	10,400	
variable overhead	4,000	17,400
Contribution		£7,600

Still keeping to the premise that the £8,000 allocated fixed costs are merely a reallocation of existing fixed costs from other work, then the total profit of the firm should increase by £7,600 if the order is accepted. However, if additional fixed costs of £8,000 happened to be incurred on this contract, then it would not be a viable proposition.

Let us now consider an extreme case of over-capacity in an industry where competing firms are struggling to survive and new business is fought for most fiercely. This could apply to many cyclical industries such as construction, shipbuilding, and ship repairing, or in other industries where technological change makes existing operations uncompetitive.

Example

Imagine a ship repair yard which is short of work with many men idle but receiving a guaranteed wage. Tenders are invited for an immediate repair to a damaged ship which will take a few weeks to complete. Rumours on the grapevine suggest that another firm is tendering on the basis of direct labour and material costs plus only half of the normal fixed overhead charge. Is it still worth competing?

The approach to take in this situation is to consider the extra costs which will be incurred if the tender is accepted. These extra costs will include all direct materials; any wage payments in excess of the guaranteed amount; direct expenses and variable overheads. A tender price in excess of these costs but below that of the other firm will be worthwhile. If, say, only a quarter of fixed overheads were recovered in addition to all the above costs, then a positive contribution will be made towards the fixed overheads and guaranteed wages. Both these latter costs have to be paid so that a smaller loss will be incurred taking on the repair job than going without it.

Obviously, neither firm can continue very long tendering for work well below total costs, but in the short term this situation can exist from time to time in certain industries. If demand does not pick up, then such firms must find new product lines or leave the industry.

A further possibility is that spare capacity does not exist to take on a special order without foregoing existing work. In this case we compare the contribution earned from the special order with the contribution foregone on the existing work that must be displaced. In both cases the fixed costs are ignored as they remain constant and are incurred irrespective of which work is undertaken.

Even if the contribution from the special order is potentially higher, we may not necessarily proceed with it. Giving up regular work, for a more profitable one-off opportunity that may never be repeated, is not necessarily good business.

Maximizing Profit from Scarce Resources

If firms are short of work then the allocation of scarce resources
to the most profitable product lines is never a problem. There are
always enough resources to go round. By scarce resources we
mean the particular factor(s) of production that limit the firm's
growth at this moment in time, in much the same way as the key
or limiting factor mentioned in the context of budgeting.

Scarce resources can be one or more of the following:

- Space
- Equipment
- Skilled labour
- Raw material
- Working capital

When resources are insufficient we need to know how best to
allocate them to product lines. Where there is only one scarce
resource at any one moment in time, then products should be
placed in rank order by the amount of contribution they earn for
every unit of that scarce resource.

Example

A firm makes only three products and has no space to expand further.
Its management wishes to know which products are the most profitable
so that it can concentrate its sales promotion accordingly. The following
information is available:

	A £000	B £000	C £000	Total £000
Sales	300	150	400	850
Less:				
direct labour	20	20	30	70
direct materials	100	60	100	260
variable overheads	30	10	30	70
allocated fixed overheads	75	25	155	255
Total costs	225	115	315	655
Profit	£75	£35	£85	£195
Space occupied (sq. metres)	3,000	1,000	6,000	10,000

In this situation the scarce resource is space and, therefore, the firm should aim to make the most profitable use of that space. This will be achieved, not by calculating the profit per square metre, but by calculating the contribution per square metre. The reasoning here is that fixed overheads are always somewhat arbitrarily apportioned to product lines. It is also the case that as soon as the volumes in the product mix change, then the profit does not change pro rata because of the very nature of fixed costs.

The information should therefore be presented in a marginal costing format to arrive at the contribution per square metre on each product:

	A	B	C	Total
	£000	£000	£000	£000
Sales	300	150	400	850
Less: variable costs	150	90	160	400
Contribution	£150	£60	£240	£450
Contribution ratio	50%	40%	60%	53%
Space occupied (sq.m)	3,000	1,000	6,000	10,000
£ Contribution per sq.m	£50	£60	£40	£45

Without any scarce resource we should rank the three products in order of their contribution ratio, which is the order CAB. When we take the scarce resource of space into account, and aim to maximize the contribution earned in that space, the contribution per square metre ranks the products in the different order of BAC.

A firm facing this situation should endeavour to switch productive resources away from Product C to Product B primarily or, failing that, from C to A. Sales promotion and marketing effort should be biased to this end, but there is obviously no point in producing products, however profitable they may seem on paper, if there is no demand for them.

Another point to bear in mind is if the individual products comprise a product range where demand is not discrete, but is either competitive or complementary. In the former case, the promotion of the most profitable product will reduce demand for the other less profitable products in the range, to the benefit of the firm overall. In the latter case, demand for all three products may move in step with each other, so that one product should not be promoted in isolation.

Multiple Scarce Resources

The above analysis was based on the premise that only one scarce resource existed at the time. It is perfectly feasible for more than one limiting factor to exist concurrently, say, when both space and skilled labour hours were insufficient for potential demand. When we consider also machine capacity and working capital requirements, it could be possible to have two, three or more scarce resources to consider at any one time.

Faced with this resource allocation problem we still proceed by identifying the contribution from each product line for each scarce resource separately. The operational research technique of linear programming is then used to decide how many of each product to make. When only two scarce resources exist, this is done by expressing mathematical equations in a graphical form and interpreting the graph to find the optimum solution. Should more than two limiting factors exist concurrently, then a computer programme will rapidly find the optimum solution. Reference should be made to a suitable book on operational research techniques for managers if you need to pursue this topic further.

Closing Down a Department/Product

Another situation which is often confusing to management is when consideration is being given to the closure of a segment of the total operation. This decision epitomizes the difference between the absorption costing and marginal costing approaches and, as we shall see, it is the latter which we apply in this context.

Consider the following situation:

Example

Imet Ltd manufactures three products, A, B and C, of which the first two are making acceptable profits but C has been losing money for some time. The most recent results for last month were:

	A £000	B £000	C £000	Total £000
Sales	60	120	90	270
Less: total costs	42	99	93	234
Profit/(loss)	18	21	(3)	36

The directors have considered a number of possible courses of future action but, meanwhile, have no new products available. Nor can they sell more of product A or B without drastically reducing the selling price. The immediate decision is whether to drop product C and apparently save £3,000 per month.

On investigation the accountant has found that the total costs of all products include £54,000 of common fixed costs apportioned £12,000, £24,000 and £18,000 respectively. The fixed costs of £18,000 presently borne by product C will continue, irrespective of whether that product is made or discontinued.

A more helpful analysis of the situation is to set out the contribution made by each product to the total fixed costs incurred by the firm and the overall profit achieved:

	A £000	B £000	C £000	Total £000
Sales	60	120	90	270
Less: variable costs	30	75	75	180
Contribution	30	45	15	90
Less: fixed costs				54
Profit				£36

The directors of Imet Ltd can now conclude that it is better to continue selling Product C for the moment because it is making a contribution of £15,000 towards fixed costs. If Product C is discontinued the contributions from the remaining two products will not change, neither will the fixed costs incurred by the firm. Discontinuing Product C immediately is not advisable as profits will fall by £15,000 to only £21,000 as follows:

	A £000	B £000	Total £000
Sales	60	120	180
Less: variable costs	30	75	105
Contribution	30	45	75
Less: fixed costs			54
Profit			£21

Having identified the basic approach to product closures let us make it more realistic by now assuming that all fixed costs are not common to all products, but that some of the £54,000 is specific to individual products. These specific fixed costs are known as direct fixed costs and we will take them to be £5,000, £13,000 and £6,000 respectively, leaving £30,000 of common fixed costs. When specific fixed costs are deducted from the product contribution we get what is referred to as the 'segment margin':

	A £000	B £000	C £000	Total £000
Sales	60	120	90	270
Less: variable costs	30	75	75	180
Contribution	30	45	15	90
Less: direct fixed costs	5	13	6	24
Segment margin	25	32	9	66
Less: common fixed costs				30
Profit				£36

When considering a product or department closure it is not usually the product's total contribution which is lost when the activity ceases, but the segment margin, which takes into account the saving of direct fixed costs. If we consider Product C in the above example, then its contribution of £15,000 will cease when it is dropped. Also the direct fixed costs of £6,000 applicable solely to that one product line will be saved. The combined effect is the loss of the segment margin amounting to £9,000, which means a drop in overall profits of that amount. Such action is not advisable until such time as other products can be introduced which would yield a greater segment margin from the use of the same capacity.

Leaving aside this drastic surgery, let us look at some management decisions that are concerned with changing the existing product mix.

Product Mix

Very often managers need to make decisions regarding possible changes in the sales volume of their firm's products. To do this effectively they need information on the profitability of the present mix of products to compare with the profitability of any proposed mix.

Our measure of profitability is the concept of contribution which leaves fixed costs to one side, on the grounds that such costs are common to all possible sales mixes and will not vary in total. Consider the following:

Example

The following data relates to the three products of a company:

	Products		
	A	*B*	*C*
Selling price per unit	£40	£52	£50
Variable cost per unit	£32	£46.8	£35
Per cent of total unit sales	30%	50%	20%

Management have realized that the present sales mix does not result in the maximum possible profit. A suggestion is being considered whereby the following revised sales mix would be adopted – A 30%, B 30%, and C 40% – and they wish to know the percentage change in aggregate contribution and whether or not it is favourable.

(LCCI)

As we are not told the absolute level of sales we must proceed by calculating the weighted average contribution for each of the two alternative product mixes, as follows:

	A	B	C	Total
Contribution per unit	£8	£5.2	£15	–
Weightings in original mix	0.3	0.5	0.2	1.0
Contribution × weight	£2.4	£2.6	£3.0	£8.00
Weightings in proposed new mix	0.3	0.3	0.4	1.0
Contribution × weight	£2.4	£1.56	£6.0	£9.96

The increase in the average contribution per unit from £8 to just under £10 is an increase of about 25% and would be reflected in the aggregate contribution to exactly the same extent.

Sometimes management are faced with various options when considering a change in the product mix, so that each option has to be evaluated in terms of its contribution to profit. The following example again illustrates the point that some fixed costs may be specific to one product line as opposed to other fixed costs which are common to all products. As explained earlier, when specific fixed costs are deducted from a product's contribution we get what is known as its segment margin.

Example

The Robbit Plating Company has the following budgeted figures for its various processes next year:

	Process A £000	Process B £000	Process C £000
Sales value	480	480	160
Variable costs	432	384	120
Fixed costs (allocated)	24	36	50

The company is concerned about Process C and several alternatives are being considered:

Alternative 1	Cut C's selling price by 10%. It is estimated that this will increase C's unit sales by 40%.
Alternative 2	Substitute a new Process D for C. Estimated sales are £140,000 in the first year. Variable costs are estimated at 55% of sales. Fixed costs directly attributable to C of £10,000 will be eliminated but

£16,000 additional fixed costs directly attributable to D will be incurred.

Alternative 3   Eliminate C entirely. This will reduce the fixed costs attributable to C by £10,000.

Alternative 4   Convert C into a special finish by adding additional treatments, which will secure a price increase of 20%. The additional costs incurred will be 10% of the new increased price.

Management wants to know the effect of each alternative on the profit of the company and their ranking in order of preference.

(Certified Diploma)

None of the four options concerns Process A or B so these two can be ignored in the sense that whatever contribution they currently make will continue at the same level. We shall therefore examine each alternative course of action in turn.

Alternative 1   A cut of 10% in the unit sales price will reduce current sales from £160,000 to £144,000 with variable costs remaining at £120,000 to give a revised contribution of £24,000. A 40% increase in volume will yield a 40% increase in the contribution, i.e. an extra £9,600 profit.

Alternative 2   The original contribution from C of £40,000 will be lost but the direct fixed costs of £10,000 will be saved, giving a segment loss of £30,000 on C. The new Process D will yield a contribution of 45% of the £140,000 sales amounting to £63,000. This is reduced by the direct fixed costs of £16,000 to leave a segment margin of £47,000. Overall, this gain of £47,000, less the lost £30,000 on Process C, leaves an extra £17,000 profit. This information is presented again under the heading of differential costing later in the chapter.

Alternative 3   The elimination of Process C entirely without a replacement loses the segment margin of £30,000.

Alternative 4   The original sales value of Process C will rise from £160,000 to £192,000 with the special finish. Variable costs will amount to the original £120,000 plus the additional £19,200, making £139,200 in total. This yields a contribution of £52,800 which is £12,800 more than the original contribution from Process C.

To summarize and rank the four alternatives in order of attractiveness we can say:

Alternative 2	Increases profit by £17,000
Alternative 4	Increases profit by £12,800
Alternative 1	Increases profit by £9,600
Alternative 3	Reduces profit by £30,000

Differential Costing

When alternative courses of action are being compared, it is useful to set the alternatives side by side and examine the difference between them. It is not surprising, therefore, that this approach is referred to as 'differential costing'. It is, however, a wider approach than pure marginal costing because it takes all costs and revenues into account.

Example

We will use the same information in the Robbit Plating Company example above for the second alternative mentioned. This proposal replaces their existing Process C by a new Process D. Using a differential costing approach now, we can set out the information as follows:

	Process C £000	Process D £000	Difference £000
Sales	160	140	20
Variable costs	120	77	43
Contribution	40	63	23
Direct fixed costs	10	16	6
Segment margin	30	47	17

Our conclusion from this differential cost analysis is that the new Process D will yield £17,000 more profit for the Robbit Plating Company than the existing Process C. This is, of course, the same conclusion we came to previously.

Make or Buy Decisions

The question of whether to manufacture a component or to buy it in from another firm is one often faced by manufacturing firms. Other sectors may face the same decision regarding a particular service, for example the choice between in-house or specialist market research. The answer may not just be decided on financial grounds but, obviously, the effect on profits is of major importance.

Assuming first that a firm is already making the component and has spare capacity, then the buying-in costs should be compared with the costs that would be saved if production ceased. These costs would normally include the variable costs plus any direct fixed costs. Any common fixed costs allocated to this component's manufacture will continue irrespective of make or buy.

Example

An offer has been made by another company to supply your firm on an annual contract with a certain component for the sum of £40,000 per annum.

The annual costs of your production of components have been budgeted as follows for the coming year:

	£
Materials	14,000
Labour	12,000
Variable overheads	3,000
Direct fixed overheads	6,000
Fixed overheads (common)	12,000
Total Cost	£47,000

We should never make the comparison of the £47,000 total cost of manufacturing with the buying-in cost of £40,000. This is because the allocation of £12,000 common fixed costs will not be saved should production cease. All other costs, totalling £35,000, might be saved depending on whether labour can be deployed elsewhere. A comparison of this £35,000 avoidable cost with the offer of £40,000 is the correct one to make, so we should conclude that it is cheaper to make it ourselves.

This conclusion may well be different if we are working to full capacity, when buying in the component would release capacity to do other work. Let us assume now that the same labour could be used to do other work that would earn us a contribution of £19,000.

This becomes the opportunity cost for labour and increases our avoidable costs to £42,000, which is now in excess of the £40,000 offered by the other firm. Whether this £2,000 saving is sufficient to warrant buying-in is debatable, when security of supply, labour relations and other factors are taken into account. If we assume now that your firm has not previously used the component, then the buying-in cost should be compared with the costs of own manufacture in a similar way. In the above example the additional costs incurred by manufacturing are £35,000, which is cheaper than the buying-in alternative costing £40,000.

Summary

Marginal costing is probably the most useful technique for managers to appreciate. This chapter has examined a wide variety of essentially short-term decisions of a one-off nature. Such decisions have been concerned primarily with the best use of a firm's existing resources in terms of their profit outcome.

At the heart of the marginal costing technique lies the concept of 'contribution' which takes only sales revenue and variable costs into account. In some circumstances direct fixed costs specific to an individual product are considered to identify the segment margin.

Common fixed costs are never relevant in decisions concerning special prices; the best use of scarce resources; closure of a product/department; and changes in the product mix.

In the next chapter we examine decisions with a longer outlook, where capital is invested in equipment or projects that have an expected life of many years.

13. Investment appraisal I

Capital is not free. The owners of firms and financial institutions require a return on their investment in the company. In its turn the company must earn a return on assets at least equal to the cost of capital. To do otherwise will not satisfy the providers of that capital and will make the raising of future capital more difficult, if not impossible.

Firms need to set a minimum required rate of return against which the profitability of proposed new investments is measured. This required rate must be at least equal to the cost of the different types of capital used in the business.

There are two main sources of new capital for new investments. Firms can either borrow the money, usually from a financial institution, or they can obtain it from the owners, either through a 'rights issue' of new shares or by retaining profits. Most firms use a mix of owners' and borrowed capital when the relationship between the two is known as 'capital gearing'.

A company is said to be highly geared when it has a large amount of borrowed capital relative to owners' capital. It is lowly geared when the proportion of borrowed capital is small. The relationship between these two sources of capital can be expressed by calculating each source as a proportion of the total capital, as the following example shows:

Example

	Low gearing	High gearing
Owners' capital (share capital + retained profits)	90%	50%
Borrowed capital	10%	50%
Total capital	100%	100%

New projects must be financed by new capital. We therefore need to look at the cost and mix of new capital to calculate the minimum required rate of return on any new investment. Also, we must bear in mind the effects of taxation on each type of capital as they differ in this respect. We will first examine the cost of borrowed capital, then the cost of equity, and weight the different proportions to get an overall cost.

Cost of Borrowed Capital

The cost of borrowed capital can be regarded as the effective rate of interest which has to be paid on new loans to get them taken up by investors at par. Such rates of interest vary over time in sympathy with interest rates obtainable on alternative investments. They also vary slightly, according to the size of the loan and the degree of risk attached to the particular firm.

Because interest is an allowable expense for tax purposes, a 35% rate of corporation tax reduces the rate of interest by about one third. For example a rate of interest of 10% would only cost a firm 6.5% in effect, after tax relief.

Cost of Equity

The equity of a company is its risk capital, embracing ordinary share capital and retained profits, both of which can be regarded as having the same cost. Companies retain profits to short circuit paying out all the profits with one hand, whilst asking shareholders to buy new shares with the other.

Put simply, the cost of equity is the return shareholders expect the company to earn on their money, which will vary from industry to industry and from one company to another. It is the investors' estimation, often not scientifically calculated, of the rate of return which will be obtained both from future dividends and an increased share value.

Unfortunately, simple concepts are not always so easy to apply in practice. The cost of capital is a favourite battlefield for academics with no one agreed practical solution. One common approach to calculate the cost of equity is:

$$\text{cost of equity} \quad = \quad \frac{\text{current net dividend}}{\text{current market price}}\ \%\ +\ \%\ \begin{array}{l}\text{average annual}\\\text{growth rate}\end{array}$$

Example

If, say, the annual dividend is 20p and the market price £2 per share, with a growth in profits averaging 10% per annum, this gives:

$$\text{Cost of equity} \quad = \quad \frac{20\text{p}}{£2}\ \%\ +\ 10\%$$

$$\quad = \quad 20\%$$

As new projects are financed by a mix of borrowed capital and equity capital we now need to combine them together to calculate the weighted average cost of capital at the desired level of capital gearing.

Weighted Average Cost of Capital

Let us assume Canny Ltd attempt to keep their gearing ratio of borrowed capital to shareholders' funds in the proportion of 30:70 when measured in terms of their current market value. The nominal cost of new capital from these sources has been assessed, say, at 10% and 20% respectively. We now need to take account of the tax relief on interest, the cost of each type of new capital, and the target mix of types to calculate the overall cost as follows:

Type of capital	Proportion		After-tax cost		Weighted cost
18% loan capital	0.3	×	6.5%	=	1.95%
Shareholders' funds	0.7	×	20.0%	=	14.00%
Total	1.0				15.95%

The resulting weighted average cost of about 16% is the minimum rate which Canny Ltd will accept on proposed investments. Any investment which is not expected to achieve a 16% return is not a viable proposition for this firm. We now want to link this concept of cost of capital to the decision of whether a new investment is worthwhile or not.

Investment Appraisal

Investment appraisal is concerned with decisions now which will have long-term effects. It concerns whether, when and how to spend money on capital projects. Such decisions are important ones for the company involved because often large sums of money are committed in an irreversible decision, with no certain knowledge of the size of future benefits. If this measurement is done badly, it can hamper a firm's growth and employment prospects for years to come, and may lead to an inability to attract new investors.

Types of Investment Situation

There are a number of basic situations where an appraisal takes place:

- Expansion – where we assess the worthiness of expanding existing product lines by acquiring more fixed assets and working capital.
- New product/diversification – where we assess the viability of the more risky investment in totally new products.
- Cost saving – where we assess the profitability of a cost-saving scheme: for example, when an investment in a new machine automates an existing manual process.
- Alternative choice – where we decide between alternative investments to achieve the same ends: for example, choosing between two or more models of a machine we wish to acquire for any of the above purposes where their financial characteristics differ.

- Financing – where we compare the cost of purchasing an asset outright with the alternative cost of leasing.

All the above investment situations have the same common approach. In each case we must decide whether the benefits we get from the initial investment are sufficient to justify the original capital outlay.

Example

Suppose a printing firm is considering buying a binding machine for £9,000 which will reduce labour costs on this activity by £3,000 every year, for each of the five years the machine is expected to last. What the management of this firm have to consider – and this is no easy task – is whether a return of £3,000 every year for five years justifies the initial investment of £9,000. In the next chapter we shall consider the risk that the savings may not amount to £3,000 per annum and/or the machine may not last five years. For the moment we will assume that we do know these values with certainty.

We measure the worthiness of investment proposals by building simple financial models of the expected events. Using the binding machine example above we can set out the expected events as cash inflows (+) or outflows (−) at the end of each year of the machine's life, starting at Year 0 which is now:

Financial model of the binding machine project

	£
Year 0	− 9,000
Year 1	+ 3,000
Year 2	+ 3,000
Year 3	+ 3,000
Year 4	+ 3,000
Year 5	+ 3,000
Total profit	+£6,000

There may be some investment situations where no benefits are quantifiable in money terms. For example, the government may require firms to invest in fire detection and alarm systems in all their premises. In this case firms have no choice, and although there will be benefits in employee welfare these are not readily quantifiable in cash terms.

Even in this kind of situation an appraisal technique could be used to help us make the choice between competing systems which have different financial characteristics. In the case of the fire detection and alarm systems, one supplier's equipment may have a high capital cost but a low maintenance cost over a long life. An alternative supplier's equipment may have a low capital cost but high maintenance costs over a short life. We need to formalize this information to make a rational judgement.

Cash Flows

All appraisal methods require an estimate of the yearly cash flows attributable solely to the project under review. Typically, there will be an initial cash outflow on a project, being cash spent on the physical assets such as buildings, plant, vehicles, machinery and the like. If any of these items needs replacing before the project ends, then a cash outflow will also occur in a later year.

Other cash outflows may occur through the firm building up stocks or giving credit to its customers. These working capital items will be cash outflows at the beginning of the project or at some subsequent date, if increased in amount. At the end of a project the working capital is released and becomes a cash inflow at that time.

Cash inflows occur, for example, from sales revenue less their wage and material costs. No deduction from such income is made for depreciation as the total asset cost is shown as a cash outflow at the time of purchase. Where cost-saving projects are concerned, the cash inflow each year is the value of these cost savings, again without charging any depreciation. It is worth emphasizing at this point that profits which accrue from cost-saving investments are just as valuable as profits from investments which extend the firm's output.

At this stage all cash flows are expressed in £s of Year 0 purchasing power, and inflation is ignored. An explanation of how to deal with inflation follows in the next chapter, but first we need to review the four main methods used to appraise investment projects.

Appraisal Methods

Two of the methods we cover are relatively crude measures of the worthiness of any investment and this sums up their weakness. The remaining methods are much more precise as they are both based on yearly interest calculations. They are easy techniques to understand and, with the help of modern calculators or computers, are not difficult to implement. The advantage of interest-based methods of appraisal is that only these methods can adequately incorporate working capital requirements, tax payments and allowances, inflation and risk.

Payback Method

Simplicity is the keynote of this investment appraisal method. Payback measures the number of years it is expected to take to recover the cost of the original investment.

As an illustration, let us assume that the board of directors of the printing firm mentioned earlier set a maximum period of two years within which any investment must be paid back. Payback in the binding machine example will take exactly three years to complete and the investment will be rejected:

Financial model of the binding machine project

	Yearly cash flow £	*Cumulative cash flow* £
Year 0	− 9,000	− 9,000
Year 1	+ 3,000	− 6,000
Year 2	+ 3,000	− 3,000
(Maximum payback period allowed: 2 years)		
Year 3	+ 3,000	NIL
Year 4	+ 3,000	+ 3,000
Year 5	+ 3,000	+ 6,000
Total profit	+£6,000	+£6,000

One disadvantage of this method is that cash received after payback is completed is totally ignored. Nor does the payback method attempt to measure this total profitability over the whole life of the investment and other methods have to be introduced to do this. However, payback is still used and can yield useful information as an indicator of risk, but is best used in conjunction with another method.

Rate of Return Method

The rate of return used to be the main method of investment appraisal as it purports to measure exactly what is required: namely, the annual profit as a percentage of the capital invested.

An average profit is calculated by taking the total profits earned on the investment over the whole of its life and dividing by the expected life of the project in years. Profit in this context is after charging the total cost of the investment, or wholly depreciating it in accountants' terminology. This total profit is more easily understood as the total cash inflows less the total cash outflows over the whole life. Referring back to the binding machine example we get:

$$\text{Average profit} \quad = \quad \frac{£6,000}{5 \text{ yrs}} \quad = £1,200 \text{ p.a.}$$

The average investment is normally regarded as half the original investment on the grounds that if it will be wholly depreciated by the end of its useful life, half-way through its life the investment will be half depreciated. Referring again to the binding machine example:

$$\text{Average investment} \quad = \quad \frac{£9,000}{2} \quad = £4,500$$

Combining the average profit of £1,200 and the average investment of £4,500 gives a rate of return of 27% per annum for each of the five years.

A disadvantage of this method is that the calculation can give misleading results. Provided total profits were £6,000 over the five years, the return will be 27% irrespective of whether the pattern of cash flows increased, decreased or just stayed constant, as in the example. The method does not take the yearly incidence into account. Nor will this method help rank projects whose lives vary as, say, when a project giving a 27% return for five years is compared with another project giving a 20% return for seven years.

True Rate of Return

The profitability of an investment should be measured by the size of the profit earned on the capital invested. This is what the rate of return method attempts to do without perfect success. An ideal method will not rely on averages but will relate these two factors of profit and capital employed to each other in every individual year of the investment's life.

Example

£20,000 mortgage at 12% p.a. repayable over 10 years

Year		Annual cash flow £	Interest payment at 12% p.a. £	Capital repayment £	Capital balance outstanding £
Year	0	−20,000			20,000
	1	+ 3,540	2,400	1,140	18,860
	2	+ 3,540	2,263	1,277	17,583
	3	+ 3,540	2,110	1,430	16,153
	4	+ 3,540	1,938	1,602	14,551
	5	+ 3,540	1,746	1,794	12,757
	6	+ 3,540	1,531	2,009	10,748
	7	+ 3,540	1,290	2,250	8,498
	8	+ 3,540	1,020	2,520	5,978
	9	+ 3,540	717	2,823	3,155
	10	+ 3,540	379	3,155	+ 6

A useful analogy can be made with a building society mortgage. In this situation the borrower pays to the society a sum of money each year. Part of this sum is taken as interest to service the capital outstanding, leaving the remainder as a capital repayment to reduce the capital balance. The profitability of the investment from the society's viewpoint can be measured by the rate of the interest payment, assuming that the yearly capital repayments have paid off all the mortgage.

The example on the previous page sets out the yearly cash flows of £3,540 required on a typical mortgage of £20,000 repayable over ten years with interest at 12% per annum on the reducing balance. The small surplus remaining at the end of ten years is negligible given the size of the annual cash flows.

This building society is getting a true return of 12% p.a. on the reducing capital balance of the mortgage.

Present Value

The calculations involved on proving the building society's return on investment to be 12% are somewhat laborious. A simpler method is used in practice based on the principles of compound interest. Suppose £1 was invested one year ago at interest of 10% per annum. After one year the sum has grown to £1.10. If the £1 was invested two years ago it would have grown to £1.21 with the first year's interest reinvested for a second year. Compound interest measures the future value of money invested some time in the past.

It is equally possible to look at money in the reverse direction, namely, the present value of money receivable at a future point in time. The present value of a future sum of money is the equivalent sum now that would leave the recipient indifferent between the two amounts. The present value of £1 receivable in one year's time is that amount which, if invested for one year, would accumulate to £1 in one year's time. Using a 10% rate of interest, £1 receivable in one year's time has an equivalent value now of £0.909 because £0.909 invested for one year at 10% will accumulate to £1.

The following is an extract from the present value table shown in Appendix 1 alongside the compound interest factors at the same rate of interest:

	Present value of £1 receivable in a future year with interest at 10%	Future value of £1 with compound interest at 10%
Year 0 (now)	1.000	1.000
1	.909	1.100
2	.826	1.210
3	.751	1.331
4	.683	1.464

The relationship between the factors is that one is the reciprocal of the other for the same year. For example:

$$\text{In Year 4,} \quad 1.464 \quad = \quad \frac{1}{.683}$$

Returning to the building society mortgage example, this was shown to have a true rate of profitability of 12%. This can now be proved using the simpler present value approach shown below:

Example

Calculation of the rate of profitability of a £20,000 mortgage repayable over 10 years with interest at 12% p.a. using present value factors:

	Annual cash flow £	Present value factors at 12%	Present value £	Present value £
Year 0	− 20,000	1.000		− 20,000
1	+ 3,540	.893	+ 3,161	
2	+ 3,540	.797	+ 2,821	
3	+ 3,540	.712	+ 2,520	
4	+ 3,540	.636	+ 2,251	
5	+ 3,540	.567	+ 2,007	
6	+ 3,540	.507	+ 1,795	
7	+ 3,540	.452	+ 1,600	
8	+ 3,540	.404	+ 1,430	
9	+ 3,540	.361	+ 1,278	
10	+ 3,540	.322	+ 1,140	+ 20,003
				+ £3
				(negligible)

To do this the cash flows are tabulated yearly and brought back (discounted) to their present value by the use of present value factors. In effect, interest is deducted for the waiting time involved. The remaining cash is therefore available to repay the original investment.

The profitability of the investment is measured by the maximum rate of interest which can be deducted, whilst leaving just enough cash to repay the investment. This rate of interest is the same 12% as found when we calculated the interest and capital repayments previously on the mortgage principle. We can still say that the true rate of profitability on the investment is 12%.

The effect of using present value (PV) factors on the future cash flows is to take compound interest off for the waiting time involved. If a higher rate of interest than 12% had been applied, then not all the capital would be repaid over the ten year life. If a lower rate of interest than 12% had been used, the capital repayments would be larger each year as the present values would be larger. This would result in the mortgage being repaid in less than the ten years stipulated.

Both the methods of calculation explained above arrive at the same conclusion, although at first sight they may not appear related. That they are related can be seen by comparing the capital repayments in the former with the inverted present values of the latter which are almost identical, apart from rounding off differences. This will always be the case in examples with constant annual cash flows. The present value approach will also give correct results with any fluctuating pattern of annual cash flows.

Net Present Value Method

We can now use this present value approach to assess the profitability of investment projects.

Example

The directors of E. Ltd are considering investing £150,000 on a press to make and sell an industrial fastener. Profits before charging depreciation (i.e. cash inflows) are expected to be £60,000 for each of the first four years tapering off to £40,000 in Year 5 and only £20,000 in Year 6, when the press will be scrapped. E. Ltd normally require a minimum rate of return of 20%.

The cash flows can now be set out and multiplied by the present value factors at 20% to discover whether this project is viable or not:

Calculation of the net present value at 20%

	Annual cash flow £	PV factors at 20%	£	PV £
Year 0	−150,000	1.000		− 150,000
1	+ 60,000	.833	+ 49,980	
2	+ 60,000	.694	+ 41,640	
3	+ 60,000	.579	+ 34,740	
4	+ 60,000	.482	+ 28,920	
5	+ 40,000	.402	+ 16,080	
6	+ 20,000	.335	+ 6,700	+ 178,060
			NPV	+ £28,060

The net present value (NPV) surplus of £28,060 means that the annual cash flows are big enough to allow more interest to be deducted and still repay the original investment. This investment is therefore worthwhile as it more than fulfils the requirement of a 20% return.

The word 'net' in net present value means the sum of the negative and positive present values, and this method of investment appraisal is widely known as the 'net present value method' or 'NPV method' for short.

Discounted Cash Flow Yield Method

The NPV method answers the question of a project's viability when tested against the minimum required rate of return for that particular company. This required rate is alternatively referred to as the criterion rate, or cut-off rate, being 20% in the above example. But sometimes managers want to know not just whether a project is viable, but what rate of return they can expect to earn on it.

To answer this question the NPV method is taken a stage further. The annual cash flows are discounted again at a higher trial rate of interest. Such trial is an educated guess but a higher rate rather than a lower rate is chosen, because it was a surplus NPV, as opposed to a negative one, which previously occurred.

Assuming a trial rate of 30% was chosen, then the annual cash flows can be discounted by the present value factors at 30%:

Calculation of the net present value at 30%

	Annual cash flows £	*PV factors at 30%*	£	*PV* £
Year 0	−150,000	1.000		− 150,000
1	+ 60,000	.769	+ 46,140	
2	+ 60,000	.592	+ 35,520	
3	+ 60,000	.455	+ 27,300	
4	+ 60,000	.350	+ 21,000	
5	+ 40,000	.269	+ 10,760	
6	+ 20,000	.207	+ 4,140	+ 144,860
			NPV	− £5,140

As there is a deficit net present value of £5,140, the rate of return is less than 30%. This is because too much interest has been deducted to allow all the capital to be repaid.

If, instead of going to an estimated trial rate of 30%, the annual cash flows had been repeatedly discounted at 1% intervals from the 20% required rate, then a zero net present value would have been found at approximately 28%. This is the true rate of return on the project and is known as the 'discounted cash flow yield'. In other words, the DCF yield is the solution rate of interest which results in a NPV of zero.

Interpolation

It would be a tedious task to adopt the above suggestion of

successive discounting at 1% intervals, but fortunately this is not required. The NPV calculations at 20% and 30% yielded a surplus of £28,060 and a deficit of £5,140 respectively. This provides sufficient information to estimate the DCF yield reasonably accurately by interpolation, which can then be proved by calculation.

A quick way to interpolate is to calculate the change in the NPV that equates to a 1% change in the discount rate as follows:

$$\text{Change in NPV of } 1\% = \frac{\text{Total change in NPV}}{\text{Total change in interest rate}}$$

$$1\% = \frac{28,060 + 5,140}{10\%}$$

$$1\% = £3,320$$

The discount rate of 30% resulted in a deficit NPV of £5,140. A reduction of 1% in the discount rate will reduce this deficit by approximately £3,320 and, therefore, a reduction of about 1.5%

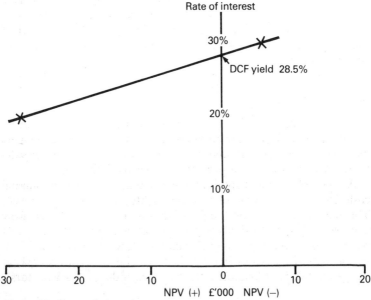

Figure 11: Interpolation chart

will be required to give an NPV of zero. The DCF yield can therefore be estimated at 28.5% which should then be tested for accuracy, after which a more precise interpolation can be made if necessary.

Another interpolation method takes the form of a simple graph with the rate of interest on the vertical axis and the net present value on the horizontal axis. The NPVs from the trial at the company's required rate and the further guesstimate are then plotted against their respective interest rates and the two plots joined by a straight line.

The approximate DCF yield is where the straight line intersects the vertical axis at a zero NPV. If the two plots are far removed from the actual rate of return, the interpolation may not be quite accurate and again it should be proved by a final calculation. (See *Fig. 11*)

It is mathematically possible to express the DCF yield to one or more decimal places. Although one decimal place may be justifiable, there is usually no case for further precision. This is because the basic data on which the calculations are performed are only estimates of future events. To calculate the DCF yield to, say, three decimal places, gives an impression of precision which is illusory.

Other Short Cuts

The interpolation techniques described earlier are obvious short cuts in the search for the solution rate of interest. Some managers may have access to calculators or computers which can rapidly answer the question of a project's rate of profitability.

Another short cut is applicable where there is a constant annual cash flow in every year of a project's life, starting at year one. This method is based on the principle that if a constant cash flow is multiplied by individual PV factors, the total present value will be the same as if the constant annual cash flow had been multiplied by the sum of the individual PV factors. This will always apply if we ignore the rounding-off differences on individual PV factors:

Example

	£1,000	×	0.870	=	£870
+	£1,000	×	0.756	=	£756
=	£1,000	×	1.626	=	£1,626

If the sum of the individual PV factors had to be arrived at by literally adding up the individual factors, this might be thought to be a long short cut! Fortunately, a table exists with all the adding up done for the reader and the total of any number of separate yearly factors can be read off at a glance. Such a table is shown in full in Appendix 2 as the cumulative present value of £1 per annum.

A cumulative PV table can be used as a short cut to both the NPV and DCF yield. Because the cumulative table applies only to constant annual cash flows this technique is usually used for rule of thumb calculations on a project's profitability.

Very often managers or industrial engineers want a quick guide as to whether it is profitable to pursue a certain course of action. This can easily be done using a cumulative PV table when the cash flows are constant. A more comprehensive evaluation incorporating taxation, grants, working capital changes, etc. can be done later.

Example

Take a proposal to introduce a forklift truck costing £50,000 to handle palletized stock in a warehouse. This can be expected to yield an annual saving in labour costs of £18,500 after deducting truck running costs. The equipment is expected to last six years and the company regards a 25% return before tax as a minimum requirement.

Calculation of the NPV at 25% on a forklift truck project

	Annual cash flow £	*Cumulative PV factor at 25%*		*PV* £
Year 0	− 50,000	1.000		− 50,000
1–6	+ 18,500	2.951		+ 54,594
			NPV	+ £4,594

Because there is an NPV surplus we conclude that the project will satisfy the required rate of return of 25%.

The above method quickly calculates the NPV but can be used to even greater effect in finding the DCF yield. In this case we require the cumulative PV factor to be first calculated, and then looked up on the line of the relevant year of the cumulative PV table.

$$\text{Cumulative PV factor} = \frac{\text{Cost of investment}}{\text{Constant annual return}}$$

$$= \frac{\text{£50,000}}{\text{£18,500}}$$

$$= 2.703$$

Looking along the year six line of the cumulative PV table for 2.703, we find 2.700 at 29% which is therefore the size of the DCF yield.

Comparison of Appraisal Methods

Four methods of investment appraisal have been discussed so far and useful conclusions can be drawn by examining the ranking of three sample projects by these four methods:

Appraisal methods compared

	Project A	Project B	Project C
	£	£	£
Year 0	− 200,000	− 200,000	− 200,000
1	+ 20,000	+ 80,000	+ 60,000
2	+ 40,000	+ 60,000	+ 60,000
3	+ 60,000	+ 60,000	+ 60,000
4	+ 60,000	+ 40,000 + 240,000	+ 60,000
5	+ 60,000		+ 40,000
6	+ 68,000 + 308,000		+ 20,000 + 300,000
Total profit	+ 108,000	+ 40,000	+ 100,000
Payback period (ranking BCA)	4.33 years	3 years	3.33 years
Rate of return (ranking ACB)	18%	10%	16.7%
NPV @ 12% (ranking CAB)	− £884	− £12,580	+ £15,100
DCF yield (ranking CAB)	12%	8.5%	15%

The payback method selects Project B as the most attractive investment but ignores the short life remaining after payback is completed. This is taken into account, however, by the DCF yield method which shows up Project B in its true light as the least profitable of all three projects.

The rate of return method selects Project A as the most profitable simply because the average profit per year is more than in the other two projects. When the timing of those profits is taken into account then Project A is shown to give a DCF yield, or true return, of only 12% compared with its undiscounted rate of return of 18%.

When Project A is compared with Project C on the DCF yield method, the extra £8,000 profit on Project A does not compensate for the slow build-up of the project. Even though total profit is this £8,000 less on Project C, the project is more profitable than Project A because discounting emphasizes the value of the earlier high returns.

In short, payback can yield useful information but must not be used by itself. Either discounting method will give more accurate results than the rate of return method when assessing the profitability of an investment over its whole life. However, firms may sometimes calculate the rate of return expected in the first year of operation and compare this with the actual return earned for monitoring purposes. This monitoring or post-audit appraisal is an important part of project investment.

Summary

This chapter started with the premise that the cost of capital employed in the business is the minimum required rate of return that needs to be earned on new investments.

The profile of any investment can be expressed in terms of money flowing in and out of the firm year by year. These yearly cash flows form the basis for a number of techniques aimed at deciding the worthiness of any planned investment.

These techniques start with the simple idea of the payback period, which although useful, does not look at the total profitability over the whole life. We also found that the return on capital technique did not cater for the individual yearly timings of cash flows and, therefore, did not accurately measure the rate of profitability.

We finally homed in on discounting techniques as being the most comprehensive when dealing with variations in yearly cash flows and being most accurate in calculating the true rate of profitability.

There are two main discounted cash flow techniques. The net present value method tells us if a certain minimum level of profitability is likely to be attained. The DCF Yield method goes a stage further and tells us the expected rate of profitability on the proposed investment.

This ends the review of basic discounting techniques. The next chapter goes on to examine ranking, followed by the special situations of capital rationing and the choice between mutually exclusive projects. It then explains how taxation, inflation and uncertainty are incorporated in capital investment appraisals.

14. Investment appraisal II

The previous chapter described the basic appraisal techniques which can be used to decide whether long-term investments are viable or not. The situations described there were based on a number of limiting assumptions, namely that:

- Unlimited capital was available
- Investments were not mutually exclusive
- Company tax payments/allowances did not apply
- Inflation did not exist
- All data could be estimated precisely

We now want to relax these limiting assumptions one by one to see what happens in the real world that firms inhabit. The virtues of discounted cash flow appraisal methods were emphasized at the end of the previous chapter, notwithstanding that empiric evidence points to payback remaining the most popular criterion.

These virtues of discounting techniques are now enhanced as we relax each of the above assumptions, because only yearly cash flow models can cope with the complexities.

Ranking

There are two ways to rank projects in order of attractiveness. The simplest is to rank them by the size of their DCF yields. Alternatively, when only the NPV method is used, we rank projects by the size of their 'profitability index'. This is calculated by dividing the NPV inflow by the NPV outflow:

$$\text{Profitability index} = \frac{\text{NPV inflow}}{\text{NPV outflow}}$$

Example

When an investment costs £100,000 initially (outflow) and the NPV of its inflows total £110,000, then its profitability index is:

$$\text{Profitability index} = \frac{£110,000}{£100,000} = 1.10$$

Any project is viable when the profitability index exceeds 1.00, but its relative profitability against other projects can be measured by the size of the index number. There is, however, one exception to this rule when dealing with mutually exclusive projects, as discussed later in the chapter.

Capital Rationing

Care must be taken when ranking in the situation where capital is insufficient to undertake all projects and has to be allocated to the most profitable ones. The selection of projects should be based on the profitability index of the competing projects for those scarce funds. This will ensure that the maximum £ inflow is earned for every £1 outflow.

Example

A firm has £200,000 capital to invest in some of the following projects:

	Cost	Profitability index
Project A	£36,000	1.27
B	£73,000	1.08
C	£120,000	1.52 *
D	£48,000	1.36 *
E	£36,000	1.15
F	25,000	1.78 *

The projects selected will be * F, C and D ranked in order of their profitability index and using £193,000 of the £200,000 capital available. The remaining projects are rejected as they earn less present value inflow for every £1 initially invested than the projects selected. If capital was not the only scarce resource at this time, then resort must be made to linear programming in a similar way to that described in Chapter 12.

Mutually Exclusive Projects

In certain situations a choice has to be made between alternative projects. By alternatives we mean where the selection of one investment automatically rules out the other, as in the case of a choice between two machines to perform the same function.

Such projects are called mutually exclusive investments and the choice should be based on the one which gives the highest NPV surplus, or lowest NPV deficit if the appraisal considers only costs.

Example

A decision has been made to install a machine to automate a manual process. Two possible machines have been identified with differing purchase costs and estimated savings over a ten year life:

	Purchase cost	Annual saving	NPV at 15%
Machine A	£25,000	£6,000	+ £5,114
Machine B	£35,000	£7,500	+ £2,642

In this case machine A will be selected as it yields the highest NPV surplus over and above the 15% cost of capital used in the present value calculations.

In some situations we may be examining costs only, with a view to minimizing the overall cost of fixed assets, like machines or buildings, over their whole life. This accords with the ideas of terotechnology which aims to pursue economic life cycle costs.

In cases where we are trying to identify the most economic asset to use from a number of choices, we base our selection on the one with the lowest total present value cost. This entails discounting all future operating and maintenance costs back to their present value at the firm's cost of capital and adding this sum to the original capital cost.

Example

You are advising a company which proposes to erect a new factory building. Two types of construction are being considered, the costs of which are detailed below. The company's cost of capital is 10% and the life of each type of construction is estimated at 20 years with no residual value at the end of that period. Which type of building would have the lowest cost over its life?

Construction:	*Type A*	*Type C*
Cost of building	£700,000	£944,000
Maintenance costs (net of tax) at each period	£100,000	£110,000
Maintenance period	every	every
	3 years	8 years
		(RICS)

The approach to this problem is to bring the periodic maintenance costs back to their present value by discounting at the appropriate 10% PV factors. When the original cost is also included we get a total PV for the whole twenty years and the design with the lowest overall PV should be selected:

	Type A *Cash flow*	*PV factor*	*PV*		Type C *Cash flow*	*PV factor*	*PV*
Year 0	−700,000	1.000	−700,000	Year 0	−944,000	1.000	−944,000
3	−100,000	.751	− 75,100	8	−110,000	.467	− 51,370
6	−100,000	.564	− 56,400	16	−110,000	.218	− 23,980
9	−100,000	.424	− 42,400				
12	−100,000	.319	− 31,900				
15	−100,000	.239	− 23,900				
18	−100,000	.180	− 18,000				
		NPV	−£945,700			NPV	−£1,019,350

The lowest total PV of the two alternatives considered is that of the Type A building and this will be the preferred choice. Any number of alternative designs can be considered in this way.

Taxation

Cash flows on any project will be incomplete if we do not build the tax effects into the yearly figures. There are two aspects to taxation, one being negative and the other positive. The negative side is the payment of tax on profits whilst the positive side is the receipt of tax allowances on certain new assets which effectively reduce the tax payments.

Corporation tax is the system of taxation which applies to profits of all limited companies and nationalized industries, as opposed to income tax which applies to the profits of the self-employed and partnerships. Differences between the two systems are confined mainly to the tax rates and the timing of the tax payments, as the tax allowances are the same in both cases. We shall concentrate our attention on the former.

The profit on which corporation tax is levied is not identical with the profit disclosed in the firm's profit and loss account, but is an adjusted figure after some costs have been disallowed and allowances inserted. The main difference is that the Inland Revenue disallow any depreciation that a company has charged to its profit and loss account and substitute capital allowances instead:

Example

	£
Profit as per profit & loss account	1,900,000
Add back: depreciation	400,000
	2,300,000
Deduct: capital allowances	440,000
Taxable profit	£1,860,000

Corporation tax payable then becomes £1,860,000 multiplied by the current rate(s) of tax.

It is, therefore, never possible to reduce the size of the company tax bill by increasing the depreciation charge, because whatever figure is charged, the Inland Revenue will add it back. However, it would be manifestly unfair if companies were disallowed depreciation and given nothing in its place, hence the system of writing down, or capital allowances.

Capital Allowances

The Inland Revenue have their own system of depreciation allowances which are called capital allowances, or writing down allowances. These are generally available to firms which buy new fixed assets of the specified categories, although some allowances are restricted to specific industries only.

Rates of capital allowances at April 1986 were:

- Industrial buildings (qualifying industries only) — 4% p.a. on a straight line basis
- Plant & machinery, office equipment, all motor vehicles (all industries) — 25% p.a. on a reducing balance basis

We shall take the 25% capital allowance on plant and machinery as an example as this applies to all fixed assets other than buildings and to all industries. The effect of the reducing balance method is that an asset is never fully depreciated at any moment in time and when sold or scrapped any unclaimed allowances are claimed later.

The amount of tax actually saved by getting an allowance is the capital allowance for the year multiplied by the rate of tax. This tax saving becomes a cash inflow for that particular year.

Example

A firm buys a computer installation for £80,000 and claims 25% capital allowance. The rate of corporation tax is 35%:

Calculation of capital allowance × Rate of tax = Tax saved

	£			£
Purchase cost of computer	80,000			
Year 1 – 25% allowance	20,000	× 35%	=	£7,000
Balance at end Year 1	60,000			
Year 2 – 25% allowance	15,000	× 35%	=	£5,250
Balance at end Year 2	45,000			
Year 3 – 25% allowance	11,250	× 35%	=	£3,937
Balance at end Year 3	33,750			
	etc.			

Tax Payments

Unlike income tax on our salaries which is collected monthly at source under the PAYE system, companies make tax payments on their yearly net income (profit) on only two or three occasions, which fall mainly in the following year. Although the total corporation tax liability is based on the profit for the year when that is finally calculated, tax is collected in stages before that time by reference to the size of the interim and final dividend payments.

These timings differ from one company to another and it is a generally agreed convention that tax payments are included in the yearly cash flow following the year the profit was made.

The taxable profit in any year is the profit from sales before charging either interest or depreciation. Interest is not deducted because the discounting process performs this function and tax relief is taken into account in the calculation of the cost of capital. As we have seen, capital allowances take the place of depreciation. If the investment was of a cost-saving nature then these cost savings increase profit and are therefore still taxable. Again, no charge for either interest or depreciation should be offset against the cost savings.

We now want to see how tax savings from capital allowances and tax payments on the profit arising from the new investment are built into the yearly cash flows. We then proceed with the discounting process using present value factors as before.

Example

A firm is considering buying a machine which costs £80,000 and is expected to last five years, when its scrap value will be about £2,000 only. Taxable profits are estimated to be £40,000 each year and the rate of corporation tax is 35%. Capital allowances of 25% on the reducing balance can be claimed but no allowances are available on the £30,000 working capital required. The cost of capital is 18% and this is regarded as the minimum requirement.

Year	Capital cost	Taxable profit	Tax payment on profit	Tax saved by C.A.	Annual net cash flow	18% PV factors	PV
	£	£	£	£	£		£
0	−80,000				−110,000	1.000	−110,000
	−30,000						
1		+40,000		+7,000	+47,000	.847	+39,809
2		+40,000	−14,000	+5,250	+31,250	.718	+22,438
3		+40,000	−14,000	+3,937	+29,937	.609	+18,232
4		+40,000	−14,000	+2,953	+28,953	.516	+14,940
5	+30,000	+40,000	−14,000	+2,215	+60,215	.437	+26,314
	+2,000						
6			−14,000	+1,661	−12,339	.370	−4,565
						NPV	+£7,168

Our conclusion is that this project is viable as it results in a surplus NPV after discounting at the required rate of 18%. This surplus is understated slightly as there are unclaimed tax allowances to come later which are not included in the above appraisal.

You will have noticed how working capital has been included in the above cash flows. Firms need to earn a return on this capital just as much as on the capital tied up in fixed assets. By subjecting the initial outflow of working capital and its eventual release to the discounting process, we ensure that the firm earns sufficient cash to service the capital tied up in stocks and debtors.

Inflation

Up to this point we have ignored inflation and its effects on the future cash flows of projects being appraised. Inflation brings two additional problems to project appraisals. It increases the uncertainty surrounding the value of future costs and revenue and it also influences the required rate of return through its effects on the cost of capital.

When describing how to incorporate both these aspects in appraisals it is useful first to distinguish between the real rate of return on a project and its nominal rate of return. A simple example may clarify this difference between real and nominal rates of return:

Example

Suppose an investor receives an income of £100 per annum on an investment of £1,000, then his nominal or apparent rate of return is 10%. If inflation is zero then his real rate of return will also be 10% as he can spend the £100 interest each year and still keep the spending power of his £1,000 capital intact. If, however, inflation is running at 6% per annum he needs to reinvest £60 of his interest to keep the value of his capital intact and can only spend the remaining £40. This £40 can be described as a real return of 4% on his investment. In approximate terms we can therefore say:

Real return   =   Nominal return   —   Rate of inflation
   4%   =   10%   —   6%

At high rates of return/inflation this approximate relationship may need refining and the more accurate relationship is now shown using decimal notation:

$$\text{Real return} = \frac{(\text{Nominal return } 1.10) - 1}{(\text{Rate of inflation } 1.06)}$$

$$= (1.038 - 1) = 0.038 \times \frac{100}{1} \% = 3.8\%$$

Turning now to individual project appraisals we need to know whether the yearly cash flows have been inflated year by year or not. If they have been inflated year by year then the DCF yield is the nominal return expected from that investment. The real return will be the nominal DCF yield minus the general rate of inflation.

When the yearly cash flows are not inflated year by year but are expressed in the constant terms of Year 0 £'s, then the DCF yield is the real return expected from the investment.

At appraisal time we are therefore faced with a choice. We can express future cash flows at their inflated values and find the nominal rate of return. Alternatively, we can express the future cash flows in Year 0 £'s and find the real rate of return.

Our choice is influenced by the way management express the target rate of return and whether we see the future cash flows keeping pace with inflation or not. Firms are tempted to express their cost of capital in nominal terms because interest rates and the cost of equity are expressed in nominal terms also. This means we should inflate the yearly cash flows, possibly at different rates for different items, and find the nominal DCF yield.

An alternative approach, if we expect the yearly cash flows to more or less keep pace with inflation, is to find the real DCF yield on the cash flows expressed in constant Year 0 £ values. We then convert this real DCF yield to a nominal DCF yield by adding the estimated rate of inflation.

Risk and Uncertainty

It would be unrealistic for us to assume that the future events expressed in yearly cash flows will occur exactly as predicted. The nature of investment appraisal is such that we are dealing with an uncertain future with the risk that one or more of income, costs, tax, inflation or project life may vary from our estimate. Some writers differentiate between risk and uncertainty along the lines that risk can be quantified but uncertainty cannot. It is intended here to use the terms synonymously.

When projects are overwhelmingly profitable it does not matter which appraisal techniques are used as they are viable on any test we care to apply. Most projects, however, are more marginal and subject to a greater degree of uncertainty.

It is here that discounting techniques come into their own by taking into account each year's cash flow over the whole life of the project. This allows us to manipulate the data to answer 'what if' questions and generally apply financial modelling techniques.

Computers have an obvious role here when we are dealing with reiterative calculations on raw data.

The more substantial a project is, relative to the size of the firm, the more sifting should be done before approval is given. We are now going to examine various approaches to risk and uncertainty ranging from a crude payback criterion at one extreme to portfolio theory at the other.

Payback was described in the previous chapter as a relatively crude technique used to measure the viability of investments. This is performed by counting the number of years it takes to recover the original investment using either discounted or undiscounted cash flows.

Sometimes firms use payback in a slightly different context to reduce the risk element in a project by setting a maximum allowable payback period. When this is applied to cash flows discounted at the firm's cost of capital it ensures that the minimum required return is always achieved and that cash is quickly generated for reinvestment.

If we can assume that events in the coming year or two can be forecast with a high degree of certainty then it also reduces the risk element. This is because distant cash flows are multiplied by relatively small present value factors and, conversely, a higher weighting is given to more immediate cash flows.

These advantages are sufficient for many firms, and payback remains one of the most popular appraisal techniques. We should be aware, however, of its potential weakness in selecting less profitable projects by its concentration on quick returns.

Example

	Project A	*Project B*
Year 0	−10,000	−10,000
1	+ 4,000	0
2	+ 4,000	+ 4,000
3	+ 4,000	+ 4,000
4	+ 4,000	+ 4,000
5	0	+ 4,000
6	0	+ 4,000

7	0	+ 4,000
8	0	+ 4,000
Payback period	2.5 years	3.5 years
DCF yield	22%	25%

If the maximum payback period was set at three years then Project A would be selected rather than the more profitable, but slow starting, Project B.

Instead of pinning all their faith on the DCF yield resulting from the expected cash flows, firms sometimes calculate two further sets of cash flows based on pessimistic and optimistic assumptions respectively. The DCF yields are calculated for all three sets of cash flows and give a better perspective of the range within which the return on investment will fall.

Example

DCF yields on different sets of cash flows

	Pessimistic	Expected	Optimistic
Project A	22%	27%	40%
Project B	− 12%	12%	21%
Project C	− 3%	20%	40%

If this company required a return of say, 20%, then Project A will be approved as it satisfies the 20% required return in all conceivable circumstances. It is very unlikely Project B will be approved, however, as only in the most optimistic circumstances will the 20% criterion just be satisfied. Project C is more difficult to evaluate as the possibility of a small loss has to be balanced against the possibility of a very high rate of return of 40%.

The main drawback of this method is now apparent. It does not quantify the degree of optimism or pessimism assumed in the sets of cash flows. A statistical technique that can be applied to overcome this weakness is contained in probability theory.

Example

A firm is considering buying new equipment costing £80,000 which has an expected life of ten years and is also expected to save £17,600 in operating costs each year when compared with existing methods. It is thought that at worst these savings would not fall below £11,600 per annum and at best that they would not exceed £23,600 per annum. The project manager has assigned subjective probability factors to various estimates of savings which are used to calculate the expected or weighted average DCF yield:

Annual saving	Probability factor	DCF yield	DCF yield × probability
£11,600	.05	7%	0.35%
£13,600	.15	11%	1.65%
£15,600	.25	15%	3.75%
£17,600	.33	18%	5.94%
£19,600	.15	21%	3.15%
£21,600	.05	24%	1.20%
£23,600	.02	27%	0.54%
	1.00		16.58%

The weighted average or expected DCF yield turns out to be 16.58%, which would be satisfactory if the required return was set at a lower level. If the required return was, say, 20% this project would not be satisfactory as the expected DCF yield at 16.58% is significantly less. Only the last three possible cash flows yield a return in excess of 20% and their combined probabilities or level of confidence in a satisfactory outcome is only 22%.

On a more complex project, like an expansion scheme to sell a new product, we can apply probability factors to each constituent item making up the cash flows. In this case we would use computers to perform the hundreds of reiterative calculations and there are appropriate programmes dedicated to this task.

Another approach is to recognize that different kinds of investment carry different degrees of risk and should therefore be set different target rates of return. A simple approach to this idea is to add an extra discount rate, called a 'risk premium', to the basic cost of capital, so setting different target rates of return for different risk categories of investment.

The risk premium may vary according to the risk category of the investment under review and is based on a subjective assessment of the risks involved. The following example illustrates this approach:

Risk category	Example	Cost of capital	Risk premium	Target rate of return
No risk	Financing decision	15%	–	15%
Low risk	Cost saving – existing technology	15%	3%	18%
Medium risk	Expansion – new markets, existing technology	15%	10%	25%
High risk	Expansion – new markets, new technology	15%	20%	35%

In practice, investors demand a higher return on more risky investments than on less risky ones. By using the risk premium approach firms are giving recognition in their individual investment apraisals to what investors themselves practise when investing in individual companies.

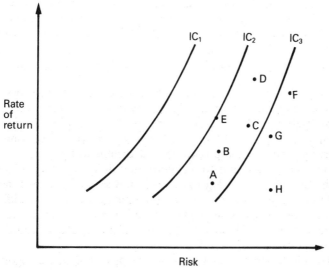

Figure 12: Portfolio selection

An extension of this idea is found in what is referred to as 'portfolio theory', where a collection of investments is described as a portfolio. Many portfolios can be constructed from different combinations of investments.

The risk level of each portfolio is measured by the variability of possible returns about the mean expressed in standard deviations. Investors' attitudes to 'risk versus return' can be expressed on indifference curves. In Figure 12, any point on indifference curve IC_1 gives a higher return, or lower risk, than its equivalent point on IC_2 which itself is preferred to IC_3.

When we add various alternative portfolios assigned the letters A–H on to the same graph, the selected portfolio will be the one which reaches the highest possible indifference curve. This is indicated on Figure 12 as portfolio E, which is the closest to IC_2, with no portfolio reaching IC_1. (See *Fig. 12*)

Portfolio theory goes on to say that it is not the individual project risk that matters but its effect on the overall portfolio's risk. Therefore, when we evaluate a risky project we need to correlate the individual project risk to that of the existing portfolio it would join if accepted.

A branch of portfolio theory called the 'capital asset pricing model' states that we should calculate the net present value on a new project at a composite discount rate comprising:

(a) a rate of interest representing the risk-free cost of capital plus
(b) a risk premium or discount determined by the correlation of the risk on the individual project to the risk on the whole existing portfolio it would join. This is referred to as the beta factor.

One further approach to risk in the context of investment appraisal is that of sensitivity testing. This takes the form of recalculating the NPV or DCF yield assuming a different value for any one variable in the cash flows.

Example

A firm requires a minimum return of 15% on any new investment and is proposing to buy a new machine costing £20,000 which is expected to save £5,000 each year of its ten year life. This project may be sensitive to any reduction in the expected life or annual saving.

First the DCF yield is calculated on the expected events which turns out to be 21%. Next an arbitrary percentage change in one variable is taken and the DCF yield recalculated to get an estimate of sensitivity. If, say, the estimated life was 10% less at only nine years then the DCF yield would still be 20% and, therefore, this project is relatively insensitive to length of life. This would not be the case, however, with short-life projects of only a few years.

The sensitivity test is repeated for a 10% reduction in the annual savings reverting to the original expected life of ten years. This reduces the DCF yield from the original 21% to only 18%, so we conclude that this project is more sensitive to inaccuracies in the savings estimate than to those of estimated life.

Many other techniques are available to deal with risk including the 'minimax criterion' and decision tree analysis coupled with probability theory.

Summary

The previous chapter dealt with the basic theory of investment appraisal with emphasis on the production of yearly cash flow models for both payback and discounted cash flow calculations.

These models have been extended in this chapter to examine certain situations where further manipulation is required. First, we examined the possibility of capital being scarce and the need to maximize its return by selecting projects with the highest profitability index.

Another situation that can arise requires us to choose between alternative (mutually exclusive) projects, which we do by selecting the one with the highest NPV surplus or lowest NPV deficit as appropriate.

In the real world of taxation and inflation, private sector companies need to incorporate their effects in the cash flows of projects and think their way through whether to set the target in real or nominal terms.

Finally, we spent some time looking at a variety of approaches to the problem of uncertain data which exists with nearly all projects. All of the above ideas are to help us make the best decision now on capital spending, the consequences of which may be with us for many years to come.

Notwithstanding this scientific approach there is still a place for management art and subjective judgement. When these are reinforced by a quantitative assessment of the costs and benefits, as described above, then the outcome is surely improved.

Appendix 1: Present value of £1

n Year	5%	6%	7%	8%	9%	10%	11%	12%	13%	14%	15%	16%	17%	18%	19%	20%	21%	22%	23%	24%	25%	26%	27%	28%	29%	30%	35%	40%
0	1.000	1.000	1.000	1.000	1.000	1.000	1.000	1.000	1.000	1.000	1.000	1.000	1.000	1.000	1.000	1.000	1.000	1.000	1.000	1.000	1.000	1.000	1.000	1.000	1.000	1.000	1.000	1.000
1	.952	.943	.935	.926	.917	.909	.901	.893	.885	.877	.870	.862	.855	.847	.840	.833	.826	.820	.813	.807	.800	.794	.787	.781	.775	.769	.741	.714
2	.907	.890	.873	.857	.842	.826	.812	.797	.783	.769	.756	.743	.731	.718	.706	.694	.683	.672	.661	.650	.640	.630	.620	.610	.601	.592	.549	.510
3	.864	.840	.816	.794	.772	.751	.731	.712	.693	.675	.658	.641	.624	.609	.593	.579	.564	.551	.537	.524	.512	.500	.488	.477	.466	.455	.406	.364
4	.823	.792	.763	.735	.708	.683	.659	.636	.613	.592	.572	.552	.534	.516	.499	.482	.467	.451	.437	.423	.410	.397	.384	.373	.361	.350	.301	.260
5	.784	.747	.713	.681	.650	.621	.593	.567	.543	.519	.497	.476	.456	.437	.419	.402	.386	.370	.355	.341	.328	.315	.303	.291	.280	.269	.223	.186
6	.746	.705	.666	.630	.596	.564	.535	.507	.480	.456	.432	.410	.390	.370	.352	.335	.319	.303	.289	.275	.262	.250	.238	.227	.217	.207	.165	.133
7	.711	.665	.623	.583	.547	.513	.482	.452	.425	.400	.376	.354	.333	.314	.296	.279	.263	.249	.235	.222	.210	.198	.188	.178	.168	.159	.122	.095
8	.677	.627	.582	.540	.502	.467	.434	.404	.376	.351	.327	.305	.285	.266	.249	.233	.218	.204	.191	.179	.168	.157	.148	.139	.130	.123	.091	.068
9	.645	.592	.544	.500	.460	.424	.391	.361	.333	.308	.284	.263	.243	.225	.209	.194	.180	.167	.155	.144	.134	.125	.116	.108	.101	.094	.067	.048
10	.614	.558	.508	.463	.422	.386	.352	.322	.295	.270	.247	.227	.208	.191	.176	.162	.149	.137	.126	.116	.107	.099	.092	.085	.078	.073	.050	.035
11	.585	.527	.475	.429	.388	.350	.317	.287	.261	.237	.215	.195	.178	.162	.148	.135	.123	.112	.103	.094	.086	.079	.072	.066	.061	.056	.037	.025
12	.557	.497	.444	.397	.356	.319	.286	.257	.231	.208	.187	.168	.152	.137	.124	.112	.102	.092	.083	.076	.069	.062	.057	.052	.047	.043	.027	.018
13	.530	.469	.415	.368	.326	.290	.258	.229	.204	.182	.163	.145	.130	.116	.104	.093	.084	.075	.068	.061	.055	.050	.045	.040	.037	.033	.020	.013
14	.505	.442	.388	.340	.299	.263	.232	.205	.181	.160	.141	.125	.111	.099	.088	.078	.069	.062	.055	.049	.044	.039	.035	.032	.028	.025	.015	.009
15	.481	.417	.362	.315	.275	.239	.209	.183	.160	.140	.123	.108	.095	.084	.074	.065	.057	.051	.045	.040	.035	.031	.028	.025	.022	.020	.011	.006
16	.458	.394	.339	.292	.252	.218	.188	.163	.141	.123	.107	.093	.081	.071	.062	.054	.047	.042	.036	.032	.028	.025	.022	.019	.017	.015	.008	.005
17	.436	.371	.317	.270	.231	.198	.170	.146	.125	.108	.093	.080	.069	.060	.052	.045	.039	.034	.030	.026	.023	.020	.017	.015	.013	.012	.006	.003
18	.416	.350	.296	.250	.212	.180	.153	.130	.111	.095	.081	.069	.059	.051	.044	.038	.032	.028	.024	.021	.018	.016	.014	.012	.010	.009	.005	.002
19	.396	.331	.277	.232	.194	.164	.138	.116	.098	.083	.070	.060	.051	.043	.037	.031	.027	.023	.020	.017	.014	.012	.011	.009	.008	.007	.003	.002
20	.377	.312	.258	.215	.178	.149	.124	.104	.087	.073	.061	.051	.043	.037	.031	.026	.022	.019	.016	.014	.012	.010	.008	.007	.006	.005	.002	.001
25	.295	.233	.184	.146	.116	.092	.074	.059	.047	.038	.030	.025	.020	.016	.013	.011	.009	.007	.006	.005	.004	.003	.003	.002	.002	.001	.001	.000
30	.231	.174	.131	.099	.075	.057	.044	.033	.026	.020	.015	.012	.009	.007	.005	.004	.003	.003	.002	.002	.001	.001	.001	.001	.000	.000	.000	.000
35	.181	.130	.094	.068	.049	.036	.026	.019	.014	.010	.008	.006	.004	.003	.002	.002	.001	.001	.001	.001	.001	.000	.000	.000	.000	.000	.000	.000
40	.142	.097	.067	.046	.032	.022	.015	.011	.008	.005	.004	.003	.002	.001	.001	.001	.000	.000	.000	.000	.000	.000	.000	.000	.000	.000	.000	.000
45	.111	.073	.048	.031	.021	.014	.009	.006	.004	.003	.002	.001	.001	.001	.000	.000	.000	.000	.000	.000	.000	.000	.000	.000	.000	.000	.000	.000
50	.087	.054	.034	.021	.013	.009	.005	.003	.002	.001	.001	.001	.000	.000	.000	.000	.000	.000	.000	.000	.000	.000	.000	.000	.000	.000	.000	.000

Note: The above present value factors are based on year-end interest calculations.

Appendix 2: Cumulative present value of £1 per annum

Year	5%	6%	7%	8%	9%	10%	11%	12%	13%	14%	15%	16%	17%	18%	19%	20%	21%	22%	23%	24%	25%	26%	27%	28%	29%	30%	35%	40%
1	.952	.943	.935	.926	.917	.909	.901	.893	.885	.877	.870	.862	.855	.847	.840	.833	.826	.820	.813	.807	.800	.794	.787	.781	.775	.769	.741	.714
2	1.859	1.833	1.808	1.783	1.759	1.736	1.713	1.690	1.668	1.647	1.626	1.605	1.585	1.566	1.546	1.528	1.510	1.492	1.474	1.457	1.440	1.424	1.407	1.392	1.376	1.361	1.289	1.224
3	2.723	2.673	2.624	2.577	2.531	2.487	2.444	2.402	2.361	2.322	2.283	2.246	2.210	2.174	2.140	2.106	2.074	2.042	2.011	1.981	1.952	1.923	1.896	1.868	1.842	1.816	1.696	1.589
4	3.546	3.465	3.387	3.312	3.240	3.170	3.102	3.037	2.974	2.914	2.855	2.798	2.743	2.690	2.639	2.589	2.540	2.494	2.448	2.404	2.362	2.320	2.280	2.241	2.203	2.166	1.997	1.849
5	4.329	4.212	4.100	3.993	3.890	3.791	3.696	3.605	3.517	3.433	3.352	3.274	3.199	3.127	3.058	2.991	2.926	2.864	2.804	2.745	2.689	2.635	2.583	2.532	2.483	2.436	2.220	2.035
6	5.076	4.917	4.767	4.623	4.486	4.355	4.231	4.111	3.998	3.889	3.784	3.685	3.589	3.498	3.410	3.326	3.245	3.167	3.092	3.021	2.951	2.885	2.821	2.759	2.700	2.643	2.385	2.168
7	5.786	5.582	5.389	5.206	5.033	4.868	4.712	4.564	4.423	4.288	4.160	4.039	3.922	3.812	3.706	3.605	3.508	3.416	3.327	3.242	3.161	3.083	3.009	2.937	2.868	2.802	2.508	2.263
8	6.463	6.210	5.971	5.747	5.535	5.335	5.146	4.968	4.799	4.639	4.487	4.344	4.207	4.078	3.954	3.837	3.726	3.619	3.518	3.421	3.329	3.241	3.156	3.076	2.999	2.925	2.598	2.331
9	7.108	6.802	6.515	6.247	5.995	5.759	5.537	5.328	5.132	4.946	4.772	4.607	4.451	4.303	4.163	4.031	3.905	3.786	3.673	3.566	3.463	3.366	3.273	3.184	3.100	3.019	2.665	2.379
10	7.722	7.360	7.024	6.710	6.418	6.145	5.889	5.650	5.426	5.216	5.019	4.833	4.659	4.494	4.339	4.192	4.054	3.923	3.799	3.682	3.571	3.465	3.366	3.269	3.178	3.092	2.715	2.414
11	8.306	7.887	7.499	7.139	6.805	6.495	6.207	5.938	5.687	5.453	5.234	5.029	4.836	4.656	4.486	4.327	4.177	4.035	3.902	3.776	3.656	3.544	3.437	3.335	3.239	3.147	2.752	2.438
12	8.863	8.384	7.943	7.536	7.161	6.814	6.492	6.194	5.918	5.660	5.421	5.197	4.988	4.793	4.611	4.439	4.278	4.127	3.985	3.851	3.725	3.606	3.493	3.387	3.286	3.190	2.779	2.456
13	9.394	8.853	8.358	7.904	7.487	7.103	6.750	6.424	6.122	5.842	5.583	5.342	5.118	4.910	4.715	4.533	4.362	4.203	4.053	3.912	3.780	3.656	3.538	3.427	3.322	3.223	2.799	2.469
14	9.899	9.295	8.745	8.244	7.786	7.367	6.982	6.628	6.302	6.002	5.724	5.468	5.229	5.008	4.802	4.611	4.432	4.265	4.108	3.962	3.824	3.695	3.573	3.459	3.351	3.249	2.814	2.478
15	10.380	9.712	9.108	8.559	8.061	7.606	7.191	6.811	6.462	6.142	5.847	5.575	5.324	5.092	4.876	4.675	4.490	4.315	4.153	4.001	3.859	3.726	3.601	3.483	3.373	3.268	2.825	2.484
16	10.838	10.106	9.447	8.851	8.313	7.824	7.379	6.974	6.604	6.265	5.954	5.669	5.405	5.162	4.938	4.730	4.536	4.357	4.190	4.033	3.887	3.751	3.623	3.503	3.390	3.283	2.834	2.489
17	11.274	10.477	9.763	9.122	8.544	8.022	7.549	7.120	6.729	6.373	6.047	5.749	5.475	5.222	4.990	4.775	4.576	4.391	4.219	4.059	3.910	3.771	3.640	3.518	3.403	3.295	2.840	2.492
18	11.690	10.828	10.059	9.372	8.756	8.201	7.702	7.250	6.840	6.467	6.128	5.818	5.534	5.273	5.033	4.812	4.608	4.419	4.243	4.080	3.928	3.786	3.654	3.529	3.413	3.304	2.844	2.494
19	12.085	11.158	10.336	9.604	8.950	8.365	7.839	7.366	6.938	6.550	6.198	5.877	5.584	5.316	5.070	4.843	4.635	4.442	4.263	4.097	3.942	3.799	3.666	3.539	3.421	3.311	2.848	2.496
20	12.462	11.470	10.594	9.818	9.129	8.514	7.963	7.469	7.025	6.623	6.259	5.929	5.628	5.353	5.101	4.870	4.657	4.460	4.279	4.110	3.954	3.808	3.673	3.546	3.427	3.316	2.850	2.497
25	14.094	12.783	11.654	10.675	9.823	9.077	8.422	7.843	7.330	6.873	6.464	6.097	5.766	5.467	5.195	4.948	4.721	4.514	4.323	4.147	3.985	3.834	3.694	3.564	3.442	3.329	2.856	2.499
30	15.372	13.765	12.409	11.258	10.274	9.427	8.694	8.055	7.496	7.003	6.566	6.177	5.829	5.517	5.235	4.979	4.746	4.534	4.339	4.160	3.995	3.842	3.701	3.569	3.447	3.332	2.857	2.500
35	16.374	14.498	12.948	11.655	10.567	9.644	8.855	8.176	7.586	7.070	6.617	6.215	5.858	5.539	5.251	4.992	4.756	4.541	4.345	4.164	3.998	3.845	3.703	3.571	3.448	3.333	2.857	2.500
40	17.159	15.046	13.332	11.925	10.757	9.779	8.951	8.244	7.634	7.105	6.642	6.234	5.871	5.548	5.258	4.997	4.760	4.544	4.347	4.166	3.999	3.846	3.703	3.571	3.448	3.333	2.857	2.500
45	17.774	15.456	13.606	12.108	10.881	9.863	9.008	8.283	7.661	7.123	6.654	6.242	5.877	5.552	5.261	4.999	4.761	4.545	4.347	4.166	4.000	3.846	3.704	3.571	3.448	3.333	2.857	2.500
50	18.256	15.762	13.801	12.234	10.962	9.915	9.042	8.305	7.675	7.133	6.661	6.246	5.880	5.554	5.262	5.000	4.762	4.545	4.348	4.167	4.000	3.846	3.704	3.571	3.448	3.333	2.857	2.500

Note: The above present value factors are based on year-end interest calculations.

Appendix 3: Glossary of terms

Absorption costing A system of costing where cost units (i.e. products) absorb indirect costs in addition to the allocated direct costs.

Acid test see **Liquidity ratio**

Activity ratio Used in standard costing to express the actual work produced as a percentage of the budgeted work for the same period when both are expressed in standard hours.

Apportionment The process of splitting an indirect cost into smaller parts to charge to various cost centres.·

Asset Any possession or claim on others which is of value to a firm. See also Fixed assets and Current assets.

Balance sheet A statement of the financial position of a firm at a point in time showing the assets owned and the sources of finance.

Batch costing A type of job costing where a batch of identical products is treated as an individual job for costing purposes. The unit cost is found by dividing the total batch cost by the number of units produced.

Break-even chart A graph showing the break-even point where the total cost line intersects the sales revenue line.

Break-even point The level of output, or sales value, at which total cost equals total revenue.

Budgetary control A system of detailed financial plans to meet corporate objectives over a future period of time, not exceeding one year.

Capacity ratio Used in standard costing to express the actual hours worked as a percentage of the budgeted standard hours.

Capital allowance The Inland Revenue's equivalent of a company's depreciation charge. Allowances are granted on purchases of certain new fixed assets, and reduce taxable profits.

Capital employed All sources of finance excluding current liabilities. Sometimes called net capital employed.

Capital expenditure Expenditure on fixed assets with a life expectancy of more than one accounting period.

Capital gearing The relationship of borrowed capital to either shareholders' funds or total capital employed.

Cash budget A monthly plan of future cash receipts and payments showing the cumulative balance.

Common fixed cost A fixed cost which does not relate to any one cost unit but is incurred on behalf of multiple cost units.

Contract costing A type of job costing where all costs are accumulated on an individual contract for a building or engineering construction.

Contribution The difference between sales and the variable cost of goods sold, before charging any fixed costs.

Contribution price variance Used in standard marginal costing to evaluate any difference in actual sales price from the standard sales price for the actual quantity sold. Identical with the sales price variance in standard absorption costing.

Contribution ratio (or Profit/Volume ratio) Contribution expressed as a percentage of sales revenue.

Contribution volume variance Used in standard marginal costing to evaluate the total contribution gained or lost through actual sales volume varying from the budgeted sales volume.

Controllable cost A cost which is the direct responsibility of, and influenced by, the manager concerned.

Corporation tax Tax levied on a limited company's profit after capital allowances have been deducted.

Cost centre A physical location within an organization where costs are accumulated.

Cost classification The analysis of costs into homogeneous groups according to source, nature and ultimate destination in the costing system.

Cost code A numbering system used to describe the type, source and purpose of all costs and income.

Cost element Labour or material or expense.

Cost-plus pricing Where a percentage mark-up is added to the total cost of a product to calculate the selling price.

Cost unit Any product or service to which costs can be charged.

Cost/Volume/Profit (CVP) analysis A study of the effect of changing levels of output on profit.

Creditor Anyone to whom a firm owes money. Trade creditors are purchases bought on credit and awaiting payment in due course.

Current assets Stocks, work-in-progress, debtors and cash/bank balances.

Current liabilities Short-term sources of finance from trade creditors, bank overdraft, dividend and tax provisions awaiting payment within the next twelve months.

Current ratio A measure of liquidity obtained by dividing current assets by current liabilities.

Debt ratio Total debts expressed as a percentage of total assets.

Debtor A credit customer or other party who owes money to the firm.

Depreciation A proportion of the original (or current) cost of a fixed asset which is charged as an expense in the profit and loss account.

Differential costing The costs and/or revenues of alternative courses of action which are compared to identify the difference between them.

Direct cost A cost which can be specifically allocated to a cost unit (product), say, for example, any raw materials used or labour expended.

Direct fixed cost A fixed cost which can be specifically identified with a product line or segment of activity.

Discounted cash flow (DCF) yield A measure of the true rate of profitability expected on a project. It represents the maximum rate of interest which could be allowed to leave a net present value of zero.

Dividend cover A measure of the security of the dividend payment obtained by dividing the profit after tax by the total dividend for the year.

Earnings Profit attributable to the ordinary shareholders after interest, tax and any preference dividends have been deducted, irrespective of whether that profit is distributed or retained in the company.

Earnings per share Earnings for the year divided by the number of ordinary shares issued.

Efficiency ratio Used in standard costing to measure efficiency by expressing the standard hours equivalent of the work produced as a percentage of the actual hours taken.

Financial accounting The recording of financial transactions leading to the preparation of global financial statements: for example, profit and loss account or balance sheet. Although used by top management, these statements are also used for external reporting.

Fixed assets Physical assets kept by the firm to carry on its business: for example, buildings, plant and vehicles.

Fixed budget A budget which remains unchanged, irrespective of the actual level of output.

Fixed costs Costs which do not vary in total when the level of activity varies. Rent and rates are typical examples.

Fixed overhead expenditure variance The difference between the actual cost and the budgeted cost of fixed overheads.

Fixed overhead volume variance The under- or over-recovery of fixed overheads caused by the actual level of activity varying from the budgeted level used to set the standard absorption rate.

Flexible budget A budget which is designed to change in accordance with the actual level of activity achieved.

Funds flow see **Sources and applications of funds**

Gearing see **Capital gearing** or **Operational gearing**

Goal congruence When the objectives of an individual manager coincide with those of the organization.

Gross profit The difference between sales and the cost of sales before charging general overhead expenses.

Income gearing The annual interest charge expressed as a percentage of the annual operating profit. The larger the percentage, the higher the level of financial risk.

Incremental expenditure The additional expenditure incurred in pursuing a new project.

Indirect costs or **Overheads** Costs which cannot be identified with specific cost units.

Interest cover The number of times the annual operating profit covers the interest charge.

Interfirm comparison The comparison of accounting ratios of different firms to measure relative performance.

Internal rate of return (IRR) see **DCF yield**

Investment appraisal The use of accounting and statistical techniques to determine the worthiness of new investment projects.

Investment centre A type of responsibility centre where the manager is responsible for revenues, costs, profit and investment culminating in either a residual profit or return on capital objective.

Irrelevant costs Costs which remain unaffected by the decision under review and can therefore be ignored.

Job costing A system of costing which accumulates costs for each job separately.

Labour efficiency variance The difference between the hours taken and the standard hours allowed for the actual level of production, evaluated at the standard rate per hour.

Liabilities Money owing and repayable at some future time to shareholders or third parties, for example, banks and suppliers.

Liquid assets Cash, bank balances and customer debts which will be converted into cash in a few weeks. Essentially liquid assets are all current assets excluding stocks and work-in-progress.

Liquidity The ability of a company to pay its short-term debts when they become due.

Liquidity ratio A measure of liquidity obtained by dividing liquid assets by current liabilities.

Machine-hour rate A method of charging overheads to cost centres obtained by dividing the budgeted overheads by the budgeted number of hours.

Managed costs see **Controllable costs**

Managed cost centre A responsibility centre where the manager is responsible for giving the best level of service whilst keeping within his budget.

Management accounting The provision of detailed cost and income data to facilitate the role of managers in financial planning, controlling and decision making.

Management by exception The reporting to managers of only the significant variances from standard or budget.

Management information system Any planned system of collecting, storing, processing and presenting information to management so that effective decision making and control can take place.

Margin Either gross or net profit as a percentage of sales value.

Margin of safety The difference between the current level of activity and that needed to break even, expressed as a percentage of the current level.

Marginal costing A system of costing used for decision making which is based on the analysis of costs into fixed and variable categories.

Mark-up A percentage addition to costs to cover overheads and/or profit.

Master budget The overall budget built up from the detailed functional budgets and expressed in a budgeted profit and loss account, a budgeted balance sheet and a budgeted funds flow statement.

Material mix variance The cost difference arising from the combination of materials in non-standard proportions.

Material price variance The difference in cost between actual and standard unit purchase prices, multiplied by the actual quantity purchased.

Material usage variance The difference in cost arising when the actual quantity of material is compared with the standard quantity for the actual level of production. Both quantities are evaluated at the standard price.

Material yield variance The value of the abnormal gain or loss in process, in excess of the standard allowance.

Net capital employed see **Capital employed**

Net cash flow A comparison of total cash in with total cash out for each year, being part of an investment appraisal.

Net current assets see **Working capital**

Net present value (NPV) The value obtained by discounting all yearly net cash flows back to Year 0 value at either the cost of capital or other target rate.

Operational or **operating gearing** A measure of the effect a given change in sales will have on profit, obtained by dividing contribution by net profit.

Opportunity cost The cost of a resource in an alternative use to the one being considered.

Overhead absorption rate A basis on which indirect costs are charged to individual product lines, for example, £x per direct labour hour.

Overhead efficiency variance This variance arises in standard costing when overheads are recovered on the basis of time as opposed to units of product. It is the difference between the standard overhead cost allowed for the actual production level achieved, and the standard overhead cost for the actual time taken.

Overhead expenditure variance The difference between the actual cost and the budgeted cost of overheads.

Overheads see **Indirect costs**

Overhead recovery rate see **Overhead absorption rate**

Payback period The number of years taken to recoup the original investment.

Portfolio theory A branch of investment appraisal concerned with risk.

Present value The value now of a future sum of money after interest has been deducted by discounting at an appropriate rate.

Price/Earnings ratio A stock market yardstick used to assess the market rating of ordinary shares. It is calculated by dividing the market price by the earnings per share.

Prime costs The total of all direct labour, direct material and direct expenses.

Process costing The system of costing used when production is of a continuous nature rather than of discrete units.

Profitability A relative measure of performance found by expressing profit as a percentage of capital employed and/or turnover.

Profitability index A measure of the attractiveness of an investment found by dividing the NPV of the inflows by the NPV of the outflow. It is also used in capital rationing situations to ensure the maximum £ inflow for every scarce £ outflow.

Profit and loss account A statement of trading performance, typically for a month or a year, when sales income is compared with total expenditure which comprises the cost of sales and overheads relating to the period under review. Once the profit is computed, the statement concludes by showing its appropriation in tax and dividend payments with any balance being retained.

Profit centre A type of responsibility centre where the manager is responsible for costs and revenues and therefore profit. Managers have no authority over the level of investment in this case.

Profit margin A ratio used to measure performance, calculated by expressing gross or net profit as a percentage of sales value.

Profit/Volume ratio see **Contribution ratio**

Profit/Volume chart A chart or graph depicting profit or loss at all levels of activity.

Quick ratio see **Liquidity ratio**

Ratio A pair of figures, usually taken from a profit and loss account and/

or a balance sheet, which are related together and used as an indicator of performance. A typical example is the return on capital.

Rate of return A rather arbitrary method of investment appraisal which relates average annual profit to the capital employed.

Rate of return pricing A method of pricing where the total cost of products is enhanced by the amount of profit required to yield the desired return on capital.

Relevant costs Costs which are affected by the decision under review and which therefore must be taken into account.

Relevant range The range of activity level within which costs behave in a linear fashion.

Residual profit (Income) Used in responsibility accounting as a performance target for managers. It is calculated as a money figure of profit after interest has been charged on the capital invested.

Responsibility accounting A system of accounting used in decentralized organizations to identify costs, income, profit and investment with individual managers for the purpose of assessing their performance.

Responsibility centre A part of a decentralized organization for which a manager has responsibility. It can be a managed cost centre, a revenue centre, a profit centre or an investment centre.

Return on capital A key ratio used to measure overall performance, calculated by expressing annual profit as a percentage of the closing (or average) capital employed.

Revenue centre A type of responsibility centre where the manager is responsible for the income generated from sales.

Sales price variance The total gain or loss caused by selling the actual level of sales at a non-standard price. It is calculated by multiplying the actual sales quantity by the difference between standard and actual selling prices.

Sales volume variance The total value of the profit margins gained or lost on the difference in quantity between actual sales and budgeted sales.

Segment margin The contribution of a product line, or other segment of a business, after any direct (specific) fixed costs have been taken into account.

Semi-variable or semi-fixed costs Costs which include both fixed and variable elements and therefore neither stay constant nor move pro rata with the level of activity.

Sensitivity analysis Used in investment appraisal as a risk technique where any component in the net cash flows can be examined for its effect on the NPV or DCF yield when its value is varied from the original estimate.

Sources and applications of funds statement A financial statement for a period of time showing both internal and external sources of cash and where that cash has been applied.

Standard cost A predetermined cost which is compared with the actual cost to highlight any significant variances for investigation and analysis.

Standard cost centre A type of responsibility centre where the managers' performance is judged by their ability to operate within the standard costs allowed for their products.

Standard hour A measure of the volume of work achievable in one hour.

Standard marginal cost A type of standard cost where only variable costs are included in the standard cost specification. Fixed costs are excluded for control by budgets or other means.

Stock turnover rate A ratio used to measure the speed in weeks at which any kind of stock is used up.

Sunk costs Costs which were previously incurred and are now irrelevant to the decision under review, other than any opportunity cost they may possess.

Transfer pricing The basis for pricing goods or services transferred between different segments of an organization. It is a critical issue when the performance of the individual segments is monitored, as is usually the case.

Turnover or **Revenue** Alternative terms for the value of sales within a period of time.

Turnover of capital employed A ratio used as a performance indicator to measure the number of £ sales achieved within a year for every £1 of capital employed in the business.

Uniform costing A system of cost comparisons between similar organizations operating in service industries so that relative performance can be measured.

Variable costs Costs which vary in total when the level of activity varies. For example, the total cost of direct materials will move pro rata to the level of activity.

Variance The difference between a budget/standard and the actual cost.

Variance analysis The analysis of differences between standard costs and actual costs into their causes.

Working capital or **Net current assets** The part of a firm's total capital which is tied up in stocks, work-in-progress and debtors and not financed by short-term debts. It is equal to current assets less current liabilities.

Appendix 4: Sample questions

Chapter 1   Cost Analysis and Classification

Question with answer

1 In the establishment of a system of cost accounting, classification and coding is extremely important.

Required:
- (i) (a) Briefly explain what is meant by 'classification'
    - (b) Distinguish between 'subjective' and 'objective' classification.
- (ii) (a) Define the term 'coding'
    - (b) Give an example of a 'composite' symbol and explain its significance
    - (c) List four advantages derived from the use of coding.

(LCCI)

Question without answer

2 Cost must be classified to facilitate its arrangement in as flexible a manner as possible.

Required:
- (a) Explain the meaning of the 'classification of cost' and give some practical examples of the ways cost is classified.
- (b) Design a code number series for use in a costing system integrated with a financial accounting system. Detail some practical examples of the code numbers.
- (c) Detail four advantages of using code numbers for stock materials.

(AAT)

Chapter 2   Costing Labour, Materials and Overheads

Questions with answers

1 Wood & Bark Ltd trade in a single product and maintain a perpetual inventory. The company has valued its stock on the LIFO basis, but is now proposing to change to the FIFO method.

Their records disclose that 2,000 units were in stock at the beginning of the current period, and valued on the basis of a receipt of 5,000 units priced at £2.50, of which 4,000 had been sold before the end of the period, plus 500 from a delivery in 1980 when the cost was £2.00 per unit, plus 500 purchased in 1957 when the cost was £0.50 per unit.

The following transactions took place in the period January 1982 to June 1982:

January	– Sold	1,500 units	at £4.00 each
February	– Received	10,000 units	at £2.50 each
March	– Sold	8,000 units	at £4.00 each
April	– Received	15,000 units	at £2.60 each
May	– Received	6,500 units	at £2.70 each
June	– Sold	22,000 units	at £4.00 each

You are required:
(a) to calculate the stock valuation at 30 June 1982 using:
   (i) the LIFO method
   (ii) the FIFO method.
(b) to calculate the trading profit for the period January to June 1982 using both methods of valuation for opening and closing stocks.
(c) to reply to Mr Wood who suggests, 'In order to be consistent we should value opening stock on the LIFO basis and closing stock on the FIFO basis in the trading account'.
(d) to explain the possible reasoning behind the company's decision to change to the FIFO method at the present time.
(e) to summarize the advantages and disadvantages of the FIFO method of stock valuation.

(AAT)

2 (a) From the following information relating to component BCD you are required to calculate:

   (i) the re-order level
   (ii) the re-order quantity
   (iii) the minimum level
   (iv) the average stock held.

Maximum stock has been set at:		5,500 units
Usage per month	Maximum	1,100 units
	Minimum	900 units

Estimated delivery	Maximum	4 months
period	Minimum	2 months

(b) What do you consider to be the essential practices of efficient storekeeping? Explain by giving at least four examples.

(AAT)

3 An industrial concern manufactures three products known as P, Q and R. Each product is started in the machining area and completed in the finishing shop. The direct costs associated with each product forecast for the next trading period are:

	P	Q	R
	£	£	£
Materials	18.50	15.00	22.50
Wages:			
machining area at £5 per hour	10.00	5.00	10.00
finishing shop at £4 per hour	6.00	4.00	8.00
	£34.50	£24.00	£40.50

There are machines in both departments and machine hours required to complete one of each product are:

Machine area	4	1.5	3
Finishing shop	0.5	0.5	1
Budget output in units	6,000	8,000	2,000
Fixed overheads are:			
machine area		£100,800	
finishing shop		£94,500	

Required:
(a) an overhead absorption rate for fixed overheads using:
    (i) a labour-hour rate for each department
    (ii) a machine-hour rate for each department.
(b) the total cost of each product using:
    (i) the labour-hour rate
    (ii) the machine-hour rate, as calculated in (a) above.
(c) your comments to the factory manager who has suggested that one overhead rate for both departments would simplify matters.
(d) the fixed cost and the variable rate of overhead cost for the machining area. This has been constant over the previous five periods, and extracted from the following:

Period	Total overhead	Labour hours
	£	
1	92,600	21,300
2	86,200	18,100
3	95,250	22,625
4	105,500	27,750
5	93,200	21,600

(AAT)

Questions without answers

4 Stoker and Coke Ltd are coal merchants. During 1981 they sold 120,000 tonnes of coal. The original price was £90 per tonne which rose on 1 April to £110 per tonne. 40,000 tonnes were sold at the lower price. The rise in the selling price for coal reflected an increase from the collieries from £75 to £95 per tonne. However, shrewd purchasing by Stoker, who expected a price increase, meant that they purchased 30,000 extra tonnes at the old price, in addition to the coal sold. A further 60,000 tonnes were purchased at the new price.

The stock on hand at 1 January 1981 was 10,000 tonnes which cost £620,000. During the year, stocks never fell below 10,000 tonnes before the price rise, nor 20,000 tonnes after the price rise, although the latter stock level was reached twice – in September and on 31 December 1981. Distribution and selling costs amount to 6% of sales, and administration costs amount to £80,000 per month.

In the past, Stoker and Coke Ltd have always used the FIFO method of stock costing for accounting purposes, but Mr Coke was told that the LIFO system provides more realistic accounting information.

You are required to:
(a) calculate the net profit (ignore taxation) under both methods for the year ended 31 December 1981
(b) comment upon the different results produced by the two methods.

(Certified Diploma)

5 A factory manufactures three components, A, B and C. During week 26, the following was recorded:

Labour grade	Number of employees	Rate per hour	Individual hours worked
		£	
I	6	4.00	40
II	18	3.20	42
III	4	2.80	40

| IV | 1 | 1.60 | 44 |

Output and standard times during the same week were:

Component	Output	Standard minutes (each)
A	444	30
B	900	54
C	480	66

The normal working week is 38 hours, overtime is paid at a premium of 50% of the normal hourly rate.

A group incentive scheme is in operation. The time saved is expressed as a percentage of hours worked and is shared between the group as a proportion of the hours worked by each grade. The rate paid is 75% of the normal hourly rate.

(a) You are required to calculate the total payroll showing the basic pay, overtime premium and bonus pay as separate totals for each grade of labour.

(b) Journalize the payroll assuming: Income Tax deducted is £884.00; National Insurance payable by employee is 6% of gross pay; National Insurance payable by employer is 5% of gross pay; 12 employees are members of the Social Club whose weekly subscription is 25 pence.

(c) Summarize two advantages and two disadvantages of group incentive schemes.

(AAT)

6 A company which made one type of product had an actual output this year of 36,000 units compared with a budgeted output of 32,000 units. Sales for the year were 34,000 units at a selling price of £34 per unit, while the opening stock for the year was 5,000 units. There was no opening stock in the preceding year. Using an absorption costing system based on budgeted levels of output, unit costs for this year and the preceding year were as follows:

	This year	*Preceding year*
	£24	£22
Prime cost	£24	£22
Production overhead (fixed and variable)	5	4
Selling and administrative overhead (fixed)	1	1
Total cost	£30	£27
Profit	4	3
Selling price	£34	£30

Fixed production overhead this year was £48,000 and £3 per unit last year.

You are required:
(a) to prepare tabular income statements for this year on the basis:
    (i) that an absorption costing system is in use, based on budgeted levels of output
    (ii) that fixed production overhead is charged against revenue for the year in which the expense is incurred.
(b) to comment on the reasoning underlying the different results.

(AAT)

7   All good wage-incentive schemes should incorporate certain general principles.

You are required to list and discuss five such general principles.

(AAT)

Chapter 3   Job and Process Costing

Questions with answers

1   A specialist manufacturer of purpose-built plant engaged in three separate jobs in May 1983. The following costs were incurred:

	Job A	Job B	Job C
Direct materials purchased	£524	£671	£382
Direct labour:			
skilled, hours	158	170	16
semi-skilled, hours	316	190	30
Site expenses	£118	£170	£25
Selling price of job	£3,318	£2,750	£1,950
Completed at 30April 1983	100%	80%	25%

The following information is available:
    Direct materials for the completion of the jobs have been recorded.
    Direct labour is paid: skilled £5 per hour; semi-skilled £4 per hour.
    Site expenses tend to vary with output.
    Administration expenses total £440 per month and are to be allocated to the jobs.
    On completion of the work, the practice of the manufacturer is to divide the calculated profit on each job 20% to the site staff as a bonus,

80% to the company. Calculated losses are absorbed by the company in total.

You are required to:
(a) calculate the profit or loss by the company of Job A.
(b) project the profit or loss by the company of Jobs B and C.
(c) comment on any matters you think relevant to management as a result of your calculations.
(d) advise management whether to accept Job D which must be delivered by 30 June 1983. Job D is identical to Job B, but the customer has agreed to accept a 10% increase in the selling price. As Jobs B and C must also be delivered by 30 June, management is concerned that there may be insufficient labour available as this cannot be increased. No other orders are in prospect.

(AAT)

2   The following information relates to Process B for Period 4:
Work-in-progress at start of period – Nil.
Material transferred from Process A during the period – 2,500 kilos valued at £7,145.
Wages paid – 234.5 hours at £4.00 per hour.
Other direct costs allocated – £463.
Normal waste during processing – 5% of Process A input. This has a scrap value of 16p per kilo and is credited to the process account.
At the end of Period 4, there were 2,100 kilos transferred to finished stock, and 150 kilos remained in work-in-progress.
The work-in-progress is 100% completed so far as materials are concerned, but only 80% labour and 60% other direct costs are completed.

(a) You are required to construct:
   (i) the Process B account showing your workings clearly
   (ii) any other accounts relevant to the process.
(b) Process costing is a method of costing falling within the broader category of Operation Costing. An alternative category is known as Specific Order Costing.
   Briefly distinguish between Operation Costing and Specific Order Costing, stating any other methods of costing associated with these broader terms.

(AAT)

Questions without answers

3   On 1 October, 6,000 square metres of canvas in unfinished condition

were on hand, the cost value being £5,250 for direct material and £3,900 for wages and overhead combined.

During October a further 25,000 square metres were put into process, the material cost being £22,650. Wages and overhead together amounted to £30,525. 20,000 square metres were completed and transferred to the warehouse whilst 11,000 square metres remained in process at closing time on 31 October, being only half-finished so far as wages and overhead were concerned but complete as to material content. Output is valued on the 'weighted average' cost basis.

Required:
Tabulate the above information and calculate:
 (i) The value of work-in-progress as at 31 October
 (ii) The cost of finished output.

(LCCI)

4   A Public Works company secures a contract to build a technical college at a fixed contract price of £5 million, completion must be in time to meet the start of the educational session starting two years hence.

Work commenced on 1 July and at 31 December, the following details had been recorded in the costing records:

	£
Materials purchased	620,000
Wages paid	140,000
Other direct charges	127,000
Plant sent to site (at valuation, 1 July)	180,000
Value of work measured (to 15 December)	860,000
Cash received	774,000

Additionally you ascertain:

Materials on site not used to date	14,000
Work completed, but not measured	74,000

Plant is depreciated at 20% per annum against valuation.

Required:
(a) A contract account for the period showing the amount of profit/loss you consider should be taken to the profit and loss account.
(b) Explain why the amount taken to profit and loss account may differ from the normal profit.

(AAT)

Chapter 4 Pricing

Question with answer

1 Your company makes a single product, the Betascope.

(a) You have been asked to calculate the unit selling price by the company from the information, provided below, based on a monthly output of 1,000 units:

17 units of raw material at £7.50 per unit

125 hours of direct labour at £2.50 per hour

variable overheads at 40% of direct labour cost

fixed overhead is to be recovered at the rate of 10% of total variable cost

mark-up is 50% of total cost

(b) The company's monthly potential productive capacity is 1,000 units. For the coming month it is forecast that the factory will only produce at 80% of its potential. Also, you are informed that raw materials, wages and variable overheads are expected to rise by 15%, 10% and 5% respectively. Fixed costs of £56,500 will not alter.

Using a marginal cost approach, calculate the new unit selling price on the basis that the financial director requires the factory output to yield a constant amount of monthly profit.

(IOM Adapted)

Question without answer

2 The Flexible Tool Company manufactures and sells three industrial power drills. The company's policy is to apportion fixed overheads month by month on the basis of monthly direct labour hours. Wages are paid at a rate of £2.50 per hour. The forecast fixed overheads for November, 1985, are £14,000.

The variable unit costs relating to components and assembly for each type of drill are:

Drill Type	D 123	D 456	D 789
Parts	£15.00	£25.50	£30.00
Direct labour	5.00	7.50	10.00
Variable overhead	1.50	3.00	2.00

The company calculates its selling price by doubling the total cost (i.e. variable costs plus apportioned fixed overheads). The sales forecast for November, 1985, is as follows:

	D 123	D 456	D 789
Units	400	500	300

You are required to:
  calculate the unit selling price of each drill, showing your workings in a clear manner.

(IOM Adapted)

Chapter 5   Profit/Volume Planning

Questions with answers

1 From the following information you are required to:
(a) calculate the unit selling price.
(b) prepare the break-even chart.
(c) calculate the total profit.
(d) calculate the profit if the cost of ingredients rises by 10% and the selling price was reduced by 10%.

Autumn Products operates on a seasonal basis preparing and selling Christmas food hampers. The company's fixed costs amount to £10,000. The cost of ingredients is £80 per hamper. Each hamper costs £5 and takes 2 hours at £2.50 per hour to pack and decorate. The company anticipates selling 1,000 hampers at a unit selling price of total cost plus 40% mark-up.

(IOM)

2 The board of directors of your company is about to make a decision as to the installation of equipment which will result in the redundancy of a number of operating staff. The overall effect will be a reduction of variable cost but an increase in fixed costs, and a potential increase in production.

You have been requested to prepare notes of the points they need to consider, with special reference to the effects of operating gearing.

(Certified Diploma)

3 An electrical component manufacturer budgets to sell 36,000 units although the factory has the capacity to produce 40,000 units in normal circumstances.

Direct costs per unit are:

wages	£2.00
materials	£8.00
overheads	£4.00
	£14.00

Fixed costs for the period are expected to be £201,600.

The selling price is £20 per unit.

You are required:
(a) to calculate how many units must be made and sold in order to break even during the period. Express the information on a break-even chart for presentation to the management.
(b) to ascertain the budgeted profit for the period assuming opening and closing stocks are the same.
(c) to state the number of units to be manufactured when the amount of capital invested in this production is £330,000 and the directors require a 15% return on this.
(d) to advise the management on the results calculated in item (c) above stating any reservations you may have.

(AAT)

Questions without answers

4 G. Limited makes product H in each of its two manufacturing divisions, J in the north and K in the south.

The following trading results for two months are given for the two divisions:

		February 1984 £		March 1984 £
Division J				
Sales: units	810		960	
value		58,320		69,120
Total cost of sales		56,160		61,560
Profit		2,160		7,560

	£		£
Division K			
Sales: units	780	830	
value	56,160		59,760
Total cost of sales	51,200		53,200
Profit	4,960		6,560

Using the information given above you are required to:
(a) calculate for each division the number of units sold to:
  (i) break even
  (ii) make a profit of £14,400 per month.
(b) state which division would suffer the larger loss if sales were to fall 100 units below its break-even point.

(RSA)

5 A company manufactures one product and the results for last year are shown in the simplified profit statement given below:

			£000
Sales	20,000 units		300
Costs:		£000	
variable		150	
fixed		90	
			240
Profit			60

(a) You are required to construct a break-even chart to show the break-even point and the margin of safety.
(b) Based on the above you are required to draw separate break-even charts to indicate the effect on profit of each of the following increases in:
  (i) sales price per unit
  (ii) fixed cost per annum
  (iii) variable cost per unit
  (iv) sales volume per annum.

(RSA)

6 B. Ltd is investigating the likely sales for next year. The projection is that 75,000 units will be sold at £10.60 each. The variable costs are £4.20 per unit and the relevant fixed costs are £220,000.
  Three possible alternatives have been suggested. The managing director thinks that more could be sold if the price was reduced by 5%.

The production manager thinks that the price could be increased by 10% with only a small loss in sales. The sales manager proposes that the variable cost should be increased by 20p per unit as commission to the sales force, with a consequent saving in fixed costs of £15,000.

You are required:
(a) to calculate the levels of sales required under the first two proposals to maintain the projected profit at its original level before the proposals were considered.
(b) to show the break-even point if the sales manager's proposal was accepted, and to compare this with the break-even point before the proposals were considered.

(AAT)

Chapters 6 & 7 Standard Costing

Questions with answers

1 It has been decided that the performance of the assembly department of your company is to be measured using ratios based upon standard hours.

During two succeeding periods the following information was obtained:

	Period 1	*Period 2*
Budget production in standard hours	2,000	2,250
Actual hours worked	1,800	2,400
Actual production in standard hours	1,750	2,250

(a) You are required to produce the following for each of the above periods:
  (i) the efficiency ratio
  (ii) the activity ratio
  (iii) the capacity ratio.
(b) You are also required to comment on the figures you have produced in (a).

(Certified Diploma)

2
(a) Calculate the material and labour variances from the following data:

Standard Cost of Component XY:

material cost	£0.60 per kg
material weight to produce one component	1.5 kg

wages rate, per hour	£3.80
time required to manufacture one component	36 minutes
Standard selling price, per component	£3.50

The following was recorded in the month of May 1983:

components manufactured and sold		3,510
sales income		£12,285
materials purchased and issued	(i)	2,740 kg. at £0.58
	(ii)	2,315 kg. at £0.62
wages paid for the production	(i)	880 hours at £3.90/hr
	(ii)	1,300 hours at £3.65/hr

(b) Present the answers to the above information in a statement to management disclosing the reasons for the differences between standard and actual gross profit.

(c) A consultant recently stated that 'Past performance is the best guide to ascertaining standard costs'.
Analyse this statement in detail and indicate whether or not you agree with it.

(AAT)

Questions without answers

3 You are given the following information in relation to the month just finished:

Budget production	3,200 units	Actual production	3,050 units
Actual hours worked	25,250	Actual labour cost	£60,600
Standard labour rate per hour	£2.60	Standard hours per unit	8

You are required:
(a) to calculate
    (i)   the efficiency ratio
    (ii)   the capacity ratio
    (iii) the activity ratio.
(b) to calculate
    (i)   the labour efficiency variance
    (ii)   the labour rate variance
    (iii) the labour cost variance.
(c) to comment on the results.

(AAT)

4 F. Limited makes and sells two products, G and H, using two direct materials, J and K, and two grades of direct labour, 1 and 2.

The following information has been extracted from the standard prime cost per unit of each of the products:

		Standard price per kilogram	*Product G kilograms*	*Product H kilograms*
Direct material:	J	£3.00	30	24
	K	£4.00	15	12
		rate per hour	*hours*	*hours*
Direct labour:				
Grade 1		£2.50	20	16
Grade 2		£2.00	15	14

Direct materials received are charged to stores at standard price.

During the month ended 31 March 1985, 80 units of product G and 120 units of product H were made.

Actual data for the month of March 1985 were as follows:

	Direct material J	*Direct material K*
Stock at start, quantity	NIL	NIL
Received: quantity	6,000 kgms	3,000 kgms
value	£18,200	£11,920
Stock at end, quantity	700 kgms	370 kgms
Direct labour:	*Grade 1*	*Grade 2*
hours	3,500	3,000
wages	£8,785	£5,900

You are required to calculate:
(a) the standard prime cost per unit of each product.
(b) for the month of March 1985
    (i) total standard prime cost of actual production
    (ii) total material price variance
    (iii) total material usage variance
    (iv) total direct labour cost variance, and analyse it into rates of pay and efficiency variances.

(RSA)

5 The sales budget for the last quarter for a division of a large company which markets two similar products was as follows:

Sales budget	Units	Value
Model:		£
'Prestige'	5,000	10,000
'Superior'	5,000	7,500
	10,000	17,500

The standard variable cost per unit was 'Prestige' £1.30 and that of 'Superior' 70p. Although the two products are not completely interchangeable it is thought that one type is purchased in lieu of the other, despite being sold through different outlets.

The results for the last quarter were as follows:

Actual sales	Units	Value
Model:		£
'Prestige'	7,500	14,250
'Superior'	2,800	4,480
	10,300	18,730

The costs charged were as standard.

The management have expressed their disappointment at the results and have asked you to prepare:
(a) a standard variance analysis.
(b) suggestions as to how this stage of affairs can be prevented or anticipated in the future.

(Certified Diploma)

Chapters 8 & 9   Budgetary Control

Questions with answers

1 In the preparation of budgets it is important to separate controllable costs from non-controllable costs.
(a) Distinguish between:
    (i) controllable costs, and
    (ii) non-controllable costs.
(b) Sketch a budget statement, which is to be presented on a monthly basis, for a small workshop, showing four controllable costs and four non-controllable costs.
(c) Outline the duties of a budget committee.

(AAT)

2

(a) (i) Explain the purpose of a cash budget.
   (ii) From what principal source is the cash budget prepared?
(b) On 31 December 1984, the summary balance sheet of Kingsley &
   Dickens Ltd, booksellers, was as follows:

	£		£
Capital	10,000	Shop equipment	3,750
Creditors	5,000	Stock of books	6,000
Proposed dividends	750	Debtors	3,750
		Cash in bank	2,250
	15,750		15,750

The following transactions are anticipated for the next three months:

	Credit sales	Cash sales	Credit purchases	Cash purchases
January	£3,750	£3,500	£6,000	£500
February	4,500	1,250	5,750	250
March	5,000	3,000	6,750	250

Additionally, you are informed:
  Wages paid will be £250 per month.
  Postage and packing is to be 20% of credit sales, and paid in the month
  of sale.
  Debtors normally pay one month after books are sold to them.
  Creditors are paid one month after receipt of books.
  Shop equipment will be replaced on 1 January. The new equipment
  will cost £6,000 and payment will be made in equal instalments in
  February, March and April. The old equipment will realize £2,000 in
  February.
  Depreciation of the new equipment will be 10% per annum and charged
  to accounts monthly.
  Half the dividends proposed will be paid in March, half in July next.
  The company expects a gross profit of 33.33% on selling price.

Required:
 (i) A cash budget for three months ending 31 March 1985
 (ii) A forecast trading and profit and loss account
(iii) A forecast balance sheet at 31 March 1985.

(c) Miss Kingsley cannot understand why the cash balance does not
   equate with the profit and loss account surplus. How would you
   respond?

(AAT)

Questions without answers

3   You are contemplating leaving your full-time employment and starting a consultancy business specializing in marketing research.

You have looked into the possibility and have discovered the following facts:

(i) Your available capital is £5,000. This you would pay into your business' bank account at the beginning of June 1984.

(ii) You estimate there are 200 working days in the year. In the first six months you anticipate charging clients for the following days:

June	5	September	10
July	8	October	12
August	10	November	12

Your daily charging rate will be £150.

(iii) Your clients will take one month's credit.

(iv) Expenses, which will be recovered from clients with the fee charges, will amount to 15% of the fees charged.

These costs will be paid by you in the month in which the consultancy is undertaken.

(v) Office equipment, having an estimated life of 5 years, will be purchased in June on the following terms:

    Cost   £5,500
    Deposit   £ 500
    12 monthly instalments from July of £500 each (including interest of £83 per instalment).

(vi) Secretarial and admin. costs are likely to be £300 per month. These will be paid monthly as incurred.

(vii) Premises can be rented on the following terms:

    Premium for a five year lease   £   500
    Annual rental payable in advance on 1 June   £1,200

You are required to prepare:

(a) the cash forecast for your consultancy for the six months to 30 November 1984

(b) the profit forecast for the six months ending 30 November 1984

Work to the nearest £.   (IOM)

4

(a) Explain the term 'limiting factor'.

(b) Give an example of how it may be recognized, and explain how the cost accountant may assist management in overcoming the problem.

(AAT)

5   A company manufactures two products. Each product uses two kinds of material and three grades of labour.

The next budget period includes the following:

Budget period – 12 weeks; 5 days are worked each week and normal attendance is 7 hours per day.

Products:

	Fern	*Alder*
Budget sales (units)	1,500	3,000

Material consumption per product

	Fern	*Alder*
A (£2 per kilo)	3 kilos	2 kilos
B (£4 per kilo)	3 kilos	1 kilo

Labour cost and utilization

	Fern	*Alder*
Grade 1 (£3 hour)	2 hours	1 hour
Grade 2 (£4 hour)	2 hours	1 hour
Grade 3 (£5 hour)	1 hour	1 hour

There are employed: 16 – Grade 1, 15 – Grade 2, 10 – Grade 3.

Labour is paid a premium of 50% on basic pay for overtime.

Absenteeism and lateness (which are not paid) are expected to be 5% of time available and evenly spread over the three grades.

Labour efficiency is assessed at 75% in normal time but at 100% in overtime.

Budgeted stocks of products and materials:

	Opening	*Closing*
'Fern'	400	10 days' sales
'Alder'	600	30 days' sales
Material A	5,000 kilos	20 days' usage
Material B	1,000 kilos	20 days' usage

There is a 2% loss in material consumption anticipated.

Required for the budget period:
(a) The production quantities for the period.
(b) The direct wages cost budget. Include overtime if necessary.
(c) The direct material cost budget.

(AAT)

6   A. Ltd can produce 10,000 units of a product per month when operating at 100% capacity. The following information is obtained from the records:

Month	Sept.1981	Oct.1981
Units produced	8,800	7,300
Costs	£	£
Production labour	6,160	5,110
Heating	3,900	3,900
Security salaries	880	880
Repairs	6,480	5,580
Production material	51,040	42,340
Depreciation	7,640	7,640
Supervisors' salaries	6,880	5,980
Rent and rates	6,300	6,300
Lighting	2,336	2,006
General labour	3,696	3,066

The rate of production is 5 units per hour.

You are required to:
(a) compute the cost of production at 100%, 80% and 75% capacity, showing separately prime cost and the variable, semi-variable and fixed components of production overhead.
(b) show the overhead recovery rate per hour at 80% capacity.

(AAT)

7   'Budgets are based on sales figures, so there is no point in budgeting in a service industry or in local or central government.'
  You are required to comment on this statement in relation to your own definition of budgeting, which you should give.

(AAT)

Chapter 10   Ratio Analysis

Questions with answers

1   From the following annual accounts of New Horizons Limited you are required to calculate the following ratios and comment on the results, indicating what other information you would require.

(i) Gross profit percentage	(vi) Stock: turnover
(ii) Net profit percentage	(vii) Fixed assets: turnover

(iii) Return on total assets	(viii) Return on shareholders' funds
(iv) Quick assets ratio	(ix) Current ratio
(v) Debtors' collection period	(x) Debt ratio

Balance sheet at 30 April 1985

	£000
Share capital	450
Retained profits	240
	690
12% debentures	700
Trade creditors	620
Proposed dividend	45
	£2,055
Fixed assets net of depreciation	£875
Stock	310
Debtors	770
Bank balance	100
	£2,055
Sales for the year	£3,100,000
Gross profit	1,725,000
Expenses	805,000
Depreciation	250,000

(IOM)

2 The following balance sheets as at 31 December relate to Crocks plc, wholesale hardware merchants:

£000 1982		£000 1983
1,000	Issued share capital (fully paid)	1,000
240	Profit and loss account	200
300	Debenture stock	300
	Current liabilities:	
160	Trade creditors	200
£1,700		£1,700
1,500	Fixed assets at cost	1,500

325	less provision for depreciation	400
1,175		1,100
	Current assets:	
300	stock-in-trade	300
200	trade debtors	250
25	cash	50
£1,700		£1,700

Extracts from the profit and loss account for 1983:

	sales	3,000
	gross profit	600
	net profit before tax	300

The Trade Association has published average figures compiled from returns submitted by all members of the Association, in respect of the year 1983. Some of these are:

(i)	rate of stock turnover	10 times
(ii)	debtors' average credit time	40 days
(iii)	percentage gross profit to turnover	25%
(iv)	percentage net profit to turnover	8%
(v)	return on capital employed	15%

You are required to:

(a) write a short essay to show your understanding of (i) interfirm, and (ii) intrafirm comparisons and their purpose.

(b) comment on the performance of Crocks in comparison with the average.

(c) state two other ratios/percentages you would expect to see if you were a shareholder in Crocks and you were considering whether or not to dispose of your shareholding. Give reasons for your selection and ignore any interim or final dividends which may have been paid during the year.

(RSA)

Questions without answers

3 At the 30 April 1982, the accounts of a company showed the following actual figures for the first four months of the year:

	£
Turnover	1,200,000
Variable costs	780,000
Fixed costs	240,000
Fixed assets	400,000
Working capital	200,000

The company has financial objectives expressed in working ratios as follows:

Pre-tax profit	15% of turnover value
Pre-tax profit	30% of capital employed
Gross profit margin	35%
Margin of safety	43%

The directors require expansion and, in the final four months of 1982, have stated that expansion accompanied by cost reduction and more aggressive selling prices should result in an improved performance. Hence for this period the following changes are to be made:

(i) output to be increased by 10%. All output is expected to be sold
(ii) sales prices reduced by 5%
(iii) variable cost savings for four months, £42,000
(iv) working capital to be increased by 15%
(v) fixed assets, unchanged in value
(vi) fixed costs increased by £19,000 to cover additional insurance and other charges.

You are required to:
(a) tabulate comparative figures for the first four months and the third four months, with appropriate ratios (to the nearest whole number).
(b) state your opinion as to the worthiness of the director's proposals.

(AAT)

4 Define 'return on capital employed' and 'current ratio'. How can they be used and what factors determine each?

(RICS)

5

CHG LTD
Balance sheets at 31 December:

	1981	1982		1981	1982
Share capital	20,000	20,000	Buildings at cost	20,000	–
Capital reserves	3,000	33,000	Plant & equipment	19,200	20,000

Retained profit	12,000	15,000	Stock & work-in-		
Creditors	8,000	10,000	progress	12,000	18,000
10% loan stock	10,000	10,000	Debtors	6,400	10,800
Tax due	1,600	1,800	Cash in hand	200	41,000
Bank overdraft	3,200	–			
	£57,800	£89,800		£57,800	£89,800

(a) Explain the changes that have taken place in the balance sheet between the two years.
(b) Define working capital and compute the current ratio for the two years.

(RICS)

Chapter 11   Responsibility Accounting

Question with answer

1
(a) What are the principal types of financial responsibility centre? Describe the financial objectives of the manager of each centre.
(b) What are the main considerations which will affect the choice of the definition and measurement of these responsibility centres?
(c) What criteria should be used for deciding which measure of financial responsibility to use for each organizational unit?

(Certified Diploma)

Questions without answers

2   The directors of a business wish to institute a system of Responsibility Centre Accounting and have asked you to explain the system of responsibility accounting.

You are required to prepare an explanation with special reference to the three types of responsibility centres, namely:
   expense centre; profit centre; investment centre.

(Certified Diploma)

3   You have recently been appointed as a consultant to a small engineering company with a sales turnover of £80m. The directors have been considering a decentralization scheme which will involve the creation of five divisions with profit responsibilities. The finance director has been quoted: 'This change will create a climate in which the divisional managers will be judged by their own performance'.

You are required to prepare a briefing for the managing director which:
(a) identifies the advantages and disadvantages of making an interest charge based on divisional capital employed.
(b) outlines any problems in defining and measuring the capital employed on which to base an interest charge.

(Certified Diploma)

4 A recent American study has shown that despite the alleged conceptual weaknesses in measuring the performance of divisions, the majority of divisionalized companies use a percentage figure of Return on Investment (ROI) and not a figure, expressed in dollars, of the Residual Income (RI) remaining after making a charge for the use of the capital invested in the division.

Required:
A description, with examples, of the alleged conceptual weaknesses and explain why, none the less, ROI (Return on Investment) is used.

(Certified Diploma)

Chapter 12 Short-Term decisions

Questions with answers

1 Your company manufactures three products, the Alpha, the Beta and the Gamma.

The following information has been given to you from the sales forecast for the month of August 1984:

	Alpha	*Beta*	*Gamma*
Forecast demand	50	150	200
Raw materials per unit	£100	£150	£80
Direct labour hours (at £3.00 per hour)	5	8	2

Variable overhead: 10% of total cost of materials and labour.

Fixed overhead is to be allocated to the products at 150% of total direct labour cost.

Selling price is calculated by adding 50% of total cost.

(a) Calculate: (i) the unit selling prices
                (ii) the contribution per direct labour hour.
(b) Prepare a forecast of the profit for the month of August in sufficient detail to measure the performance of each product.
(c) If the direct labour available in August falls below that required to produce at the forecast level, how would you allocate it in order to maximize your profit, assuming that each product may be sold independently and that the labour force can be transferred from one product to another?

(IOM)

2   Your company's sales director has just received the following statement from the company's accountant.
   Your company trades through three branches, each selling an identical product in different parts of the country.
   The sales director considers that Branch B should be closed down.

Branch	A	B	C
Units sold	5,000	6,000	3,000
Sales income	£50,000	£54,000	£45,000
Less: direct cost of goods sold	25,000	30,000	15,000
Gross profit	£25,000	£24,000	£30,000
Salesmens' commission:			
10% of selling price	5,000	5,400	4,500
Branch fixed cost	5,000	5,000	5,000
Allocation of head office fixed cost at £2 per unit sold	10,000	12,000	6,000
Total cost	20,000	22,400	15,500
Net profit	£5,000	£1,600	£14,500

You are required to:
(a) redraft the report using the marginal costing approach showing:
   (i) the contribution by branch
   (ii) the contribution per unit sold per branch
   (iii) total profit for the three branches.
(b) write a memorandum to the sales director indicating:
   (i) the benefits of marginal costing

(ii) your appraisal of the branches' performance

(iii) the loss of profit if Branch B were closed down.

(c) What steps may the branch managers take to improve the perform-ance of their branches?

(d) What steps could the sales director take to improve the performance of branch managers?

(IOM)

3   An offer has been made by a company to supply on an annual contract all the requirements for components in a section of your business, for the sum of £32,000 per annum.

The annual costs of your own production of components have been budgeted as follows for the coming year:

	£
Materials	12,000
Labour	10,000
Overheads	15,000
	£37,000

Required:

A report showing the information which you would take into account when considering such a proposition.

(Certified Diploma)

Questions without answers

4   A company manufactures four products. The following information has been provided for the last accounting period:

Product	Sales value £'000	Contribution/Sales ratio
Q	240	15%
R	300	17%
S	160	− 6.25%
T	140	5%

Total fixed costs are £60,000

(a) Required:

(i) total variable costs for all products

(ii) the net profit or loss of the company

(iii) the total contribution/sales ratio.

(b) 5,000 units of Product S were sold. Certain modifications have been proposed which would increase variable costs by £4 per unit, but the selling price could be increased to £40 per unit. It is forecast that 3,000 units could be sold in the next accounting period. Fixed cost would not be altered. Required: Your recommendation for this proposal.

(c) Define 'differential costing'.
(Your explanation should refer to calculations you have made in (b) above).

(AAT)

5   Perton Ltd manufacture special machinery to customers' orders. The cost estimation department have costed an enquiry received from Shipley Ltd at £15,200 on a total absorption cost basis, and have suggested a selling price of £17,000. Shipley decline to give an order at this price and propose that £14,000 is all they are willing to pay.

Required:
Discuss this problem from Perton's point of view. Your essay should include a description of alternative costing principles that might allow Perton to accept the order at £14,000 and an indication of the criteria which Perton might take into account in deciding whether or not to accept the order.

(RSA)

6   On a farm of 200 acres, 100 acres are used for growing wheat, 20 acres for growing kale, and the remainder is reserved for milk cattle to graze on, this area being just adequate for the size of the herd.

Annual costs of seed and fertilizer are (per acre): wheat £64, kale £60. The entire kale crop is fed to the dairy herd but, if sold, its market value would be £4,800. Other food for the herd costs £8,000 per annum.

The annual wheat crop sells for £36,000 and the milk sales realize £32,000.

As the herd is self-replenishing, no question of depreciation arises.

General costs, including farmworkers' wages, rent, rates, etc., amount to £40,000 per annum. These would not vary as a result of any re-allocation of the acreage. So far as this farm is concerned, there would be an outlet for all it could produce of wheat or kale or milk.

Required:
State how you would allocate the acreage in order to maximize its profitability, and state the additional annual profit likely to arise from the change you recommend.

(LCCI)

Chapters 13 & 14   Investment Appraisal

Questions with answers

1   The board of Pilmar Plastics Ltd is considering whether or not to replace equipment used in the manufacture of a particular type of television case. It is estimated that the remaining life of this product is five years and that at the end of that time any equipment held will be valueless. The selling price of the case is £5.00 and sales of 20,000 units per annum are expected over the next five years.

Three alternatives have been suggested by the Chief Production Engineer:

A   Persisting with the existing equipment which originally cost £60,000 five years ago and which is being depreciated at 10% per year on a straight line basis. The total annual cost of this method including depreciation is £95,000. This method has a continuing investment in working capital of £20,000.

B   Purchase of new equipment which would cost £300,000. In this case there would be a trade-in allowance of £50,000 on the old equipment. This method requires a total investment in working capital of £40,000 and the total annual cost, including depreciation, would be £82,000.

C   Sale of the existing equipment to Biret (Gloucester) Ltd for £20,000 plus a royalty of 25p on each case sold over the next five years. Biret expects to sell 20,000 units per annum. The cost of capital used by Pilmar Plastics Ltd for appraising capital proposals is 15%.

Required:
(a) Show, by computation, which of the three alternatives A, B or C offers the most attractive financial proposition for Pilmar Plastics Ltd (Ignore taxation).
(b) Comment on the implications of the information produced in your answer to (a).

(Certified Diploma)

2   Smith is a building inspector who may use his own car for which he is reimbursed at 12.5 pence per mile. He now has to decide whether to buy a second-hand car and run it for three years or buy a new car. The following alternative terms have been offered:

	Second-hand car	New car
Purchase price:	£	£
payable at once	2,500	deposit 500
end of first year		3,000
end of second year		2,000
Scrap or trade-in value:		
End of third year	250	1,000

It is expected that annual mileage will be:

	Using second-hand car	Using new car
First year	16,000	20,000
Second year	16,000	20,000
Third year	12,000	20,000

You are required to assess the relative merits of each alternative, using the 'net present value' method and the tables given below.

It is assumed that the cost of capital will remain at 10 per cent per annum throughout the three-year period and the mileage allowances will be received at the end of each of the three years.

Net present value table

Year	Discount factor at 10%
1	0.909
2	0.826
3	0.751
4	0.683

(RSA)

3 The directors of Milnthorpe Engineering plc are considering the feasibility of issuing 12% debentures at par to raise £1,000,000 for an investment to broaden their product range. The new plant is expected to produce a return of £240,000 per year indefinitely, before tax and interest charges.

The company's existing capital structure is:

	£
Issued ordinary shares (£0.50 nominal value)	3,000,000
Issued 5% preference shares (£1 nominal value)	6,000,000
Reserves	6,000,000
	£15,000,000

The current market values of ordinary and preference shares are £2.00 and £0.80 respectively, and the company's current maintainable earnings before meeting corporation tax at an effective rate of 50% are £3,840,000 per year.

Required:
(a) Calculate the weighted average cost of capital before the issue of the debentures.
(b) If there is no change in the cost of either equity or preference capital, what would you expect the market value for ordinary shares to be immediately after the issue of the debentures, and what would the weighted average cost of capital be at that time?
(c) Discuss the effect of issuing debentures on the weighted average cost of capital of a company.

(Certified Diploma)

Questions without answers

4 Your company is contemplating replacement of one of its machines. Two alternative ways of purchase have been examined:
 (i) outright purchase, and
 (ii) credit purchase over 5 years.
The machine will cost £100,000 if purchased for cash or £20,000 deposit followed by 5 equal annual instalments of £20,000 each, if purchased on credit terms. It is estimated that repairs will cost £5,000 and £10,000 during years 2 and 4 respectively and that the scrap value will be £10,000 at the end of year 5. Your company's cost of capital is 10% per annum.

Which purchase method would you advise and why?

Describe the following methods of investment appraisal:
 (i) Accounting rate of return
 (ii) Payback method.

Present value of £1 at 10% cost of capital
received at the end of year

	1	.909
	2	.826
	3	.751
	4	.683
	5	.621

(IOM)

5 Your company is about to launch a new product. This will require the abandonment of an existing line. You have been given the following information to assist you in selecting the products to abandon:

Product			Net sales income			
	Year 1	Year 2	Year 3	Year 4	Year 5	Year 6
A	£140,000	£40,000	£50,000	£60,000	£80,000	£100,000
B	80,000	80,000	80,000	80,000	80,000	
C	40,000	80,000	120,000	160,000		
New line	30,000	80,000	105,000	320,000	354,000	400,000

The cost of capital is to be taken as 10%. The present value of £1 received in the future is:

Year	1	2	3	4	5	6
	£.909	.826	.751	.683	.621	.564

You are required to:
(a) calculate the present value of the future cash flows for the four products. State, giving your reasons, which product you would discontinue.
(b) state the advantages of the discounted cash flow method of investment appraisal.
(c) compare this technique with the payback method.
(d) What other information would you, as a marketing manager, require before you make a final decision?

(IOM)

6   You have been told that the financial director in your company has identified a capital structure which he believes will minimize the long run 'average cost' of capital. This structure is:

	£'000	Cost of capital
Equity	6,000	11% net
Debt	4,000	7% gross

The cost of equity has been determined as follows:

Dividend yield	5%
Annual dividend growth rate	6%
	11%

The company is profitable and a 50% corporation tax rate is relevant.

You are a senior member of the engineering capital section, and with your team you have been examining a problem in the crimping department. The PX73 machine was purchased 5 years ago for £20,000, and was given a depreciation life of 8 years with no residual value. Although the PX73 machine could be used for 3 more years, it has been showing significant signs of wear, with a consequent adverse effect upon material and operating costs. Having regard to the rapid deterioration in the condition of the machine, your team has estimated costs for the next 3 years:

Year	1	2	3
	£	£	£
Material and operating costs	19,500	24,500	29,000
Depreciation	2,500	2,500	2,500
	£22,000	£27,000	£31,500

It is believed that a machine incorporating significant technological development features will be on the market in 3 years' time, and will inevitably be purchased by your company in order to maintain competitive edge.

However, your team has suggested that a modified crimping machine could be purchased for use over the next 3 years pending the availability of the superior machine. The modified machine would cost £28,500 but would have no market value in 3 years' time. The existing machine has no current sale value. The use of the modified machine will, your team believes, give rise to the following costs:

Year	1	2	3
	£	£	£
Material and operating costs	13,500	14,500	16,000
Depreciation	9,500	9,500	9,500
	£23,000	£24,000	£25,500

A 100% first year tax allowance is available for the modified machine, and will be taken if it is purchased.

Required:

Having some appreciation of appraisal techniques, you decide to make an initial assessment of the data produced by your team before submitting the proposal to divisional management.
(a) Compute the average cost of capital to be used as a discount rate in project appraisal. Explain the rationale underlying the use of an average cost of capital in these circumstances.
(b) Present your appraisal of the proposal to purchase a modified machine. Taxation benefits and charges can be assumed to give rise to cash flows in the year following that in which they occur.

(Certified Diploma)

Appendix 5:   Suggested answers

These are intended to act as a guide to the main points which should be included in an answer. Reference is made to an appropriate part of the text if the answer is contained therein. I am grateful to the Association of Accounting Technicians for permission to reproduce their suggested answers, which are denoted (AAT) at the foot. All other answers are the author's own responsibility and do not necessarily reflect the views of the examining bodies concerned.

Chapter 1

1

(i) The classification of costs is the grouping of costs in a systematic way according to their nature or purpose. A subjective classification is when, say, all wage costs are grouped together for the different kinds of tasks performed within the organization. An objective classification is the cost centres or cost units to which all costs are charged. Common classifications are by:

Element	– labour, material or expenses
Behaviour	– fixed or variable costs
Function	– departments or other cost centres
Cost units	– individual product lines

(ii) Coding is the use of a numbering system to fully describe any cost (subject) and its destination in the costing system (object). All prime documents are coded before entry into the accounting system.

Most cost codes are composite codes, being compiled of separate series of numbers relating to both subject and object. For example, the composite code 96–453–271 may mean that the cost was incurred in Department 96 on Job Number 271 and 453 may refer to a particular type of material used on the job.

Financial data, when coded, can be easily input into computerized accounting systems. Each code is unique and easily understood if the coding structure is well designed. Management can obtain all the information they require in a subjective and/or objective way to plan, control and make decisions.

Chapter 2

1

(a) Stock valuation at 30 June based on LIFO valuation:
   2,000 units valued at £4,000 (1,500 at £2.50 + 500 at £0.50)
   Stock valuation at 30 June based on FIFO valuation:
   2,000 units at £2.70 valued at £5,400 in total.

(b)

	LIFO		*FIFO*	
	£	£	£	£
Sales		124,000		124,000
Opening stock	3,750		5,000	
Purchases	81,550		81,550	
	85,300		86,550	
Less: closing stock	4,000	81,300	5,400	81,150
Trading profit		£42,700		£42,850

(c) Mr Wood's suggestion must not be adopted since a consistent policy is demanded in accounting in financial statements. If this was adopted the company's profit and loss account would disclose a distorted profit figure. Mr Wood should be advised to disclose the information shown in (b) FIFO above, a profit of £42,850, as his main account, but also an accompanying note indicating that the change in stock valuation has been made and that under the basis previously adopted the trading profit would be £42,700.

(d) Accounting practice relating to stock valuation on the historical basis has been spelled out in SSAP 9 'Stocks and WIP' which infers that stock should be valued on the lower of cost or net realizable value. This may be construed as meaning that LIFO is not acceptable, and no doubt the company has been informed to this effect by its accountant. Generally acceptable methods are FIFO, weighted average and adjusted standard price.

Other reasonable explanations would also be accepted.

(e) Advantages of FIFO method.
   The technique is based on the logical assumption that materials are consumed in the order in which they are purchased. This means that it is:
   (i) Reasonably easy to administer and charge issues to production.
   (ii) Simple to explain to managers responsible for costs.
   (iii) Generally acceptable for closing stock purposes.
   Disadvantages:

(i) In times of inflation, production is charged at outdated prices.

(ii) Managers may be confused by being charged with different prices for identical materials.

(iii) It is held that the method overstates profit, and undercharges current production.

(AAT adapted)

2

(a) Re-order level   – Maximum usage in maximum delivery period
$1,100 \times 4 = 4,400$

Re-order quantity   – Maximum stock less (re-order level minus minimum use in minimum delivery period):
$5,500 - (4,400 - 900 \times 2) = 2,900$

Minimum level   – Re-order level less average usage in average delivery period:
$4,400 - (1,000 \times 3) = 1,400$

Average stock   – Alternative answers acceptable
Average of maximum plus minimum stock:
$$\frac{5,500 + 1,400}{2} = 3,450$$

or

Minimum stock plus half of re-order qty:
$1,400 + (0.5 \times 2,900) = 2,850$

(b) Essential practices of efficient storekeeping include:

(i) Efficient storage of materials for production and other uses

(ii) Effective protection of materials from deterioration and loss

(iii) Ensuring that right quantities are available as and when required

(iv) Maintenance of records of movements of materials in and out of stores

(v) Maintaining stock controls over maximum, minimum and re-order levels, ensuring variations are reported immediately

(vi) Vigilance on slow moving and obsolete stocks, reporting when suspect stocks fall into these categories.

(AAT)

3

(a) (i) $\dfrac{£100,800}{24,000 \text{ hrs}} = £4.20$ $\dfrac{£94,500}{21,000 \text{ hrs}} = £4.50$

     (ii) $\dfrac{£100,800}{42,000 \text{ hrs}} = £2.40$ $\dfrac{£94,500}{9,000 \text{ hrs}} = £10.50$

(b)   **Total cost per product**

(i) Labour hour rate

	P	Q	R
	£	£	£
Direct costs	34.50	24.00	40.50
Overheads – machining	8.40	4.20	8.40
finishing	6.75	4.50	9.00
	£49.65	£32.70	£57.90

(ii) Machine-hour rate

	£	£	£
Direct costs	34.50	24.00	40.50
Overheads – machining	9.60	3.60	7.20
finishing	5.25	5.25	10.50
	£49.35	£32.85	£58.20

(c) The factory manager has looked at the above figures and has seen that the answers are only marginally different. By combining the labour or machine hour rates, the total costs are still about the same as in the statement. A more realistic cost would be using a machine-hour rate for the machining area, and a labour rate for finishing. Departmental rates are normally used in costing practice.

(d) Hi-lo, least squares, scattergraph, etc., are acceptable methods to find the fixed cost and then variable rate of overhead cost. Using the Hi-lo method gives a fixed cost of £50,000 and a variable rate of £2 per hour.

(AAT Adapted)

Chapter 3

1

	Job A		Job B		Job C
	£		£		£
Direct materials	524		671		382
Labour – direct 158 hrs	790	170 hrs	850	16 hrs	80
– indirect 316 hrs	1,264	190 hrs	760	30 hrs	120
Site expenses	118		170		25
Administration*	237		180		23
Total costs 100%	2,933	Material	671	Material	382
80%		Other	1,960		
25%				Other	248
Selling price	3,318				

Contract profit	385	
Staff bonus 20%	77	
Profit to company	308	

Projected costs:		
B – 20%	490	
C – 75%		744
Projected total costs	3,121	1,374
Selling price	2,750	1,950
Contract profit (loss)	(371)	576
Projected staff bonus	Nil	115
Projected profit to company	£(371)	£461

*Hourly rate for recovery = £440/880 hrs = 50p

(a) Profit to company on Job A = £308
(b) Projected loss on Job B = £371
     Projected profit on Job C = £461
(c) Job B should be subject to careful scrutiny. It may be revealed that costs have escalated since contract price was agreed. Possibly a negotiated adjustment to the selling price may be feasible. Material costs are 27% of selling price compared with 18%–20% for jobs A and C. The ratio of direct/indirect hours is abnormally high on job B. Similarly site expenses appear to be excessive.

(d)

				Job D
			£	£
Selling price 2,750 + 10%				3,025
Less: variable costs:				
material			671.00	
labour – skilled 212.5 hrs at £5			1,062.50	
semi-skilled 237.5 at £4			950.00	
site expenses			212.50	2,896
Contribution				£129

Accept order if sufficient labour available in June.

		Hrs			Hrs
Skilled	A	158	Semi-skilled	A	316
	B	170		B	190
	C	16		C	30
Hours available		344			536
Required:	B	42.5	20%		47.5

C	48	75%	90
D	212.5	100%	237.5

Hours required	303	375
Surplus hours	41 hrs	161 hrs

This confirms that the order must be accepted as there is sufficient skilled and semi-skilled labour available to complete it in June.

(AAT)

2

(a)

Process B account

	Kilo	£		Kilo	Rate	£
Material from process A	2,500	7,145	Normal loss	125	16p	20
Wages		938	Finished stock	2,100	3.60	7,560
Direct costs		463	Abnormal loss	125	3.60	450
			Work-in-progress c/d	150		516
	2,500	£8,546		2,500		£8,546

Calculations:

Stock and abnormal loss

	kg	WIP	Total	Cost	Rate
Material	2,225	150	2,375	7,125	3.00
Wages	2,225	120	2,345	938	0.40
Direct costs	2,225	90	2,315	463	0.20
					£3.60

Work-in-progress

		£
Material	150 at £3.00 =	450
Wages	120 at £0.40 =	48
Direct costs	90 at £0.20 =	18
		£516

Other relevant accounts:

Normal loss account

	kg	£		kg	£
Process B	125	20	Cash	125	20

Abnormal loss account

	kg	£		kg	£
Process B	125	450	Cash	125	20
			P & L a/c		430
		450			450

Finished stock account

Process B	2,100	7,560

Profit and loss account

Abnormal loss	430

(b) Operation costing describes a system where the output is standardized and is the result of a sequence of repetitive operations or processes to which costs are charged before being averaged over the units produced during the period.

Process and service (such as transport) costing are associated with this technique.

Specific order costing applies to jobs, contracts, batches, etc., each of which is authorized by a specific special order. Job costing is applied to garage repair work as an example, contract costing with civil engineering, batch costing where batches of similar products are manufactured.

(AAT)

Chapter 4

1

(a)   **Betascope**

	per unit £	1,000 units £
Raw material 17 × £7.50	127.50	127,500
Direct labour 125 × £2.50	312.50	312,500
Variable overheads	125.00	125,000
Total variable costs	£565.00	£565,000
Fixed overheads	56.50	56,500
Total cost	£621.50	£621,500
Profit mark-up	310.75	310,750
Sales	£932.25	£932,250

Unit selling price = £932.25

(b)

The total contribution required = Fixed costs + Profit

= 56,500 + 310,750

= £367,250

The new unit contribution = $\dfrac{£367,250}{800 \text{ units}}$

= £459.06 per unit

The new unit selling price:

raw material	146.62
direct labour	343.75
variable overheads	131.25
contribution	459.06
selling price	£1,080.68

Chapter 5

1

(a) Selling price per hamper

		£ per hamper	£ per 1,000 hampers
Cost of ingredients		80.00	80,000
Cost of container		5.00	5,000
Packing labour		5.00	5,000
Fixed cost per unit	$\dfrac{£10,000}{1,000}$	10.00	10,000
Total cost		100.00	100,000
Mark-up of 40%		40.00	40,000
Selling price		£140.00	140,000

(b) Contribution 　=　Selling price − Variable costs
　　　　　　　　　=　£140 − £90
　　　　　　　　　=　£50 per hamper

Break-even volume　=　$\dfrac{\text{Fixed costs}}{\text{Contribution per unit}}$

　　　　　　　　　=　$\dfrac{£10,000}{£50}$

　　　　　　　　　=　200 hampers

The break-even chart should show the sales revenue line intersecting the total cost line at an approximate volume of 200 hampers depending on the accuracy of the drawing.

(c) The total profit is £40,000 at the anticipated volume of 1,000 hampers.

(d) The rise in ingredients costs reduces profit by £8,000.
　　The fall in selling price reduces profit by £14,000.

Both changes combined reduce total profit by £22,000 to £18,000 at the anticipated volume.

2 See text of Chapter 5 under headings 'Planning for Change' and 'Operating Gearing' for a full discussion of this question.

3 (a)

$$\text{Break-even point} = \frac{\text{Fixed cost}}{\text{Contribution per unit}} = \frac{£201,600}{£6 \text{ (i.e.20}-14)} = 33,600 \text{ units}$$

The break-even chart should show the total cost and sales curves intersecting at approximately 34,000 units.

(b)

	Profit and loss account		£
Sales 36,000 × £20			720,000
Less: wages	£2.00		
materials	£8.00		
overheads	£4.00		
	£14.00	× 36,000	504,000
Contribution			216,000
Less: Fixed costs			201,600
Budgeted profit			£14,400

(c)

Return on investment	=	15% × £330,000
	=	£49,500
Total contribution required	=	Fixed cost + profit requirement
	=	£201,600 + £49,500
	=	£251,100

$$\text{Required volume} = \frac{\text{Total contribution required}}{\text{Contribution per unit}}$$

$$= \frac{£251,100}{£6}$$

$$= 41,850 \text{ units}$$

(d) The company is not achieving the required rate of return as it is only selling 36,000 units at a profit of £14,400. To achieve a return of 15% on capital invested requires sales of 41,850 at the present selling price and cost structure. This is beyond normal capacity. Other ways to achieve a 15% return include cost reduction, increased selling price, if possible, with market research on effects, introduction of new products.

(AAT Adapted)

Chapters 6 & 7

1

(a)

	Period 1	*Period 2*
(i) Efficiency ratio	$= \dfrac{1,750}{1,800}\% = 97.2\%$	$\dfrac{2,250}{2,400}\% = 93.7\%$
(ii) Activity ratio	$= \dfrac{1,750}{2,000}\% = 87.5\%$	$\dfrac{2,250}{2,250}\% = 100\%$
(iii) Capacity ratio	$= \dfrac{1,800}{2,000}\% = 90\%$	$\dfrac{2,400}{2,250}\% = 106.6\%$

(b) The activity ratio shows that the production level was exactly in line with that budgeted in period 2, a significant improvement from only 87.5% in period 1.

   However, the capacity ratio exceeding 100% shows that this was achieved by working more hours than those budgeted whilst there was also a drop in the efficiency level during those hours from 97.2% in period 1 to 93.7% in period 2.

2

(a) Total material variance

			£
Standard cost	3,150 units × 1.5 kilos × £0.60	=	3,159.00
Actual cost	2,740 kilos × 0.58 = 1,589.20		
	2,315 kilos × 0.62 = 1,435.30	=	3,024.50
			£134.50(F)

Material price variance

		£
Standard cost of purchases 5,055 kg × £0.60	=	3,033.00
Actual cost of purchases	=	3,024.50
		£8.50(F)

Material usage variance
(Standard quantity   – Actual quantity)   × 0.60
         (5,265 – 5,055)   × 0.60 =   £126.00(F)

Total wages variance

Standard cost	3,510 × £3.80 × 0.60	=	8,002.80
Actual cost	880 × £3.90 = 3,432		
	1,300 × £3.65 = 4,745	=	8,177.00
			£174.20(A)

Wages rate variance

Standard cost of hours worked 2,180 × 3.80	=	8,284.00
Actual cost of hours worked	=	8,177.00
		£107.00(F)

Labour efficiency variance

(Standard hours required − Actual hours worked) ×	£3.80
(2,106 − 2,180) ×	£3.80
=	£281.20(A)

(b)   **Cost statement – May 1983**

		£
Sales, at standard selling price	3,510 × £3.50	12,285.00
Factory cost of sales	3,510 × £3.18	11,161.80
Gross profit at standard		1,123.20
Add: favourable variances	£	
material price	8.50	
material usage	126.00	
wages rate	107.00	241.50
		1,364.70
Deduct: adverse variances:		
labour efficiency		281.20
Gross profit, actual		£1,083.50

(c) Past performance is a method sometimes adopted in fixing standard prices, but it is not necessarily a good guide and could be misleading. It should only be used in the event of no other information with regard to expected performance being available.

Past performance includes past prices, past inefficiencies, previous conditions and methods of work. It is a concept of good management that efforts should always be made to improve past performance and, therefore, future activity should be influenced by determined and objective efforts to control cost.

Standards should be based on known future prices and efficient methods of work. Conditions should be anticipated and control features designed to enable corrections to be made where necessary.

The statement is not to be accepted.

(AAT)

Chapters 8 & 9

1

(a) (i) Controllable costs, also known as managed costs, are those which can be influenced by the actions of the person in whom control of a cost centre is vested.

   (ii) Non-controllable costs are those charges which are beyond the control of the manager of a cost centre. Generally these tend to be fixed costs, whereas controllables are usually variable.

(b)   **Budget statement**   Date . . . . .
                    Workshop – Department no.

	This month			*Cumulative to date*		
	Budget	*Actual*	*Gain loss*	*Budget*	*Actual*	*Gain loss*
Controllable costs: basic wages						
overtime premium						
direct materials						
power						
Total controllables						
Non-controllables: rent						
rates						
depreciation						
insurance						
Total non-controllables						
Total Costs						

(c)   (i) Preparation of budgets is primarily the main task and duty of the budget committee.

   (ii) Generally, one of the committee's members, usually the cost accountant, prepares and distributes a timetable for each stage of the budgeting process.

  (iii) Information must be made available to the committee and to executives and managers in the form of their functional and financial objectives.

(iv) Functional managers' co-operation is encouraged so that all objectives are capable of being summarized into master budgets.
(v) Budgets are consolidated, prepared and issued before any budget year (or other period) is started.
(vi) Actual results are compared with budget on a regular basis.
(vii) Action is taken by the committee to motivate managers to achieve budget where results are varying from targets.

(AAT)

2

(a) (i) The purpose of a cash budget is to provide information relating to future cash movements, giving sufficient notice of any surplus or deficiency of cash so that action may be taken to the benefit of the company.

(ii) The principal source of information is the operating and capital expenditure budgets of the business which are prepared in advance of the cash budget.

(b) (i) Cash budget for three months ending 31 March 1985

	January £	February £	March £
Receipts:			
sales, credit	3,750	3,750	4,500
cash	3,500	1,250	3,000
equipment		2,000	
	7,250	7,000	7,500
Payments:			
purchases, credit	5,000	6,000	5,750
cash	500	250	250
wages	250	250	250
postage & packing	750	900	1,000
dividends			375
equipment		2,000	2,000
	6,500	9,400	9,625
Cash flow	750	(2,400)	(2,125)
Opening balance	2,250	3,000	600
Closing balance	3,000	600	(1,525)

(ii) **Forecast trading and profit and loss account for three months ending 31 March 1985**

	£
Sales (credit 13,250 + cash 7,750)	21,000
Less: stock at 1 January	6,000

Add: purchases (18,500 + 1,000)	19,500	
	25,500	
Less: stock at 31 March	11,500	
		14,000
Gross profit (33.3% on sales)		7,000
Less: wages	750	
postage & packing	2,650	
loss on sale of equipment	1,750	
depreciation	150	
		5,300
Net profit		1,700

(iii)   **Forecast balance sheet as at 31 March 1985**

	£	£	£
Fixed assets			
Equipment, at cost		6,000	
Less: depreciation		150	
			5,850
Current assets			
Stock		11,500	
Debtors		5,000	
		16,500	
Less: current liabilities			
Creditors	8,750		
Bank overdraft	1,525		
Dividends due	375		
		10,650	
			5,850
			11,700
Represented by:			
Capital		10,000	
Net profit		1,700	
			11,700

(c) A cash budget projects movements of cash only, whereas the profit and loss account displays both cash and credit transactions, as it is assumed that credit will be realized in the course of time. Non-cash movements are also necessary in order to obtain distributable profits, so depreciation and loss on sale of assets have been recorded.

(AAT)

Chapter 10

1

(i) Gross profit percentage $= \dfrac{1,725}{3,100}\% = 55.6\%$

(ii) Net profit percentage $= \dfrac{670}{3,100}\% = 21.6\%$

(iii) Return on total assets $= \dfrac{670}{2,055}\% = 32.6\%$

(iv) Quick ratio $= \dfrac{870}{665}\% = 1.3{:}1$

(v) Debtors' collection period $= \dfrac{770}{3,100} \times 365 = 91$ days

(vi) Stock:turnover $= \dfrac{3,100}{310} = 10$ times

(vii) Fixed assets:turnover $= \dfrac{3,100}{875} = 3.5$ times

(viii) Return on shareholders' funds $= \dfrac{586}{690}\% = 84.9\%$

(ix) Current ratio $= \dfrac{1180}{665} = 1.8{:}1$

(x) Debt ratio $= \dfrac{1365}{2055}\% = 66.4\%$

Very few ratios have an absolute value, but are used in a relative way in intra and interfirm comparisons. Both gross and net margins are calculated using the profit before tax and interest to identify the trading profit irrespective of the capital structure in force. Both these figures seem satisfactory but knowledge of the industry is necessary. Also the return on shareholders' funds and on total assets both appear quite satisfactory.

The quick ratio exceeds the 1:1 norm and the current ratio is near the 2:1 norm, but this requirement varies widely. On the other hand, the debt ratio seems high, as two thirds of all assets are financed by debt.

Asset turnover rates also need comparisons to make any judgement, but the debtors' collection period of 91 days would seem too long for most industries, especially if credit is granted on a net monthly basis.

2

(a) Very few ratios have value in an absolute sense but must be used in a comparative way to indicate good or bad performance. These comparisons can be with own past performance and with budgeted or target ratios set by management. Both these comparisons are intrafirm, but it is also possible to compare performance on an interfirm basis. Although simple in theory, interfirm comparisons are not so easy in practice because of:

 (i) the difficulty in identifying competitors with a similar product mix.

 (ii) the need to put all financial data on to a current cost basis, if possible, so that return on capital and turnover rates are realistic.

 (iii) the need for compatibility of information between companies, e.g. the turnover of fixed assets will differ radically if one company leases and another does not.

The purpose of all ratio comparisons is to identify areas of possible weakness for further investigation and remedial action by management.

(b)

Ratio	*T.A. average*	*Crocks*
Rate of stock turnover	10 times	8 times
Debtors' average credit time	40 days	30 days
Gross profit percentage	25%	20%
Net profit percentage	8%	10%
Return on capital employed	15%	20%

Crocks return on capital at 20% is significantly higher than the 15% trade average for this key ratio. The other ratios are a mixture of good and bad. The gross margin of 20% is five points down and may be due to bad buying or low selling prices. The final net profit of 10%, however, is better than the average, suggesting that overheads are well under control. Credit control is also significantly tighter, at 30 days, than the 40-day trade average, but this is offset by a slower rate of stock turnover.

(c) The return on shareholders' funds, as opposed to return on total capital employed, helps shareholders judge if the company is earning an adequate return on their funds. Also of interest to them is the price/earnings ratio, which indicates the market rating of the shares by relating the profit earned per share in a year to the market price per share. These are just two of a number of possible ratios.

Chapter 11

1

(a) See the first two pages of Chapter 11 for descriptions of principal types of financial responsibility centre.

(b) The choice of appropriate centres will depend on the corporate strategy employed in the organization with regard to decentralization, the organization structure which reflects the degree of decentralization, and the management philosophy.

There are many behavioural implications in responsibility accounting. Authority must go with responsibility to achieve corporate objectives.

(c) The prime criterion is the promotion of 'goal congruence', so that managers, in pursuing their individual objectives, do not conflict with other managers or corporate objectives. Another criterion is the need for clear and fair financial measurements to be employed which are appropriate to the authority and responsibility of the manager concerned. Different types of responsibility centre may be appropriate for different parts of an organization.

Chapter 12

1

(a) Unit selling prices £223.50; £341.10; £155.40 respectively.
Unit contributions £97.00; £149.70; £60.80 respectively.
Contribution per direct labour hour £19.40; £18.71; £30.40 respectively.

(b)
Forecast profit for August

	Alpha £	Beta £	Gamma £	Total £
Sales	11,175	51,165	31,080	93,420
Less: variable costs	6,325	28,710	18,920	53,955
Contribution	£4,850	£22,455	£12,160	39,465
Less: fixed costs				8,325
Net profit				£31,140
Contribution ratio	43.4%	43.9%	39.1%	42.2%

Ranking of products by contribution ratio in order of preference is B; A; G.

(c) With insufficient labour to produce at the forecast levels, the products will be ranked in order of their contribution per direct labour hour.

Gamma contributes £30.40 per hour and will be produced first up to the maximum forecast demand. Any labour remaining will be used to produce Alpha which contributes £19.40 per hour. Once forecast demand of that is met, any iabour remaining will be used to produce Beta which is the least profitable, contributing only £18.71 per labour hour.

2 (a)

	A	B	C	Total
	£	£	£	£
Sales	50,000	54,000	45,000	149,000
Less: direct costs	25,000	30,000	15,000	70,000
commission	5,000	5,400	4,500	14,900
Contribution	20,000	18,600	25,500	64,100
Less: branch fixed costs	5,000	5,000	5,000	15,000
Segment margin	15,000	13,600	20,500	49,100
Less: head office fixed costs				28,000
Profit				£21,100
Unit sales	5,000	6,000	3,000	
Contribution per unit	£4.00	£3.10	£8.50	
Contribution ratio	40%	34%	57%	43%

(b) Memo to sales director

Looked at from a net profit viewpoint, Branch B is only just profitable, but it is misleading to concentrate solely on this aspect. A marginal costing approach is used to identify the 'contribution' a segment (a product line or branch) makes towards common fixed costs and profit of the firm in total.

The contribution is found by deducting variable costs only from sales revenue. Variable costs in this case are the direct costs plus salespeoples' commission.

On this basis, Branch B is contributing £18,600 towards fixed costs and profit. Even after deducting the branch fixed costs it makes a segment margin of £13,600 which would be lost if the branch were closed down and the overall company profit would fall by this amount.

Expressing contribution as a percentage of sales gives contribution ratios of 40%, 34% and 57% respectively for the three branches, whilst the total for the firm is 43%. Branch B is therefore the least profitable of the three but still worthwhile. I suggest we keep it open and try to improve its contribution and profitability further.

(c) Performance, as measured by the amount of contribution earned by each branch, can be affected by sales volume, sales price and variable costs. Sales volume and price are interlinked and the 'price elasticity of demand' for the product, if identified, will indicate whether a price rise or reduction will be favourable.

Branch C sells at £15 per unit and makes much more profit than Branch B selling twice the quantity at £9 per unit. It could be that Branch B will make more profit selling less at a higher unit price.

Greater sales volume even at the existing price will increase contribution and, therefore, profit, as fixed costs by definition will not change. Increased advertising and marketing effort should be examined for cost effectiveness in terms of the extra contribution they generate.

An increase in commission for sales in excess of a certain level may yield extra sales volume and increase contribution.

(d) The sales director should look at the introduction of responsibility accounting with branch managers being given clear financial targets at which to aim with rewards for achieving them. These could be in the form of a branch profit or a branch contribution.

The allocation of head office fixed costs on a unit basis treats them like variable costs and is a disincentive to increased volume sales. It serves no useful purpose and a branch profit or contribution, excluding such head office fixed costs, is preferred. Feedback of experience in the most profitable branch to the others may enhance their performance.

As the product is identical, centralized purchasing should be considered for bulk discounts, as should the preparation of display and advertising materials.

3 This is a 'make or buy' decision which hinges on the behaviour of the £37,000 total annual costs (i.e. whether variable or fixed). Also required is information on whether the capacity released when components are bought in can be utilized in an alternative way to make a contribution to fixed costs.

See text of Chapter 12 under 'Make or buy decisions' for full discussion of these points.

Chapters 13 & 14

1

(a) The basis of choice between these three alternatives is to select the one offering the highest NPV surplus after the yearly cash flows have been discounted at the 15% cost of capital for Pilmar.

Both the original cost of the equipment and the existing working capital are ignored as they are 'sunk costs' common to all situations. Any new investment in equipment or working capital must be taken into account, as must the sale or release of any investment at the appropriate time.

Depreciation must be excluded from costs as it is not a cash transaction.

The calculations are:

Alternative A: Net present value + £46,812

Based on sales £100,000 less costs £89,000 ignoring depreciation. £11,000 × 3.352 cum pv factor + £20,000 × .497 re release of working capital at end of year 5.

Alternative B: Net present value + £11,336

Based on sales £100,000 less costs £22,000 ignoring depreciation. £78,000 × 3.352 + £40,000 × .497 re release of working capital. Initial investment at year 0 is £270,000 (£300,000 − £50,000 + 20,000)

Alternative C: Net present value + £56,760

Based on £5,000 × 3.352 re royalties plus £40,000 released at year 0 from working capital and sale of old equipment.

(b) The NPV calculations in (a) suggest that the highest return will be found from ceasing manufacture now and selling out to Biret Ltd, taking royalties on future sales.

This alternative C yields £10,000 more present value than continuing to manufacture with the old equipment (A) and £45,000 more than would result from buying new equipment (B).

A further advantage of alternative C is that the risk element is minimized. The royalty payment is based on unit sales irrespective of changes in costs and selling prices and will vary only with demand as it would on all alternatives.

2   The choice between these two alternatives is based on the size of the NPV surplus which indicates that the second-hand car yields the biggest contribution towards annual running costs. As the expected mileage is less for the second-hand car this reinforces this particular choice. The calculations are:

Second-hand car:			*New car:*				
Year 0	−2,500		1.000	−2,500 − 500		1.000 −	500
1	+2,000		.909	+1,818 −3,000	+2,500	.909 −	454
2	+2,000		.826	+1,652 −2,000	+2,500	.826 +	413
3 +	250	+1,500	.751	+1,314 +1,000	+2,500	.751	+2,628
			NPV +£2,284			NPV	+£2,087

3 In this context, the cost of equity is taken as the earnings yield, i.e. the earnings for ordinary shareholders as a percentage of the market value of the shares. The weighted average cost of capital is based on the market value of the securities rather than their book value.

The earnings calculations are:

	Current structure £000	New structure £000
Profit pre-tax and interest	3,840	4,080
Less debenture interest	–	120
Pre-tax profit	3,840	3,960
Less 50% tax	1,920	1,980
Profit after tax	1,920	1,980
Less preference dividend	300	300
Earnings for ordinary shareholders	1,620	1,680

(a) Existing weighted average cost of capital (WACC)

	Book value	Market value	Cost £000
Equity	£9m	£12m	1,620
5% Preference shares	£6m	£4.8m	300
		£16.8m	1,920

$$\text{WACC} = \frac{£1,920,000}{£16.8m} \% = 11.43\%$$

(b) The existing cost of equity is the earnings yield, namely:

$$\frac{\text{Earnings}}{\text{Market value}} \% = \frac{£1,620,000}{£12m} \% = 13.5\%$$

The new market value is the new earnings capitalized to 100% at the existing earnings yield if there is no change in the cost of equity:

$$\text{Market value} = £1.680m \times \frac{100}{13.5} = £12.444m$$

Market value per share = £2.07 (£12.444m/6m)

New weighted average cost of capital (WACC)

	Book value	Market value	Cost £000
Equity	£9m	£12.444m	1,680
5% Preference shares	£6m	£ 4.8m	300
12% Debentures	£1m	£ 1.0m	60
		£18.244m	£2,040

$$\text{New WACC} \quad = \quad \frac{£2,040,000}{£18.244\text{m}} \quad \% = 11.18\%$$

(c) The effect of increasing the gearing ratio by borrowing has been to lower the existing WACC from 11.43% to 11.18%. This is because the cost of borrowing (net of tax relief) is substantially lower at 6% than the previous WACC. The larger the amount of new borrowed capital then the more it will reduce the new WACC.

This is only true provided the gearing ratio is not regarded as excessive by ordinary shareholders. After this level of gearing has been breached then shareholders will expect a higher return to compensate for the higher risk. At this stage further borrowing will not decrease the WACC but actually increase it because of the effect on the cost of existing equity.

Another view expressed by Modigliani and Miller is that the WACC is constant irrespective of the level of gearing. They argue that any change in the gearing ratio immediately leads to a change in the cost of equity to counter the change in financial risk. Their proposition assumes some conditions not always present in the real world and there is probably an element of truth in both viewpoints.

Index

Management

☐	**Effective Leadership**	John Adair	£2.50p
☐	**The Effective Executive**	} Peter Drucker	£1.95p
☐	**Management**		£3.95p
☐	**Under New Management**	Tony Eccles	£2.95p
☐	**Back from the Brink**	Michael Edwardes	£2.95p
☐	**How to Double Your Profits**	John Fenton	£2.50p
☐	**Inside Employment Law**	David Field	£2.50p
☐	**How to Win Customers**	Heinz Goldmann	£2.95p
☐	**Managing People at Work**	John Hunt	£2.50p
☐	**Investment Appraisal for Managers**	Graham Mott	£1.95p
☐	**Managing With Computers**	Terry Rowan	£2.95p
☐	**Guide to Saving and Investment**	James Rowlatt	£2.95p
☐	**Reality of Management**	} Rosemary Stewart	£1.95p
☐	**Reality of Organisations**		£1.95p
☐	**Bargaining for Results**	John Winkler	£2.50p
☐	**Multilingual Commercial Dictionary**		£3.95p

All these books are available at your local bookshop or newsagent, or
can be ordered direct from the publisher. Indicate the number of copies
required and fill in the form below   12
....

Name_____
(Block letters please)

Address_____

_____

Send to CS Department, Pan Books Ltd, PO Box 40, Basingstoke, Hants
Please enclose remittance to the value of the cover price plus:
35p for the first book plus 15p per copy for each additional book ordered
to a maximum charge of £1.25 to cover postage and packing
Applicable only in the UK

While every effort is made to keep prices low, it is sometimes
necessary to increase prices at short notice. Pan Books reserve
the right to show on covers and charge new retail prices which
may differ from those advertised in the text or elsewhere